Praise for *Pitching & Closing*

I never thought I'd read a book that not only explains how nuanced BD can be, but also actually gives you what you need to take teams big and small to grow their business through partnership. Impressive, and fun to read.

—Paul Murphy, CEO of Dots and Partner at Betaworks

Pitching & Closing is a must-read not only for those in business development but also for founders, CEOs, and anyone who interacts with potential clients or partners. I'll be quoting from this book for longer than I care to admit.

—Walker Williams, CEO of Teespring

In my experience, business development is a critical set of skills whether you're starting a company, running for public office, or making a sale. *Pitching & Closing* is a seminal guide to everything you want to know about how to build great partnerships.

—Reshma Saujani, Founder of Girls Who Code

Biz dev is a little like jet propulsion: everyone knows it's important to soar but most don't really understand how it works. Alex and Ellen have done us all an incredible service with this concise, actionable guide to successful business development. A must-read for anyone moving into the field.

—Kathryn Minshew, CEO of The Muse

This book is a must-read for anyone in the business of transforming professional relationships into powerful strategic partnerships.

—Adam Bain, President of Global Revenue at Twitter

Pitching & Closing does a phenomenal job of giving you a seat in the room during some of the biggest business development deals of late. Taub and DaSilva leverage experts to provide additional context for their concepts, and they do so to great effect. Anyone who reads this book will come away with a deep understanding of business development in the world of startups.

—Dylan Smith, CFO of Box

Pitching & Closing is a definitive guide to partnerships for the next generation of entrepreneurs and business leaders. This book alone will help you master the skills needed to succeed in pitching your ideas.

—Adam Braun, Founder and CEO
of Pencils of Promise

Taub and DaSilva offer a guided road map on how to be successful in business development. From developing genuine relationships through networking to pitching deals with a win-win mentality, *Pitching & Closing* offers a step-by-step model on how to forge valuable partnerships, create lasting vision, and grow your company.

This book gives an honest and insightful look at the delicate and complex handling of business development and guides readers on how to turn good ideas into great partnerships.

—Kyle Kelly, Business Development & Analysis
at Zappos.com

Alex Taub and Ellen DaSilva have written the bible for business development in startup land—a well-researched, easily accessible accounting of best practices and tips of the trade from the people who are leaders in opening and closing deals that define some of the most exciting new companies on the landscape.

—Laurie Racine, Board Member, Creative Commons

PITCHING
&
CLOSING

PITCHING
&
CLOSING

EVERYTHING YOU NEED TO KNOW ABOUT BUSINESS DEVELOPMENT, PARTNERSHIPS, AND MAKING DEALS THAT MATTER

ALEXANDER TAUB

ELLEN DASILVA

Mc
Graw
Hill
Education

New York Chicago San Francisco Athens London Madrid
Mexico City Milan New Delhi Singapore Sydney Toronto

1 2 3 4 5 6 7 8 9 0   DOC/DOC   1 2 0 9 8 7 6 5 4

ISBN   978-0-07-182237-4
MHID 0-07-182237-2

e-ISBN   978-0-07-182515-3
e-MHID 0-07-182515-0

Library of Congress Cataloging-in-Publication Data
Taub, Alexander.
   Pitching and closing : everything you need to know about business development, partnerships, and making deals that matter / by Alexander Taub and Ellen DaSilva.
      pages cm
   ISBN 978-0-07-182237-4 (hardback) — ISBN 0-07-182237-2 (hbk) 1. Strategic alliances (Business) 2. Business networks. 3. Industrial marketing. I. DaSilva, Ellen. II. Title.
   HD69.S8T38 2015
   658'.046—dc23

                                                                                    2014008761

Alex: To my beautiful wife, Liz. Thank you for being understanding during this hectic book-writing time. Without your love and support, this book would not have happened. I love you.

To my parents, Hindy and Ruby Taub: thank you for putting up with me and giving me just enough wiggle room to pursue my passions.

Ellen: To my supportive and loving family: Russell, Peggy, Emily, and Nancy. Your enthusiasm has been the guiding light throughout this project. To David, for opening my eyes to the world of tech. I am so grateful for all your love and encouragement.

CONTENTS

ACKNOWLEDGMENTS

Alex: There are a few people in the tech scene without whom this book would not have been written. Thank you, Sam Rosen and Michael Galpert, for both having a big influence on my starting a personal blog, which has led to all of this. Thank you, J. J. Colao and Tom Post, for liking my personal blog enough to make me a contributor to *Forbes.* Thank you to my former bosses, Paul Murphy, Michael Galpert, and Avi Muchnick at Aviary and Ben Milne and Charise Flynn at Dwolla. You've all taught me so much. Thank you, Michael Schonfeld, my business partner in crime and cofounder of SocialRank. Thank you, Ron Rofe, for betting on Michael and me early on and helping us at every turn. Thank you, Mom, for reading every post I have written before it goes out to make sure that things are spelled correctly. If people only knew how bad I am at grammar and spelling! Thank you to Lisa, Jean, Henry, and the Writer's House team who made everything move and had Ellen's and my backs the entire time. Thank you to Donya Dickerson at McGraw-Hill for reaching out over email back in April 2013—I'm really happy we got to do this together! Thank you to Adam Levin for introducing Ellen and me way back when. This is the fruit of your introduction. And lastly, thank you, Ellen, for making this book a reality. Your organization and persistence got this done. Bringing you onboard for this adventure was the best decision I've made.

Ellen: I want to acknowledge all of the incredible mentors on both coasts, professional and personal, who have taught me what I need to know about the world of startups, entrepreneurism, and leadership. Thank you to Lisa, Jean, Henry, and the Writer's House team, who worked tirelessly to polish the manuscript. To the McGraw-Hill team for their vote of confidence and meticulous work. Thank you to Hindy Taub for being a force behind the scenes. I second Alex's gratitude to Adam Levin, who made the fortuitous introduction and has continued to provide sage guidance. A final, special thank-you to Alex for helping me navigate the world of tech well before I left banking, teaching me the foundations of partnerships, and taking a chance a long time ago on an English major interested in tech.

We would like to thank the following individuals for helping us embark on this project. Without their input, experience, and willingness to share, this book would not have been written.

Thanks to Lisa DiMona, Jean Garnett, Henry Ginna, Donya Dickerson, Dannalie Diaz, Pattie Amoroso and the McGraw-Hill team, Alex Guttler, Andrew Ferenci, Andy Ellwood, Brian Kil, Charlie O'Donnell, Eli Portnoy, Eric Batscha, Eric Friedman, Erin Pettigrew, Gary Vaynerchuk, Itai Ram, Jared Cohen, Jared Hecht, Jeremy Lermitte, Jeremy Schwartz, Jesse Itzler, Julie Vaughn Ruef, Kristal Bergfield, Lars Fjeldsoe-Nielsen, Laurie Racine, Matt Van Horn, Maxine Friedman, Mike Ghaffary, Nam Nguyen, Nicole Cook, Phillip Eubanks, Phil Toronto, Richard Bloom, Rick Armbrust, Rob Weiss, Scott Britton, Shaival Shah, Tanuj Parikh, Tirath Kamdar, Tristan Walker, and Zeeshan Zaidi.

INTRODUCTION

Be so good they can't ignore you.

—STEVE MARTIN

THERE ARE FEW experiences more satisfying than identifying a problem and finding a solution by convincing someone to do something that he or she wasn't previously planning to do. Regardless of your industry, company size, or stage of business, the rush that comes from creating value out of a vision, connections, and research—creating a partnership—is exhilarating. And it goes almost without saying that knowing how to close a deal successfully is applicable across all professional fields: from technology startups to the legal world, and from medicine and financial services to the public sector. This book is a guide to the very best methods of achieving that exhilaration by making deals that matter.

When we talk about "making deals," we're really talking about forging partnerships between companies, organizations, teams, or infrastructures—any two entities whose integration could substantially benefit both sides. Do you need help growing your user base? Finishing an item that's on your road map? Streamlining a process to save a substantial amount of money? These are all prime opportunities for partnerships, and it's important that you recognize such opportunities. The right kind of partnership can enhance your business in ways that you may not even have imagined. But the deals that cement productive partnerships can come about only as a result of two fundamental tenets of business development: pitching and closing. Both are equally essential parts of professional experience, and mastering both is the ultimate way to quickly add value to your company.

Pitching, when successful, is done in person and involves making a strong first impression, being professional, and speaking articulately and persuasively—all skills that are crucial for success in any professional endeavor. In their purest form, pitches are presentations that one team gives to another that propose an idea of collaboration but require some convincing on both sides.

Closing, the art of finalizing deal terms and signing the deal, is that culminating moment when you've gotten the other side to say yes. Setting aside the legalities of closing deals, this is the pinnacle of deal making, when the two sides agree to partner to augment each other's product, company, or business.

Between the pitch and the hoped-for handshake or signature, many steps need to be taken and many decisions need to be made, and while there's no single perfect way to complete a deal, there are certain crucial milestones and strategies that business development professionals use on the path to closing successfully. We are here to help you navigate that path.

Why worry about pitching and closing so much, and why now? To begin with, the startup space is buzzing. With the meteoric success of companies like Google, Facebook, and Twitter, many people are trying their hand at inventing something that will change people's behavior or enhance the way they engage with the world on a daily basis. There are many books that will walk you through how to start a company, but we'll assume here that you've already got some entrepreneurial blood and just need a little guidance on how to perfect your partnership strategies. Indeed, no matter how novel your product or business plan is, you still need to learn the fundamentals of pitching and closing, and perhaps understand something about partnering with other companies along the way. After all, while the tech startup scene is filled with engineers, designers, and product employees, we can't forget their counterparts, business development professionals, whose responsibility is to run and grow the business side of the operation.

Jobs in this vague territory known as business development are highly sought after, but many business-minded tech professionals don't actually know what this term means. At the highest level, business development has three pieces to it. The first is the process of marketing, selling, and developing strategies for your company. The second is to strengthen your ties with existing partners and create new ones. The last and most important is to get to the point where you turn these transactions into repeat occurrences (which turn into sales). We believe it is important to highlight some of the key skills required and give you landmark examples of outstanding BD to make you a well-rounded business professional in the startup space.

In order to make you an expert in making business deals and strategic partnerships, we have divided the book into five parts: "Business Development," "Introduction to Partnerships," "Pitching and Closing," "Best Practices: Preparation and Execution," and "War Stories."

Part 1, "Business Development," covers the basics of business development, one of the most coveted jobs in the startup job market and one of only a handful of nontechnical roles at early-stage companies. But what does it mean to *do* business development? What's the difference between BD and sales? What makes an employee successful at her BD job, and how does one even land such a job in the first place?

Part 2, "Introduction to Partnerships," focuses on pairing your company with other companies for the benefit of both. You'll learn how to find companies for strategic partnerships, understand their business models, use the other side's motivations for your benefit, and position yourself for success. Knowing that closing a deal with the right partner can take your company to the next level is a thrilling but also daunting task, and this section covers the nitty-gritty and helps resolve those situations that can cause anxiety for those who are looking to source a deal.

Part 3, "Pitching and Closing," helps you figure out how to identify the best strategic alliances for your business and instructs you on how to go after them. The prior sections provided the necessary skills and framework; now you're ready for the execution: how to develop the most exciting and appropriate pitch, then close the deal that actually matters.

Whether you're talking about incoming dollars, outgoing services, page views, or downloads, deals that matter are deals that help the metrics that matter to you go up. After all, companies need to make money at some point if they are to have a lasting business. If you are doing deals and they aren't helping you grow your core metrics, you need to cut down the amount of time you are spending on them. You may even need to take a step back and figure out how external partnerships are going to help you accomplish your company's goals. These are the only deals that matter.

We also delve into the legalities of drafting contracts, and finally talk about how to maintain a deal once it is closed.

Part 4, "Best Practices: Preparation and Execution," reveals tips and tricks that the pros use. We'll show you how to introduce someone properly and professionally, how to reach out to a person you don't know (and actually get him or her to respond!), and how to deal with rejection. This section draws most heavily on our experience and that of successful business professionals with business development and partnership experience. Some of these best practices were learned the hard way; others are tips and tricks passed down from mentors, colleagues, and friends.

Part 5, "War Stories," documents discussions with and profiles of business development and partnership professionals, company founders, and venture capitalists to chronicle the multifaceted process of making deals (both well-known and little-known) that mattered in a big way. This is where all the theoretical knowledge acquired in the first four sections comes to life. We've done extensive research on the individual examples and collected firsthand accounts from the business development executives, founders, and CEOs involved to get the inside story on how each deal transpired. We include details on who the related parties were, why the deals came to fruition or fell apart, and how the deal creator pitched the deal and negotiated the terms. We hone in on the moment when the pitch was successful and the other party said yes.

Our goal with this book is to help you understand how to position yourself to get that all-important closing signature (and even help you navigate the legalese behind it). We explain why people say yes and why they say no. We tell you stories, some famous and some not, about people saying yes and no. We give you the metaphorical sword and armor for pitching and closing in all aspects of your life. When you finish this book, you will be ready to go out to battle. You will be so ready that it will be very hard for people to say no to you. And if they are saying no, you will immediately identify the appropriate strategies learned here and be able to come back and convince them to say yes.

You will learn about business development and partnerships through stories, anecdotes, and best practices from current and former employees at organizations such as Google, Facebook, Apple, Amazon, Twitter, Dropbox, PayPal, AOL, Uber, Yelp, Yahoo!, Spotify, Kickstarter, Dell, eBay, Waze, Salesforce, Disney, MTV Networks, Sony BMG, American Express, Foursquare, Constant Contact, Dwolla, GroupMe, Lyft, Tumblr, Path, Aviary, AppNexus, Hunch, Fab.com, SinglePlatform, Contently, StellaService, Digg, Estimote, MessageMe, Squarespace, NetJets, Andreessen Horowitz, Union Square Ventures, First Round Capital, and more.

After this book ends, your learning will still continue. *Pitching and Closing* is the starting point, but your pitching and closing skills can always be refined.

We will continue to interact with you on PitchingandClosing.com, as well as through our Twitter account, @PandC. We will share our favorite articles from around the web, offer new tips as we discover them, and show you anything else that we think will continue to help your pitching and closing education. We hope you enjoy the book, but remember, this is just the beginning.

Now let's go close some deals.

PITCHING
&
CLOSING

PART 1

BUSINESS DEVELOPMENT

WE'LL START BY walking you through the basics of business development—what it entails and who does it—to serve as a foundation for understanding how pitching and closing really work.

CHAPTER 1

WHAT IS BUSINESS DEVELOPMENT?

WITHIN THE TECH startup industry, the term *business development* is a buzzword. The ears of nontechnical individuals who are interested in the technology world often perk up when they hear the term, but what does it actually mean? There are three core aspects of the definition of business development (BD), and we will elaborate on these and build upon the basic tenets of BD throughout the first section of this book.

1. *Business development is the process of marketing, selling, and developing strategies for your company.*
2. *Business development professionals work to strengthen their ties with existing partners and to create new ones.*
3. *Business development precedes sales.* The goal of a business development professional is to identify growth opportunities for your business, test and implement them, reproduce the deals, and then develop a standard process (which ultimately leads to building a sales team).

Let's dissect each of the core aspects of BD and the expectation for each.

Business Development Is the Process of Marketing, Selling, and Developing Strategies for Your Company

BD is a function that necessitates wearing many hats. Seeking strategic partnerships with other companies requires selling the idea of a relationship, marketing the company, and developing growth initiatives. This is a more glamorous way of saying that BD professionals at smaller companies constantly strive to do whatever it takes to help run the business side of their company.

Marketing and market research are often conducted for the product or platform that the company is offering. Most of the time, a marketing team's job is to help support the BD team with anything related to the launch of a product or partnership. A common example of this is creating marketing and promotional materials for a product launch. Sometimes, early in a company's development, a BD employee will take on some of the functions of a marketing professional and set the stage for adding a full-time marketing individual to the team. A great example is Kristal Bergfield, a former marketer turned BD, and former head of business development at StellaService. Prior to her most recent experience, she worked in business development at American Express. Bergfield used her previous marketing experience (specifically involving relationship building and management) at Waggener Edstrom when soliciting and working with partners.

As a BD professional, you will be responsible for presenting, selling, or pitching (or whatever you'd like to call it) the company and its products. For a BD professional, strategic business planning means thinking critically about the potential growth of the business and trying to develop activities that will set it on the right course. This can often mean conducting analysis about the best ways to grow the numbers that are important to your team (user acquisition, revenue growth, and other metrics) or simply figuring out the best markets to target. For example, the BD team would decide whether the company should focus its efforts on developing a certain type of business model or looking for partnerships in a particular industry. The team would also solicit feedback from prospective partners about a potential product idea or market strategy to assess interest and viability before even building the product.

Business Development Professionals Work to Strengthen Their Ties with Existing Partners and to Create New Ones

BD is built on a foundation of strong relationships with a wide range of other professionals at various companies and in various industries. As a result, a critical part of the role is being savvy about building, expanding, and tapping into your network in order to generate business. Business development professionals strive to be only one degree of separation from any other business, big or small, in industry. These connections can mean the difference between resolving an issue in a matter of hours or days, rather than needing weeks or months! If you have access to user services and support at consumer-facing enterprises (for example, if you know someone at Facebook who can help you resolve a problem with a product or get access to a new product), it maximizes efficiency and helps get things done.

Business Development Precedes Sales

The goal of a business development professional is to identify growth opportunities for the business, test and implement them, reproduce the deals, and then develop a standard process (which ultimately leads to building a sales team). This tenet is at the heart of BD, and it is what separates the legendary deal makers from the amateurish ones.

BD precedes sales, and a person who is successful in BD will typically do a similar deal three or four times before putting together a standard practice and creating a sales team around it. As a BD professional, you are expected to close deals with other companies, ordinarily focusing on a specific sector or vertical segment, then establish a standardized deal-making process with a policy on cadence and agreements, and eventually put together a sales team to grow the business within that sector. Once you begin to scale out a specific vertical sector (and have a sales team in place), it is time to go on to the next thing. As a BD professional, you will move on to identify new opportunities for your business, continuing to "sell" the company's direction and new products into uncharted territory while looking for the next product or vertical segment that will hit a home run and merit building a sales team around. The best BD employees ultimately turn what they are working on into sales, and the cycle continues.

BD Vision

The combination of acumen in identifying the right partnership and remaining attuned to potential partnerships at all times is critical for setting up the right kind of deals. We have termed this foresight and way of thinking *BD vision*, which we will vernacularly define as the ability to anticipate and spot opportunities in every corner of life. Having BD vision means being acutely aware of potential matches, knowing that if you speak to one person who has a great idea and connect that person with someone else who could benefit from that idea, a successful partnership will be made. People with BD vision are generally very helpful individuals, always seeming to connect the right people at the right time.

How does one "get" BD vision? Some people believe that it is an innate ability; others believe that developing the mindset takes time and practice. Those who have BD vision often take a step back from every situation and assess the potential outcomes of introductions, partnership suggestions, and other networking possibilities. This kind of thinking is not limited to special functions or events, but takes place in casual interactions at the watercooler, at social outings with friends, or during professional lunches.

BD vision is used to help oneself, but it is critical that you first understand how you can best help others. Company mandates and goals are different, so you need to dig in if you are to really understand what kinds of opportunities are most helpful to your friends, partners, and acquaintances. Some people need to connect to the right distribution partners; others need an investor who is a good fit to lead their round. Someone else might want help getting in touch with a great tech blogger to cover a new product announcement. It is all situational. And it is the responsibility of the BD professional to become strategically creative.

A big piece of having BD vision is doing whatever it takes: everything within reason to get something done. This could be something like flying to another state on a whim for a face-to-face meeting to go the extra mile for a prospective partner to close a very important deal. For example, a BD employee might move mountains to help a prospective partner (in person) with a press meeting or an investor pitch in order to show commitment before the prospect agrees to partner with you. BD vision is about dedication and accomplishing major tasks together in many creative ways.

CHAPTER 2

TYPES OF BUSINESS DEVELOPMENT

DEVELOPING A BUSINESS through strategic partnerships is a process that can take many forms. The focus of the team, the types of partnerships involved, and the backgrounds and skills that are needed all depend on the interest and attention of the company and its business model. As a result, there are a few different types of business development, but they are all rooted in the principle that partnerships augment businesses and clients.

There is a big difference between working in BD for a company that is focused on getting new users, for a company that is looking for new business clients, and for a company that is looking for new business clients who will offer their users a product. There are three distinct types of BD: business-to-consumer (B2C), business-to-business (B2B), and business-to-developer (B2D), also known as B2B2C (business-to-business-to-consumer).

Business-to-Consumer

B2C refers to consumer-facing companies, which are those companies that deal directly with people who buy products or use services. Companies like Facebook, Twitter, Foursquare, Instagram, and Tumblr, in addition to retail companies like Amazon and Wayfair, operate in the business-to-consumer space. For these companies, the foundation and key to success is a broad user base, and the company develops its products to satisfy its consumers.

There are several revenue models for business-to-consumer companies. The two most popular are advertising and selling goods or services to consumers. Advertising is the most popular model for companies like Twitter, Facebook, and Google since the individual user, rather than a business, is the customer for the product. The company uses the customers' data to help advertisers provide better-targeted ads. On the other side of the equation are companies like Amazon, Birchbox, and Warby Parker, which sell physical products directly to consumers. There are some companies like Netflix that have a subscription model in which a user is charged a periodic (daily, monthly, or annual) fee to subscribe to a service.

Other times, consumers dictate the monetization of a business. This typically happens in community-based consumer companies and is possible only if you have a loyal and enthusiastic user base. The best example of a community-based consumer company is Reddit, a social news and entertainment website where registered users submit content in the form of either a link or a text post. When users spend a lot of time on a website, they put a lot of emotion into their interactions. Companies like Reddit make revenue several ways, including the sale of products and services, subscriptions for premium offerings, donations, and, in the past few years, advertising as well.

Another example of a B2C revenue model is the company Pinterest. Pinterest is a website and mobile app where you go to discover new things and collect virtual items. It is the twenty-first-century version of a scrapbook or pin board. There is a lot of commerce on Pinterest, and the site has experimented with monetizing by getting a portion of the sales of any product that is clicked on or purchased when the user goes from Pinterest to a retailer's site. These are known as classic cost-per-click (CPC) and cost-per-acquisition (CPA) models.

For a B2C company, the goal is to grow the business as quickly as possible. Companies that are able to scale and unlock the viral components of their web or mobile app by drawing the highest number of users usually become the front-runners in their space, regardless of first-mover advantage. This means that B2C companies and their founders feel the need to focus on building the best product, team, and vision simultaneously. Once these companies reach scale, the business model usually takes care of itself. For example, Google became a dominant search company before it figured out its business model or its monetization strategy, which ultimately took the form of advertising. The company, founded in the late 1990s, launched its search product as we know it today in 1998.

On the other hand, the monetization pieces known as AdSense and AdWords weren't launched until 2003. In Google's case, it focused on developing and enhancing its core product to scale for an ever-expanding consumer user base, then shifted its attention to monetization once it felt confident of its product.

When companies aren't selling a product, more often than not, the consumer is the product. B2C companies can be free, but that freedom comes with a price. While companies like Facebook, Tumblr, and Twitter are free, the number one way to monetize the business is through giving the user's information to advertisers. On the other spectrum of B2C, companies like Warby Parker sell a physical good or service that is immediately consumed by individuals.

A prime example of B2C monetization is Facebook. The social media site reached hundreds of millions of users before it seriously attempted to monetize. Similar to many other tech companies that focus on a consumer product, Facebook spent its early years developing and perfecting its product while cultivating a strong core user base. On the other hand, monetization came relatively late in the game, and Facebook reported its first revenues in 2006, two years after the site began to take off.

Josh Elman, a partner at Greylock Partners, a leading venture capitalist in Silicon Valley and a former product lead at companies including Facebook, Twitter, Zazzle, and LinkedIn, rejects the idea of focusing immediately on a company's monetization potential. Indeed, Elman has worked at companies with multimillion- and even multibillion-dollar valuations that have yet to earn a cent. Elman notes that there are four great questions that will help the inquirer arrive at a premonetization valuation:

1. Is there a new behavior here that can get 100 million or more people engaged?
2. Is the product evolving in a way that ensures that people are increasingly committed?
3. Will the growth be sustainable?
4. If the product succeeds at scale, are these key behaviors monetizable? Often, monetizing is not the most difficult problem; growing and maintaining a large user base by changing standard user behavior is the hardest challenge for a B2C company.

Business-to-consumer companies often grow slower than business-to-business companies because they need a critical mass of users, so BD and partnerships are often initially carried out by a founder. The founder knows his company better than an outside hire, and often 10 or 20 engineering, product, and design hires take place before that company hires another person who focuses on the business.

Companies that focus on their consumers have BD teams with the mandate to grow the user base. Therefore, the BD team actively solicits distribution deals. This means that you are looking to add high-quality users by teaming up with other companies that have overlapping demographics and/or geographics. These distribution deals consist of either a legal agreement between two parties to handle distribution of a product *or* two companies agreeing to promote each other to their respective user bases. The end goal is to get new users and usage of your product.

A great example of a B2C partnership is Facebook and Spotify. When Spotify launched in the United States, Facebook encouraged its hundreds of millions of users (at the time) to use the service. Spotify had a great product and was looking for scale, and Facebook had scale and was looking to offer its users a great music service. Spotify now has tens of millions of monthly active users, due largely to its partnership with Facebook.

Distribution deals aren't solely digital. There are some highly successful and innovative distribution deals that revolve around physical goods. One such example is Warby Parker and the Standard Hotel. Warby Parker is a New York–based vintage-inspired prescription eyeglasses company, and the Standard Hotel is a group of boutique hotels functioning as a subset of Andre Balazs Properties. The Standard Hotel added Warby Parker newsstands in Miami and Los Angeles to sell glasses. Warby Parker even made some limited-edition sunglasses that can be purchased only at these physical locations.

In addition, business-to-consumer companies typically build an application programming interface (API) for other companies to leverage. They know their user base and audience based on information they have gathered through transacting with those users; other companies often want to take advantage of the data and information that the company has collected to build their own third-party products.

APIs and BD

Having an interface that allows programmers to build on top of a B2C company's platform doesn't completely replace the need for BD positions. It does, however, remove the necessity of having a massive partnerships team that coordinates with any developer who wants to use the API to build a third-party site. These third-party users, in addition to the regular consumers, often influence the developmental direction of the core product. This will be covered in greater detail in Chapter 8, "APIs and BD."

Business-to-Business

Business-to-business companies are those that offer their services to other businesses, rather than to individual consumers. For example, Salesforce, Box, and Atlassian are all companies that develop products for other enterprises.

BD roles are scarce in B2B companies because these institutions are already focused on selling directly to other businesses. In the case of B2B companies, a head of sales or a monetization leader can often fill the traditional roles of business development professionals. The job of the head of sales, in most cases, is severalfold: to ensure that salespeople evangelize for the product, to keep a finger on the pulse of product utilization, and to remain cognizant of changes that may be necessary to attract and retain customers. The sales leader can also be responsible for identifying key business alliances or partnerships, filling this traditional business development need. BD and strategic partnerships are needed until you reach the level of transactions at which salespeople become necessary. Once the product or offering becomes saleable, then business development moves on to the next product.

While the monetization leader of a B2B company can often fill in for a business development team, there are quasi–business development roles that may exist at B2B companies if the job becomes cumbersome for someone in sales. These business development professionals, instead of sourcing deals and forging strategic partnerships, direct their attention to relationship management. When a B2B company has a large number of strategic clients running special initiatives with the company management or with the product, it sometimes requires individuals to manage the relationships with these clients. These professionals continuously listen to the partner or client, report back to the company's product professionals, and present an improved product that incorporates client feedback when applicable. These professionals are also keenly aware that if they are unable to incorporate the client's feedback into their product, it is likely that a competitor will.

One enterprise company that is known for engaging in business development with smaller companies is Salesforce. If the partnership is mutually successful, Salesforce will either continue the relationship or acquire the company. For example, Heroku, the cloud platform as a service (PaaS), began partnering with the CRM company and was eventually acquired by Salesforce in 2010. Heroku allows developers to deploy code and manage their apps without needing to think about servers or systems administration, and more than one million applications have been built using Heroku. The acquisition of Heroku was a way for Salesforce to continue providing support for (and gaining access to) the next generation of app developers.

Another example of a B2B company is Box, the cloud data storage company. Box targets the enterprise market, encouraging companies to buy licenses to the service that enable their employees to upload material, share files, and collaborate using its site and servers. It interfaces with companies directly instead of with consumers, and many of its partnerships involve partnering with other enterprises. One of its most recent partnerships is with a company called MobileIron, a mobile device management system that allows remote wiping of information from a mobile device. In the case of Box, adding such a service to its platform enhances the company's security offering, making it a viable choice for businesses that are concerned about employees misplacing devices that could have sensitive information on them.

Business-to-Business-to-Consumer or Business-to-Developer

Business-to-business-to-consumer firms, otherwise known as business-to-developer companies, are companies that power a particular feature on an unaffiliated product. B2B2C is a mouthful, but these companies indirectly touch consumers, who ultimately benefit from the service. Other businesses serve as the necessary intermediary. What are these companies exactly? SendGrid (an email deliverability service), Stripe (web and mobile payments, built for developers), Aviary (photo editing web and mobile API), and Twilio (voice, VoIP [voice over Internet Protocol], and SMS [short message service] applications via a web API) are examples of business-to-developer companies, which focus their attention on providing developers with the tools they need to simplify their own processes.

A BD team gets built out at the early stages of such a company's existence, driven by the need to sell to a product team or a developer. Some people call it the "powered by" solution. The trick with B2B2C/B2D is to build a scalable product and developer portal so that interested parties can easily get what they need and integrate the product as quickly as possible.

The unique thing about the B2B2C/B2D space is that the best offerings are simple to integrate and scale well. This is great for these types of companies, since their partnerships require only a few key employees to source and maintain developer allies and can manage some of the most successful deals.

Twilio, a company that we previously mentioned, is a communications company that, according to its website, "enables phones, VoIP, and messaging to be embedded into web, desktop, and mobile software." Companies like Airbnb, Intuit, and Hulu use Twilio to augment their offerings and interface directly with consumers. Airbnb, for example, uses Twilio as a way to enable hosts and guests to communicate over the phone without revealing each other's phone numbers. Intuit, a payroll software company that processes payroll for millions of businesses, uses Twilio's secure SMS feature to add a layer of security to its website. Video-streaming site Hulu built its premium phone support center on Twilio. All of these are prime examples of a successful business-to-business-to-consumer company.

When selling to other businesses, especially if it requires the tech team to integrate a technology solution that will be seen by users, it is best to have someone technical on your BD team. Lots of companies call this the "developer evangelist" role. This role is key to the success of any B2B2C offering, as this person is solely responsible for everything technical with regard to any integration.

The process of building a BD team for a B2D company is a unique one in that if you find the right first employee, you can go a long way without needing to build out a large team. The truth of the matter is that the first hire or two will have to act in a quasi-product role. Your goal is to talk to as many potential partners as you can. You need to ask them what they think of your existing offering, what they would need in order to make it work for them, and what the chances are of their integrating it if you deliver what they need.

Looking at all these types of BD at different companies should give you a strong understanding of what would be expected in a BD role at a startup company. Next we will talk about what the makeup of a BD team at a startup looks like and how to set yourself up for success.

CHAPTER 3

BD Team Structure

THE NEED FOR companies to enter into partnerships depends on the type of company involved, and the business development teams of different companies can have a diverse makeup as a result. While there is a general need for certain skills, each individual company will create a BD team that is best suited to its potential partnerships' needs. That being said, there are certain key elements that are usually needed when forming the perfect BD team at an early-stage company.

Founding Members and Initial Team Building

The first key player on the business development team is often a coach or tribe leader, usually a senior or founding member of the company and often a C-level executive. Having a BD team with one member continues until the initial person reaches his capacity. Once he reaches the point of needing a second pair of hands, the company usually hires a more junior BD employee to work with the business-focused founder. If the founder or founders are all technical, then this junior person would partner with the most senior business-focused individual. In those rare cases in which none of the early employees focus on the business, it is necessary to hire a director of BD or a general manager.

What are the credentials needed for such a role? Ideally, this candidate should have prior industry experience, a preexisting network, and ideas on how to grow the business side of the operation. This employee must be effective within 30 days of hire. This means coming in with a clear vision of the types of partnerships needed and a concrete network of partners that can be included to create a strategy. If the company already has a product that entices users or businesses, a seasoned BD professional should be able to close several deals and implement the partnerships within a reasonable period of time.

On the other hand, if the product is not ready or is not in a state in which users can enjoy it, a more senior BD professional can hit the ground running by doing market research to find out what needs to be added to or changed about the product. She will do so by talking to members of her network who are knowledgeable about the industry and to a cross section of the general user base to collect feedback, then relaying this information to the product and technical team so that it can make changes.

The second hire, a junior employee, should be a high-potential candidate who doesn't necessarily need prior experience in a BD role. This person's job is to support those team members who actively solicit deals, pitch the product, structure the partnerships, and finally, close the deals. This support takes the form of partner management, administrative tasks, and team organization. The role of the junior member is no less significant or meaningful than those of the other players, as this person serves as the spine of the team, helping to build presentation decks, keeping the deal pipeline orderly, and maintaining external relationships. This role becomes a stepping-stone to career advancement or being a vertical leader in the future if things fall into place.

The role of the junior-level BD member is an interesting one in that the candidate needs no true prior experience. Junior employees can almost literally come from any background and can benefit from having a variety of skills. What is most important is that the junior BD member and the founder or head of BD have a strong working relationship. Usually, the senior person takes the entry-level BD hire under her wing to learn the skills necessary to eventually run a piece of the business.

There are three major skills that allow a junior BD professional to excel. The first is to be a quick learner. If someone tells you something once, you should be able to quickly recall that piece of information. But if you make a human error once, it never happens again. The second is being a self-starter. For the most part, you will be a sponge soaking up knowledge. You will be given tasks, but at the same time you need to be aware of what needs to get done. There is no better kind of junior BD employee than one who gets things done with minimal direction. The third skill is being a problem solver. The big thing about being a junior BD professional is that you need to anticipate problems and solve them before they even arise. This is a difficult skill to have. It takes time to hone. But having the innate ability to predict issues and solve them is very important.

The junior BD employee will start by learning from the lead BD employee, but the faster she learns to be self-sufficient, the better her chances of success. She has access to the entire team internally, and given that startups are meritocracies (or at least try to be), junior BD people can become BD-leads in no time. If you can prove yourself by bringing in and closing deals, there is nowhere you can't go.

Jared Hecht learned about business development during his time at Tumblr, and as a cofounder, led the deal side at the beginning of GroupMe's existence. He says that there is no particular way for a junior person to study business development. Hecht argues that being great at business development means understanding how to solve problems strategically. "I think that the most important thing for people who start in business development, operations, strategy, and marketing is to develop a proficiency in learning how puzzle pieces fit together to make things work. The goal of someone who is pigeonholed into a BD position and wants to start a company should be to develop a comprehensive understanding of his deficiencies and turn them into competencies before taking the plunge."

Next, a mid-level person could be hired, in between the director-level position and the junior person. This third BD team member can be someone with an existing network of professionals related to the company's space and with enough domain knowledge to hit the ground running and liaise with C-level executives both at the company and at partnership organizations. She must also have the presentation skills to do this. This hire comes only if your important metrics are trending in the right direction.

C-Level Executives and the BD Team

The direction of the BD team needs to come from the COO, the general manager, or a vice president of business development. Think of the COO as the coach of a team who makes the executive decisions on which plays to run and determines the overarching team strategy. The head of BD is like a star pitcher who is surrounded by a team of seasoned players. It is the job of the pitcher to actually pitch the ball correctly, the way it is the job of a senior-level BD professional to actually conclude the deal, but the coach guides the team's goals, points out moments of opportunity, and ultimately leads the team to victory.

In general, most BD professionals have autonomy when it comes to managing partners and maintaining existing relationships. As a non-C-level executive, you must get new initiatives approved by a CEO or founder only if they are taking up a majority of your time and not allowing you to carry out your other tasks.

Alternative Team Makeups

As described previously, the second member of the BD team is often a junior BD employee to help the head of BD take on more deals. Alternatively, some companies strategize by hiring a second employee for the team who serves as a counterpart to the head of BD, focusing on a separate vertical segment or type of partnership. For example, payment companies may have an initial need to partner with e-commerce companies, but a secondary desire to align with gaming companies. The two realms require different areas of expertise and different networks, and thus might necessitate two senior-level BD employees.

Secondary Hires and Enhancing the Team

When rounding out the rest of the BD team beyond the first two key hires, there are several factors to consider. The first is that the team members should all be at the same location. Having one member in San Francisco, another in New York, and yet another in Seattle can become a major disaster and require a large amount of unnecessary overhead. Teams need to be in the same office, day in and day out. This may seem counterintuitive, since geographic diversity could also mean diversity of networks and Rolodexes. But it can also be divisive for a team that needs to work closely together as both internal and external partners.

If the company is at a stage in which it is entering into a large number of business partnerships, it will eventually become necessary to segment the BD team vertically. For example, at Aviary, the BD team was trying to partner with social networks, dating websites, blogging platforms, marketplaces, and more. Eventually, it became difficult for people to manage partnerships with different types of companies, so it made sense to reorganize the team vertically, with each individual member of the team focusing on a specific sector or group of businesses. When team members are focusing on individual sectors, otherwise known as being verticalized, it is crucial to have one central leader, which is ordinarily the head of BD or the COO. In addition to the team leader and the vertical experts, there is the developer evangelist.

Depending on the type of partnership the company seeks to develop, a BD team may also need an engineer or more technical person to serve as the developer evangelist. That role could also be taken by a person who focuses on product integrations.

Itai Ram, who worked as a new product introductions program manager at Apple and as the director of product management at Vidyo, focuses on product integrations. He says, "BD and product have an important relationship when it comes to enabling long-term and strategic growth of the company. While BD provides the general business direction and strategy objectives, it is up to the product team to recommend whether a partnership will make sense from a product offering, user experience, and overall product road map perspective. A lot of times there will be cases in which significant amounts of money are at stake, but the benefit to the user is, at the end of the day, negligible."

The Developer Evangelist

The job of a developer evangelist on a BD team is to liaise with partners and potential relationships at the technical integration level to provide hands-on guidance for using the company's platform, tapping into the application platform interface (API), or developing helper libraries to expedite integrations. This person can be especially helpful when pitching (or even closing) potential partnerships, since he can provide technical know-how on how the partnership can be structured from a logistical level. She knows what is technically possible and what is needed from various partners.

Companies that need a developer evangelist typically have a technical product to integrate. For example, companies like Facebook, Google, and Twitter all rely heavily on technical partnerships with other companies that build on top of the platform they provide. Without a developer evangelist, there would be no one to translate the technical needs of the partner companies.

A developer evangelist provides a mix of tech support (help for companies that are integrating the offering) and technical pitching and sales. Developer evangelists present at developer conferences and hackathons. Their background should be engineering-based so that they can help code and build applications (web and/or mobile), but also know how to tell a story. We discuss this role in more depth in Chapter 8, "APIs and BD."

CHAPTER 4

BUSINESS DEVELOPMENT
VERSUS SALES

BD IS A COVETED role for many people who are interested in the business side of the technology space. Some people, especially those coming from banking or management consulting roles, believe that BD means business strategy or business operations. People coming from marketing or sales roles can sometimes confuse BD with sales.

While these distinctions aren't exactly incorrect, they don't provide the whole picture. BD is often confused with sales because it involves pitching a product or offering and winning over a client for the mutual benefit of both parties. Sounds kind of like sales, right?

The Distinction Between BD and Sales

The biggest difference between BD and sales is that BD precedes sales in the process of growing a company and a business. The main function of a BD professional is to identify a potential transaction or relationship and repeat it as many times as possible in different iterations. Once a particular type of deal has happened a few times, a BD professional's job is to standardize the process and turn it into something that can be handed off to a sales team (whether the BD professional helps build out the sales team or not). Sales professionals, conversely, are hired only after a steady source of revenue has been identified and scaled to clients en masse. Once you have a sales team in place, there are goals concerning how many emails and calls they are expected to conduct, conversion of pitches to deals, and quotas (a specific number that you need to achieve in order to perform well). Sales professionals don't identify creative opportunities outside of their domain of expertise. Rather, within the confines of their mandate, sales professionals work on tweaking their sales pitches or tailoring them to the appropriate audience.

Matt Van Horn, former vice president of business at Path and at Digg, jokes that "BD is sales without a quota. I see BD as the business problem solver for an organization that often does many hard to measure projects but also plenty that are easy to measure. But overall, BD fixes things; it solves problems."

To illustrate Van Horn's point, imagine a payments company that has a great product that works extremely well for the education space, particularly tutoring. Once this niche market has been identified, the BD individual would seek to close deals with a targeted number of tutoring companies. Once she has proved the concept and the fit, the company might consider hiring a sales team focused on the tutoring vertical segment to bring on tons of companies. The company will have language and a process formalized, goals will be set, and compensation based on performance will be put in place.

Andy Ellwood, who was the vice president of sales at Marquis Jet before running business development teams at Gowolla and Waze, also believes that the distinction between BD and sales is about the goals and the end result rather than the skills required to do the job. "I am less and less convinced that there is a difference between BD and sales, just different deliverables as to what is considered a 'sale.' BD efforts typically have a longer timeline to close and more variables to work through in a product offering to get to a 'yes.' Sales efforts are more easily replicated and can lead to a decision more quickly because the 'product' comes as is. But, aside from timing and the measurable 'ask' (revenue or distribution), it is all just a different take on the same skill set. And what happens to the BD person? He or she becomes a trailblazer for another industry or type of partnership and starts the entire process again."

At the most basic level, BD requires a bit of creativity. Sales, on the other hand, takes a preexisting model that has been proven through a number of deals and can be quickly replicated by a team of employees.

How BD and Sales Differ at Different Types of Companies

As we saw in Chapter 2, "Types of Business Development," BD and its relationship to sales depends on the type of company. We mentioned previously that BD roles at B2B companies are scarce. Sales positions, on the other hand, are slightly more abundant. This construct is intuitive given the nature of the business: *selling* a product that businesses use and almost always must purchase means that there is a scale required that involves many salespeople.

By contrast, B2C companies that seek strategic distribution partnerships have a serious need for a BD professional before they hire salespeople. Indeed, a company's founder often takes the helm when it comes to strategic partnerships for early-stage B2C companies. Sales comes into play later in the game, especially when the company has an advertising-based monetization platform (Google, Facebook, and Twitter, for example). A B2C company might use strategic partnerships for the purpose of testing out different avenues of distribution before spending time on putting together a sales team and achieving sustainable monetization.

At B2D or B2B2C companies, BD is crucial early in the business and product life cycle. As at a B2C company, the BD individual acts as a partnership leader with a focus on product integration. Strategic partnerships in these cases focus on enhancing and tweaking the product. As a result, BD team members have their ear to the ground to listen to what prospective partners are looking for in the product, so they also serve as a product feedback loop for both the product and engineering teams.

BD "Sales" Versus Sales "Sales"

Every startup is always selling something. But selling does not necessarily mean sales. Instead, these companies are selling their vision for growing their user bases or their products to various audiences, including investors, press, prospective employees, and other companies for potential partnerships. But this kind of pitching does not involve selling a concrete product and therefore does not constitute "sales" in the traditional sense. In fact, most of this selling doesn't even bring in direct revenue!

On the contrary, sales is a very structured process in which the goods or services being sold have been tested and are applicable to a specific audience.

Traditional sales exists solely to drive direct, top-line revenue and to grow the business from a monetization perspective.

Who Does the Pitching?

The word *selling* can be interchangeable with the word *pitching*, which is ordinarily conducted by whoever is presenting or leading the partnership. This could be the founder or it could be the lead business development person, but it is almost always someone who has a holistic perspective on the company and the business. As mentioned in the previous chapter, "BD Team Structure," the person doing the pitching can be almost anyone on the BD team.

Marketing

A note about marketing, which does not usually enter into this process. It is conducted in conjunction with the sales process rather than at the pitching or strategic partnership level, except in rare circumstances.

Business development and marketing are not mutually exclusive. While the nature of the jobs of a BD professional and a marketing professional can be very different, partnerships themselves can become a marketing strategy for a particular brand.

For example, when he was in the music industry as the senior director of marketing at Arista Records, Zeeshan Zaidi, cofounder of the startup Host Committee, worked with Starbucks to develop partnerships between coffee shops and artists. According to Zaidi:

> A classmate of mine from business school worked at Starbucks, and she put me in touch with an executive named Tim Ziegler from the music division, and we spoke over a few months about the possibilities. We finally crafted a comprehensive marketing partnership that included Starbucks selling Sarah [McLachlan]'s new CD in their stores and selling her music digitally on its website, Sarah creating a special "Artist's Choice" playlist of some of her top influences which would be sold as a CD in Starbucks stores, and lots of print advertising by Starbucks pushing the promotion.

This deal solved a major problem my company was facing—how to amplify our marketing push given our limited resources. It was a huge win for both sides. We got lots of marketing support from a major retail force where our target audience lived. Starbucks got exclusive content and an association with a superstar artist, which not only generated a halo effect but drove traffic into its stores. In addition, we created such a compelling partnership that Starbucks turned it into a formal program, which it then repeated with many other major artists.

CHAPTER 5

NETWORKING

A BIG COMPONENT of business development is partnering with other people, companies, and organizations for the mutual enhancement of products and services. As a result, networking is an integral part of BD, especially in the early stages of your company's existence. Networking is equal parts art and science, and there are particular types of networking that serve BD professionals differently than other fields.

Physical, in-person networking is the cornerstone of meeting other people, but in the BD realm, there is a shift toward digital networking. Unlike networking in most other fields, BD networking encourages connecting online as much as it does connecting in person, and we will delve into this topic later in the chapter.

There is a networking strategy for those professionals who are seeking to break into the BD space and are doing their networking with the intention of finding a job. This kind of mingling is not dramatically different from the second type of networking, which is conducted for the purpose of expanding your potential partnership base and your contact list in general. There is a saying in BD that a person is only as valuable as her network, and it is true that without such a network, a BD professional will have difficulty sourcing high-value deals and getting in front of the right people. To combat this, there are several tactics and styles of networking that can be carried out, even without a large jumping-off point.

Professional Networking Events

The first step to successful networking is determining the correct events to attend. This seems like an obvious point, but regardless of whether the purpose is job seeking or partnership outreach, time is valuable and should not be wasted on the wrong events. The best way to determine the right kind of BD events is to use your judgment and consider the motives: if a professional is looking to expand his network, an event that attracts individuals in a particular field of interest, company, or organization is ideal. Networking events like these are often part of a series of recurring events and provide many opportunities to meet the desired demographic (think of a monthly meet-up or breakfast). If the goal is to build the largest network possible, attending two, or even three, of these events each week will help BD professionals get recognized and known by regulars.

Another good way to determine whether an event will be worthwhile is to check the guest list. Most broadcasted events use systems like Eventbrite for RSVPs, and the guest lists are often publicly available. There is no harm in checking who might be attending the event, and if the list has enough people that you'd like to meet, it is probably worth attending.

While these methodologies often yield the most efficient results, combing through RSVP lists isn't always a sustainable solution. Social media is an incredibly effective way to scale networking, and using it will also make the process a two-way street. By using Twitter to follow influential people in the space, it is easy to find out when and where they will be attending an event. The same may apply for a company Twitter handle that broadcasts information about events. Following companies on Eventbrite or Facebook has the same effect.

Selecting, RSVPing, and showing up at a networking event is only half the battle. Before the event begins, it is crucial that you become educated about what is out there: what companies or industries will be represented, and what current events are taking place in that space. This current news knowledge involves reading and recalling product announcements, funding news, trend stories, acquisitions, partnerships, and public blunders. Once you have familiarized yourself with the space, it is important that you turn to more specific industry leaders for thought-provoking and specific insights.

Once the pre-event education recon has taken place, it is time to enjoy the actual networking function and maximize the use of your time at the event. Here are some important factors for success at a networking event.

1. Stay Focused and Find the People You Preidentified

The easiest way to do this is to spot them in the crowd and introduce yourself. When you introduce yourself, remember not to mention that you know who they are before they introduce themselves (it's the difference between charming and creepy).

2. Have a Punchy and Memorable Introduction

Err on the side of reintroduction. Networking opportunities can be overwhelming, and people amass a great number of connections at such events. Having a memorable self-introduction that includes more than simply your name ensures having an exciting initial conversation and provides grounds for a follow-up. For example, stating your name and your company or another piece of identifying information with which you can be associated is a simple starter topic and will often lead to fruitful conversations. In addition, the two pieces of information can form an associative memory for the other party. And, unless you see or speak to someone relatively frequently, it is safe to assume that a reintroduction is necessary.

Keep in mind that an introduction can change depending on the theme or nature of the networking event. It is important that you curate and express the right facts when you are meeting individuals. For example, if a networking event revolves around a particular theme or vertical segment, it is important for you state your relationship to that theme or segment.

3. Go with the Flow and Meet New People, Especially Unexpected, Unidentifiable New Faces

It is very important to meet new faces at events, regardless of whether or not you have previously researched them. Critical connections can be made in the most unexpected places, and chances are that at a networking event for tech professionals, there are other like-minded individuals. Meeting new people, especially outside of your existing network, is the best way to grow your network and open up new pockets of contacts.

4. No-Shows Are Opportunities for Offline Catch-Up

RSVPs can be misleading at times, and if someone has RSVPd yes but never showed up, or if she left before you were able to speak with her, it is perfectly fine to send that person an email (search online for or guess her email address) with a short note of introduction, mentioning your desire to meet and connect with her after the event. Ask to sit down over coffee or to tell her about your company or yourself in another setting.

5. Never, Ever Interrupt

It is by no means appropriate in any professional situation to interrupt two people who are talking to each other, but this is especially important at a networking event. If two people are engaged in conversation, respectfully wait for a pause or lull in the conversation before interjecting. This may seem like more of a general etiquette lesson, but it is important nonetheless.

6. Ask for a Business Card and Carry Your Own

The whole purpose of attending these events is to build a network, so it is critical that you have a means of following up. Providing others with a business card gives them a reason to remember the conversation or the connection made.

In addition, always provide a professional business card with your company-issued email address. A personal business card is a no-no in this game. If possible, try to ask for a standard-size business card. Too often, companies, especially in the tech space, offer smaller or more compact business cards to employees because they look edgy or are more practical to carry, but in reality those cards get lost far too easily when they are handed out.

Laurie Racine, cofounder of Startl, an education technology advisory and accelerator focused on nurturing talent and products for the next generation of education, is a master of making connections:

> We can all learn how to exercise the various "social muscles" that make it relatively easy to put together the people around us that we, in twenty-first-century parlance, call our network. Personally, if I had to prioritize which behaviors I have found most helpful in building my connected world, I would say this:
>
> 1. *Know when to talk and when to listen.* Meeting people online, at events, at the office, or at random doesn't matter. It's important to find out what another person is doing, first—what that person cares about and what he is working on—and then relate that back to your own frame of reference.
> 2. *Be generous and be collegial.* It's amazing what erring on the side of generosity can do. I am not suggesting that you should be a door-

mat, but offering to make introductions for others leads to others being more willing to make introductions for you.

3. *Be intellectually curious.* Being a jack-of-all-trades is not always a bad thing. The more you know about a variety of topics, even at a cursory level, the better you will be at connecting the intellectual dots. Follow the gray matter.

4. *Be fearless.* Put yourself out there; get into situations that are outside your intellectual comfort level. Don't try to be the smartest person in the room. Hell, don't be afraid to be the least-informed person in the room. Just be in the room.

Follow Up

After the event has concluded, it is critical that you reach out and maintain your connections. Using the business cards you collected, promptly send a short email thanking that person for taking the time to connect with you and set a concrete time and topic for potential follow-up. Adding those new connections on LinkedIn shortly after the event can also ensure the longevity of the connection.

Alternative Forms of Networking

Every event, small or large, should be treated as a networking opportunity, regardless of the forum. Networking has only become more ubiquitous, and therefore more important, with the Internet. Having a perfected introduction can come in handy in the most unlikely places (at the gym, at a party, in the grocery store, and in many other nonprofessional settings). Having a personal or company pitch ready at the drop of a hat can be the primary reason for closing a partnership deal.

Events can often be prohibitively expensive or exclusive. Brian Kil, business development and partnerships employee at Dwolla, suggests that volunteering can be a good alternative to signing up for an event. "Many of the best events are invitation-only, costly, or both. By volunteering, you can enter these semiexclusive events without having to pay anything or know anyone."

Other alternative forms of networking events, apart from the strict meet-and-greet forums, are things like Skillshare, Udemy, and General Assembly classes, subject-matter speaker series, or even product launch events. Keeping a finger on the pulse of these will also open doors to other people and events that are of interest, and will cultivate and define the perfect BD network. The following are alternatives to standard networking.

Start a Blog

Maintaining a written, thoughtful online presence can allow the author to network with the people who read the blog. It is common for blog readers to reach out to talk to the author based on posts they have read, and these are people with whom it is worth connecting. It usually means that the person either likes technology, startups, or BD or is generally engaged with and passionate about the subject matter.

Many of the business development professionals and founders we profile later in the book got their start by blogging. Eric Friedman, director of revenue operations at Foursquare, got his job at Union Square Ventures after the people there were impressed by his online presence, which included his blog. He used his blog as an outlet for expressing his opinions about the world of digital media agencies. Scott Britton, former BD lead at SinglePlatform, uses his blog to share his work with those who are interested and believes that broadcasting it is important. Finally, Charlie O'Donnell of Brooklyn Bridge Ventures is known for his blog, which has been credited with getting many people jobs and talent introductions.

In general, blogs are a creative outlet through which you can express your opinions about the world around you, become a subject-matter expert and disseminate your wisdom, or make predictions about the future. Blogs don't necessarily have to focus on business or partnerships—in fact, they are often more interesting if they have real-world applications or stories. They should provide a window into your brain.

In addition to writing a blog, you should be engaged with others' blogs by staying active in the comments section of relevant blogs and sites. Many thought leaders, founders, and venture capitalists in the tech space have regularly maintained blogs and even respond to comments posted on their sites. A well-reasoned, thought-provoking response can garner the attention of other leaders and can be a launchpad.

Teach or Attend a Class

There are several types of postgraduate professional development courses. Skillshare, General Assembly, and Udemy are three of the places where such classes are offered, and they are among the best places to network. Attending, or even teaching, a course can provide possibilities not only for learning and professional skill building, but also for meeting interested, like-minded individuals.

Get Active on Twitter

Twitter is a place where the world stage is accessible to anyone, and almost anyone who has a Twitter handle is accessible for conversation on the platform. Since Twitter is an interest network with an asymmetric follow model, it is a great place to connect with like-minded individuals. It is easy to follow thought leaders and disrupters in a space and even engage with them in a single tweet. It is a great place to have conversations and network with people without necessarily needing to go out and do physical networking.

Engage and Use Early-Adopting Community Platforms

Becoming an active early adopter of an idea or a platform can have the same effect as networking in a small room of powerful players. These platforms can either provide an opportunity to get in touch with key people (for example, venture capitalists who have invested in the idea or platform and thought leaders) or to make a splash and get known for being great on the platform. This often sparks dialogue and can even serve as the foundation for offline connections.

Networking is the cornerstone for much of what happens in the BD world. Mastering these skills can mean gaining the BD vision, becoming a strategic partnership master, and even making deals that matter.

Turntable.fm was a site that was popular from 2010 through 2013. It allowed anyone to be a virtual DJ or listen to others' DJ sets. While Alex worked at Aviary, he used Turntable.fm one night, and one of the people in the same room decided to strike up a virtual conversation with him. It turned out that the other person was working on a photo-sharing mobile app and was looking for editing and filter tools but didn't have the means to build them in-house. Alex and he set up a call the next day, and he began integrating Aviary's API into his product. Early adopting can mean setting up a network, even if unrelated, that can turn into business deals.

Events and BD

Much of networking, as described previously, takes place at events. But one of the ways in which you can grow your network and meet new people is by starting and running your own events.

It doesn't matter whether you start the event yourself or get involved with an already existing event. Simply being at the center of the event helps you to be good at networking, and by extension BD. By starting or volunteering at an event, you get access and exposure to things you wouldn't otherwise be involved in.

Organizing or Getting Involved with Events

Organizing an event is the best way for a BD professional to submerge herself in the BD community (or any community, for that matter). Doing so often involves collaboration with other BD professionals and attracts like-minded individuals. Organizing or even attending an event can also be an ideal way to merge two points of interest, whether this involves an overlap between a personal and a professional topic or a harmony between two unrelated industries. For example, dog owners who are also technology professionals may have more in common than meets the eye, and organizing a BD professionals event for dog owners may bring together people with common interests. This is a fantastic way to expand a network and make meaningful connections.

Running Events as a Business

Whether this means putting together a business conference for an industry of interest (organized by a particular company) or a technical event like a hackathon, running events as a business could be a boon for the company that is doing it. For example, Aviary, a photo-editing company, announced in April 2012 that Flickr would be integrating Aviary's photo editor onto its site. This deal was a crucial strategic partnership for Aviary, since it would allow it to tap into Flickr's enormous user base and expand the reach of its product. And the way this partnership came about was through a fortuitous tech event.

In August 2011, Aviary hosted an event called Photo Hack Day in which photo-based technology companies were encouraged to build or enhance products. When Aviary announced that it was hosting the event, there was a great outpouring of interest from photo companies of all sizes, including Flickr.

During the event, Flickr and Aviary had unlimited access to each other's teams, from engineers to people on the business side. They began preliminary discussions of integrating the two technologies during that hackathon weekend, and the conversation picked up after the introductions at Photo Hack Day.

In January 2012, with unexpected but favorable timing, Aviary's biggest competitor, Picnik (which had been acquired by Google in 2010), shut down, as Google was looking to consolidate its products. Flickr happened to be a partner of Picnik, and a deal became a reality when Flickr was looking for alternative solutions because of Picnik's shutdown.

The partnership was a great win for both sides, since Flickr had a need that it was seeking to fill, and Aviary was looking to grow its user numbers. When you are looking for partnerships in one specific industry, putting together hackathons or industry-specific events for BD introductions can do wonders for expanding a business network.

Whether it be personal, professional, or as a business, events and BD go hand-in-hand. A business development individual can gain recognition or build a reputation by organizing events month after month. A business can reap tangible results by organizing events. There is no better way to become the center of attention in your industry and grow your network.

CHAPTER 6

INTERNATIONAL BD

UNTIL NOW, WE have primarily discussed BD in the United States and the cultural assumptions that go with it. BD is, of course, an international game as well. With tech companies popping up all over the globe, partnerships that reach across borders are becoming increasingly common.

For starters, it is critical to keep a finger on the pulse of the general BD market. But as mentioned in the section in Chapter 1 titled "BD Vision," if you are to be as savvy as possible, it is also important that you keep an eye on international BD transactions and noteworthy events. Certain industries and subvertical segments develop at different paces in different countries, and at the very least it is critical that you understand different interests' business patterns in other key markets.

Countless companies have launched internationally and found out that there is a vast population of people who are waiting to consume their product. There are many endeavors, including the ubiquitous social networks, that were initially duds in the United States but hits internationally, since they resonated with the culture and consumers there. Twitter is a great example of a company that rocketed on the international level. Social attitudes concerning information sharing differ across borders, and companies can find varying degrees of success depending on the local culture.

For example, Lars Fjeldsoe-Nielsen, former head of mobile at Dropbox and current mobile lead at Uber, finds that whenever he does deals, he must be cognizant of cultural nuances and differences so as not to offend anyone. "I find it necessary . . . to be the buffer between partners and my company. A lot of cultural differences are lost in translation."

Part of the key to international BD is having a product that can be tailored to various markets. For example, Twitter is able to curate and localize its platform for each country because of the asymmetric follow model and the number of local celebrities who are on the platform. On the other hand, even Facebook, despite its years of dominance, still has big holdout countries like Russia and Japan because of competitors VK and Mixi, respectively. Localized companies in countries like China, which blocks U.S.-based social media, essentially imitate the models of American companies.

Companies that are considering entering new markets, especially internationally, must take cultural nuances into account. Many companies that are just starting to monetize overseas and want to enter markets that have high barriers to entry call upon reseller partners. These teams are affiliated third parties that help sell the company's product, and often have teams dedicated to doing so, but remain separate entities. This is common in Latin American markets other than Brazil and Asian markets other than Japan, which are more nuanced. Companies set revenue goals for this third party and a timeline for the relationship, and if the goals are met, the partnership is successful.

Eric Batscha of Knewton, an adaptive learning platform that personalizes educational content, has had extensive experience doing deals across international lines. He spent time living in Beijing when he worked as an account manager at Yahoo!, and he has led many international deals. Batscha describes the best advice he has received for conducting these transactions and also advises that in addition to understanding the cultural nuances, you still have to have a fantastic product for both regions:

> The best advice I got when I was first thinking about doing business internationally was, "Just come here." Seemingly banal enough guidance, it has paid dividends throughout my career as I've worked in China and throughout the Asia-Pacific region. Whether it was to find a job or to close a deal, my success rate dramatically increased when I was on the ground. Being face-to-face with a potential partner is always better, whether you are talking to a media executive in New York City or a brand manager at a detergent company in Guangzhou, China.
>
> Particularly in Asia, maybe because of how far you are geographically from "the west," local and expatriate professionals alike view you as a "visitor." How could you know about their business if you've spent

only a few weeks in their market? They don't care about how much market research you've done online or with third parties. Why would they trust you with their multimillion-dollar budget if you can just get on a plane and be gone in 14 hours?

By the same token, if you do move to Asia or make the investment to spend six months or more in a market, you are granted a veneer of credibility: "You must care about my business if you are willing to come all this way and stick around." That credibility goes only so far, however. Your product still has to work and deliver value.

CHAPTER 7

FINDING YOUR BD MENTOR

ONE OF THE most important reasons to network in any field is to find a mentor or sponsor who can serve as a guide during various professional junctures and can also provide key introductions when necessary. BD professionals, in particular, have several potential career paths available to them and thrive on building relationships with others. This combination makes having a BD mentor all the more beneficial.

Mentors Versus Sponsors

Traditionally, the difference between mentorships and sponsorships is that mentorships are professional relationships, in which the mentor provides advice and guidance about professional matters. Sponsors, a term coined by Sylvia Ann Hewlett in her book *Forget a Mentor, Find a Sponsor*, are those who go to bat for a professional individual, providing him with the proper connections and finding moments to promote or advance his career wherever possible. In the world of BD, the former may be the one to provide guidance and overall career recommendations concerning the types of companies to work for, teams to join or build, or skill-building opportunities. The latter will provide a relationship that could be the catalyst for deal-related introductions, promotions, or even alternative job opportunities.

How to Find a BD Mentor or Sponsor

The most obvious place to turn for a BD mentor is someone who is directly on the BD team, a boss or manager. As mentioned in Chapter 3, "BD Team Structure," this person could be the COO of the company, the head of BD, or even the leader of a division, depending on the size of the company.

When you are looking for a mentor, it is best not to explicitly ask someone to be your mentor, but rather to let it happen organically. Often, a more senior individual will take an interest in a junior professional with whom she has worked on a project or who has been assigned to the same team. It is natural for a mentor to be a superior at the same company, since mentoring often occurs during professional interaction. For BD professionals, an important mentor to seek out is the head of BD or the COO of the company. These senior individuals can accelerate a junior BD member's role on the team, provide career paths, and serve as role models.

For those who are interested in a long career in the BD space, it is also important to cultivate mentor or sponsor relationships with other members of the team within the company and with BD professionals at other companies.

When seeking out mentors who work on other teams or at different companies, it is best to think about what you need most from the relationship. There are some who have countless mentors, each one for a different industry: a mentor for fund-raising (a founder who has raised funds before and knows the game), a mentor for hiring and attracting the best talent (someone who has been successful in a hiring function), a mentor for design (a talented designer), a mentor for engineering (someone to help them scale their business), and more to help guide them along their career path.

For BD, you want to cultivate a network of mentors as well. Sarah Friar, CFO of Square, encourages people to think of this network of mentors as a "personal board of directors." In our opinion, the first should be your immediate boss to help your professional development. The next should be someone with years of experience outside of your company, so that you can learn from this person, take long-term career advice from him, and confide in him. Anything beyond that is up to you. If you want a mentor for deal closing, get one. If you want a mentor for pitching, go for it.

You don't find mentors; mentors find you. What this means is that mentors and their mentees just fit. You can't force it. You can do all the work to identify the right people, but at the end of the day, either you'll match or you won't. The best way to find the right mentors is to spend time with those people in their natural habitat. If you are looking for a design mentor, go to a design meet-up, event, or conference. If you are looking for a community manager mentor, go to some sort of community manager gathering. Once you get in front of enough prospective mentors, either you'll click with someone or you won't. You don't need to make it especially formal. A mentor can be someone you call upon every once in a while for some sage advice, or you can sit down with a mentor once every three months to connect. At the end of the day, it is up to you to cultivate and maintain these relationships.

Formal Mentorship Programs

Many more established companies have programs associated with human resources or learning and development that offer formal mentorship pairings of people within the company. These programs can be a great asset to new members of BD organizations and have significantly fewer barriers to entry when it comes to finding a mentor.

Formal mentorship programs do not necessarily focus squarely on mentoring (although plenty of them do). These sponsored mentorship initiatives can include incubators like Techstars, Y Combinator, or 500 Startups. They serve as a community or network in which members can seek mentorship from either alumni or people in the space who are designated as mentors for the program.

In most cases, formal mentorship programs assign two relevant parties, a mentor and a mentee, who are matched for specific reasons. These reasons can include shared previous experience, common interests, or simply working in related fields. Most of the time, the two have never worked together in a formal professional setting, and most of the interactions are predicated on the fact that these two people were paired intentionally. Formal mentorship programs are a great way to be introduced to members of the company in other areas and to expand your network. If cultivated correctly, these relationships can stretch beyond the duration of the formal mentorship program period and, like networking relationships, can ultimately turn into jobs or partnership opportunities down the road.

CHAPTER 8

APIs and BD

API IS A BUZZWORD often associated with technology companies that many people on the business side do not know much about. But BD and APIs go hand-in-hand, and it is critical for BD professionals to understand how an API works. When you are pitching another company for a partnership, the API can become the backbone of a product integration or a portal to a variety of information that helps sweeten the deal.

APIs for Beginners

What is an API? It stands for application programming interface, and it serves as a portal that third-party developers can use to build on top of a platform. It is a specification for how certain software components should interact with each other in order to marry two technologies. Through an API, a developer is able to extract available information or functionality that she can utilize for her own application.

APIs and BD

It might seem like an unlikely pairing, but APIs and BD have a critical relationship. APIs help speed up partnerships between two companies. They give developers the ability to grab functionality and/or build upon the platform, therefore making a partnership easier to execute.

APIs are common at business-to-consumer (B2C) companies, since these organizations have information about consumers that other developers would like to access. APIs work best in strategic partnering when the programming interface is accessible, easy to understand, and usable. For this reason, companies often work in conjunction with potential partners to develop functionality that these third parties might want to use. Doing so also allows the company to set the direction in which it wants external developers to go.

While B2C APIs are all about information, business-to-business-to-consumer (B2B2C) APIs focus on functionality. A great example of a B2B2C company with an API is Aviary, which shifted its business from a destination website for powerful photography-editing tools to a web and mobile lightweight editing platform, and it did so with developers and companies guiding it along the way. While the management at Aviary had a general idea and direction, input from both developers and companies helped to shape both the initial product and future iterations. This bet paid off in spades, as Aviary announced two years later that it had 50 million monthly active users (MAUs), leaps and bounds higher than the prepivot MAU number.

Why do companies *need* APIs? There are typically two use cases for APIs, and they are both pertinent to an early-stage technology company's BD strategy. The first is that building an API cultivates a developer community, which ultimately allows companies to extend the ability of their platform. Most of these services are free, are easy to use, and offer the company great ideas concerning what features to build next, and how.

The second is for monetization. Sometimes APIs as a service are free, but when they are monetized by other companies, the original entity asks for a royalty or a percentage of the proceeds. Most often, APIs are free for use by developers, but it is also plausible for a company to charge for use or access to its API. Twilio, SendGrid, and TokBox all charge developers and partners to use their APIs, and probably do so to weed out those who are not serious about developing on their platforms. Both use cases make it much easier for a company to get the functionality it needs and/or partner with another company without the heavy lifting of custom integrations for each partnership.

Next Step: Developer Portal

Once the API has been built and strategic partnerships are aligned, the next most important element of an API is the usability and accessibility of the API itself. In order to provide this, companies create a website dedicated to interfacing with the product, called a *developer portal*. This website houses everything that another company would need in order to get up and running with your API. The best developer portals are a one-stop shop: the goal is to have developers and other companies build on the API without ever needing to contact the company itself! This helps a company become infinitely scalable.

When APIs were a new concept, initial access to the information was very cumbersome and required specific technical abilities. But the concept of a developer portal has advanced the cause of the API, making it more accessible to a wider audience. Indeed, a big misconception about developer portals is that they are only for developers. This is not always the case. More often than not, especially as it pertains to BD deals, a business-focused or nontechnical founder of a potential partner stumbles upon the API section of the website and starts browsing the developer portal. For that very reason, companies make it very easy for nontechnical prospective partners to see from their developer portals what kinds of functionality the company provides from its API. That prospective company will be assessing whether the functionality is the appropriate fit for the company; if the developer portal is too confusing, that nontechnical founder will probably make the executive decision not to build on top of that company's platform, regardless of how great the API is for developers.

For example, at Dwolla, the developer portal has a treelike functional structure. Upon someone's entering the developer portal, the first question is whether the individual can code. If the answer is yes, the user is brought to a more technical interface that delves into API documentation. On the other hand, if the answer is no, the user is brought to the nontechnical side of the portal. This provides key talking points about why Dwolla is an appropriate partner and how the company can provide developers with successful products. It also contains answers to commonly asked questions and links to appropriate points of contact.

The developer portal is an unsung hero in the connection between APIs and BD, and can actually be the reason why two companies might partner. However, the portal alone is not enough; you still need to know the product inside and out, and understand exactly how the integration will work. Tanuj Parikh, head of business operations at Estimote, speaks of the importance of APIs when he was working on partnerships at GroupMe. "GroupMe has a public API that powers group chat functionality in third-party apps (mobile or web). We successfully pitched this API to both brands (for example, lululemon and ESPN) and developer shops (for example, Xomo and SEED Labs). In both cases, the key strategy was being product-oriented. What I mean by that is understanding the full technology stack of your product and exactly how the integration will work. This enabled our BD team to anticipate questions and concerns, heading them off throughout the entire process."

How to Attract Users to an API

Partnerships based on information sharing are predicated on the fact that the company has a usable API that attracts consumers and developers to build upon it. Indeed, most companies have difficulty persuading developers to utilize their API at the start, and there are a few methods for gaining API notoriety if that is the case.

Launch the API with a Few Companies Already Using It

Before the API is complete, it is important to have preliminary conversations with potential partners that might benefit from the API. Doing so legitimizes the API as integration-friendly. It also creates a ripple effect of companies integrating, since being able to point to active integrations helps prospective companies get over the "who is using it?" hump. Finally, developing strategic partnerships in advance can garner press, publicity, and increased awareness of both the API and the other companies that have integrated the product.

When an API is launched without a potential pipeline of companies that are interested in using it, the company should have extremely low expectations for the outcome. This often happens as a result of a mismatch between what the product offers and what users and developers want. This can be indicative of larger sustainability and scaling problems for the platform as a whole. But the worst thing that can happen is to invest resources and time building an API that no one else is interested in using.

Events

APIs help with pitching and closing and are a huge part of the future of product-related BD. Holding events helps you get companies that you want to work with all in the same room; hackathons, in particular, are a great way to showcase an API and get feedback from developers in the field as they utilize it. This is a key way to demo an API and give developers incentives to build on the platform. When you sponsor an event, most likely a hackathon, the publicity and feedback are inherent, and the API team gets real-time developer communication.

Hackathons can be successful because the focus is on the company and its potential for outside development. When the API is the center of attention, it is very easy to get many target companies or developers in the same room for a concentrated period of time, which will aid in building a meaningful relationship with each one. While hackathons seldom produce actual products that are launchable by the end of the hackathon, they are hugely beneficial in helping a company establish itself with its peers and the types of companies it would like to have as partners.

If the hackathon is hosted by another company, our advice is to participate at the lowest sponsorship level and offer a slick prize for people who use your API. This usually has the best results in terms of engagement with developers. On top of that, hackathons are a great opportunity to talk to developers about your offering and get honest feedback to make it better. Many companies use hackathons to release early versions of their API or features in their API so that they can get this key developer input.

Developer Evangelist

Although BD professionals work very closely with partners to encourage them to use the company's APIs, the intricate aspects of the integration often require someone with technical skills. The developer evangelist fulfills exactly this need: it is the job of this individual to work with both the BD team and the engineering team that is developing and managing the API, and to interface with potential developer partners. He is expected to "evangelize" the API, ensuring that users and partners understand how the platform works.

A developer evangelist works with BD professionals and engineers in general to explain the possibilities (and limits) of the company's API. He can liaise with the engineering teams of other companies and speak knowledgeably about the feasibility of collaborating, and can lend credibility to the company's efforts using the API. The developer evangelist also answers technical questions for both members of the BD team within the company and potential external partners. Finally, he can troubleshoot and triage technical problems with a partner integration.

Planning for the Future

It is important to keep in mind that the API is part of a larger business strategy that will ultimately grow the business. This means that the API and the developer portal must be treated as dynamic features of a company's platform. Therefore, it is critical to engage in constant dialogue with users of the service, and to iterate the product so that it is always something that those partners want to use.

Since APIs are often launched in stages, once the product is launched for general availability, it is more difficult to control what the service is used to accomplish. This is a delicate balancing act; sometimes companies make only a certain subset of their data available through the API, instead of permitting developers to access everything. The tactic of supplying only some information through the API is generally used when the company is afraid of having other developers build products that actually compete with the platform. The danger of taking this approach is that if the API is too restricted, it will become unusable.

Some APIs are simply portals for retrieving information, while others actually have their own functionality. These APIs, like Facebook's and Twitter's, require partners to build on top of the data they are able to obtain. Other APIs include functionality like photo editing, payment processing, or SMS texts. These interfaces can be easier for nonengineers to utilize, so consider the format before building an API.

9

A Career in BD

BD for technology companies, especially startups, is a relatively young "profession" in its current form, but its roots stem from the career trajectories of many other types of business roles. Because pitching and closing are both major elements of a job in business development, we feel that it's important to outline the stages of business development at which you begin pitching and closing, and to outline how those skills can ultimately be used. Since BD is such a popular career option for young people, we have outlined several possible tracks for professionals who are interested in carving out a career in BD.

Landing the First Job

As with any first or entry-level job, getting an offer to work in BD at a tech company is highly coveted. There are several strategies that work particularly well for lower-level opportunities at tech companies.

The first step is to find exciting and growing industries that provide the potential for job opportunities and career development. The possibilities are endless; education, fashion, healthcare, payments, social, local, photo, and video are among many industries in which technology companies are doing big things. Once you've listed 10 companies in each vertical segment that excites you, you should next identify the key employees at these companies. These are the people you would love to work for or with. BD employees are only as good as their direct bosses. A good boss can help accelerate your career a few years in a short time.

Now that you have all this mapped out, it is time to read everything you can about these vertical segments, companies, and key employees. You should be reading what they are reading, and also what they are writing. This goes for every industry, not just startups. Every sector has its own publications and thought leaders. For startups, these are tech blogs and publications like *TechCrunch, VentureBeat,* and *Fast Company,* and thought leaders who have personal blogs, such as Fred Wilson, Chris Dixon, and Mark Suster. Consume it all.

Once you've done your research and are up to date with current events in the industry, it's time to meet the people; it's networking time! As with reading, every industry has its major events. Some industries have frequent events, while others have only one or two a year. If you go to these events too early, you risk coming off as uneducated or not "with it," which is why doing research and reading is *crucial* before you start intense networking. Networking is one of the best ways to meet people and get prospects for jobs.

The dirty secret about most of the best jobs is that they are never listed. Either the employer knows whom it wants for the job, which happens more often than you might think, or there is a backroom discussion before a job is even available. In the startup world, this is typically done by investors and venture capitalists. If a company with venture capital funds backing it is planning on hiring a business employee within the next six months, the VC has foreknowledge of this. The VC is also looking to help its portfolio startups in any way possible. Couple these, and if your network has a few investors, they are the best place to start when you are looking for your first BD role.

This isn't to say that no one gets hired through traditional online applications and interviews. It's just not easy when you have no relationship with the company. Companies go to their networks first, and that network recommends people. If they can't find someone through that network, then they post the job.

One way to get noticed early on is by doing some work as an intern for a company in a BD role. Many companies hire their interns to become full-time, and those interns become important employees as the company grows. If you can demonstrate that you can be a valuable asset to a company (you do great research, you have great insights, and so on), you will get a full-time offer if the company is expanding.

Sometimes, but not always, it even makes sense to do an unpaid internship for a company. Unpaid internships are tricky because as an intern, you should balance working for free and adding enough value that the company can't function without you. This was the case with Erin Pettigrew, who began as an intern at Gawker and worked her way up through the ranks to become the vice president of business development. Make yourself indispensable and you will be hired as a full-time employee.

It is critical, especially in BD, to show passion and interest in the industry regardless of your hiring strategy. Speaking knowledgeably and passionately about an industry, a company, or the profession can make a viable candidate stand out.

Three Common Tracks for BD Professionals

Senior Leader in Business Development

One possibility for BD professionals, like people on many other career paths, is to remain in BD. These BD "lifers" tend to start their careers as entry-level professionals on the business side of a technology company and work their way into entry-level BD roles (or, if they are lucky, get hired straight into these positions).

As a junior BD professional, your job is to support the head of BD or the employee you report to (the COO, a founder, or someone else). This could involve everything from sourcing opportunities and planning growth strategies to doing research on products or vertical segments that you are interested in going into next. As a junior BD employee, it is critical that you do whatever it takes to succeed at the job. This means being highly adaptable in a constantly changing field, so risk tolerance is necessary. The junior BD individual is someone who thrives on uncertainty and can be as scrappy as necessary to solve a problem.

After spending a few years as a junior BD professional, these individuals move around between companies, helping the companies close deals and grow their businesses. While everyone has her own level of interest in conducting deals at later-stage companies, in many cases, as the company engages in more rounds of financing, the BD professional moves to an earlier-stage company to provide the same services.

Eventually, this career path can culminate in several other possible opportunities. The most natural is to be named head of BD for a company, leading the strategic initiative and guiding the company toward growth. An alternative option is to become the general manager of a company. A general manager is usually the first business-focused person at a tech company, sometimes known as "adult supervision." This person is in charge of making sure that bills are paid, conversations with appropriate strategic companies occur, and fund-raising is made a priority. Finally, a BD professional can be tapped to be the COO of a company, especially in the early stages of the company's existence, given the close ties between COOs and BD professionals.

This career path is best suited for individuals who thrive in a more operational role and enjoy the thrill of giving the BD folks direction on sourcing, closing, and collaborating with other companies. Those who choose a career path in BD can develop skills similar to those of people in sales or marketing.

A great example of someone who has made all the right moves as a BD lifer is Evan Cohen, the general manager of Foursquare. Evan has been at several companies, including Bebo, as the VP of BD. He is now at Foursquare and has definitely helped that company take its business to the next level since he joined a few years ago.

Founder of a Company

Another common route for individuals who begin in BD roles is to become the founder of a company. This is not an uncommon route, since the skills required to do BD and partnerships are entrepreneurial and are an important foundation for understanding how to set up and run a company. People in business development are responsible for thinking strategically about growing the business, monetizing the product, and envisioning a future for the platform. These skills are very similar to those required to start a company.

An early BD employee at a startup can often act as another cofounder. Strong BD employees are completely immersed in the company and its product and are required to dabble in many areas of the company in order to benefit the business, a role similar to that of a nontechnical founder. Many times, a founder who is not a good fit to become the CEO, whose responsibilities include hiring the right employees, setting the company's vision, and ensuring that cash is sustainable, ends up as the head of BD. This is a natural next step, since the types of skills needed and the perspective on the company that both jobs entail are relatively similar.

A good example of going from BD to founder is what Jared Hecht did at GroupMe. Jared worked in BD at Tumblr for almost two years before leaving to start GroupMe. The rest is history: he and his cofounder, Steve Martocci, sold GroupMe to Skype within one year for eight figures.

The big caveat for most people is: what about failure? It can happen that an individual who works in BD at multiple startups leaves to found his own company, only to fail a few years later. BD professionals should realize that this happens very often, and that indeed most startups fail. This failure does not taint a résumé and should not be considered something to be swept under the rug. On the contrary, that individual can use the failure to his advantage, seeking another role in BD at a different startup, or even joining the investing side of the industry. The most critical way to come back gracefully from a failure is to remain on good terms with investors, advisors, and other company backers, who may even be able to supply a rebound job opportunity after the fact.

Venture Capital

The final route that BD professionals commonly take is becoming a venture capitalist (VC). This is a natural move, since BD teams very frequently interact with VCs through partnerships or during strategic vision development. Venture capitalists frequently need BD professionals to work at their funds because they have experience developing businesses, have operational experience, and can perceive the strength of an investment company's potential.

A move from BD to VC takes more time and seasoning than ordinary career jumps. Very often, heads of BD are tapped to become partners at venture capital funds, since they have a specific skill set that the VCs want to acquire. Sometimes this is domain expertise; other times it is a deep network in an industry.

A great example of someone who went this route is Chris Fralic, the managing partner at First Round Capital. Chris was the head of BD at Half.com when it was sold to eBay, as well as the head of BD at Delicious when it was sold to Yahoo!

MBAs and Graduate Programs

The technology field has a very mixed attitude toward business school. Prominent individuals have been outspoken about the idea that the degree is worthless. Other influential tech leaders argue that it is critical. A consensus in the field has not yet been reached.

The reasons for not pursuing an MBA are numerous: it's expensive, it's time-consuming, and it's an opportunity cost when it comes to career advancement. It won't be an opportunity to move from one career to another. The advent of social media keeps us connected to people that we meet earlier in our lives, negating some of the networking components of pursuing the degree. Some say that the training acquired on the job is more relevant than more schooling.

But putting aside traditional arguments against getting an MBA, a BD professional might see a benefit from taking two years off to pursue an advanced degree. Those who are interested in navigating the technology and startup worlds have a few specific cases in which an MBA makes sense:

Switching industries or fields. This is a common argument of individuals who pursue business degrees. Business schools provide a blank canvas or even serve as a reset button for people who are interested in changing from one industry or job track to another. It is common for MBAs to have their first formal experiences with BD during an internship or after obtaining the degree. A common candidate for this track is someone who has not had much prior experience in the industry into which she would like to move.

Obtaining a particular network. Different schools specialize in different tracks or industries, and at a slightly more sophisticated stage in a career, individuals seek to cultivate those networks. Business school can be the perfect opportunity to network or associate with a particular group of peers or alumni in a particular industry. The same can be true of a desire to be connected to a school itself, especially if an undergraduate or even high school network was insufficient.

Rising to senior management. There are certain career tracks, even within BD, that are difficult to reach without having an MBA or formal business education. For example, senior management positions at larger tech companies, which can be as small as companies with 100 or more people, often require MBAs. Having an MBA *should* mean that the individual has the knowledge that business schools impart to their students. These degrees are valuable, and people certainly acquire both hard and soft skills during these programs. For a BD professional, the primary factor to consider when weighing the possibility of business school is whether it is worth leaving the industry for two years or whether the practical, on-the-job skills are ultimately more useful.

Talking about going to business school can be a sensitive subject in the startup world. There are many prominent people who haven't received MBAs (or even college or high school degrees), but have had tremendous success in the industry and do not think such a degree is necessary. Others will not hire professionals without them. It can be hit or miss, and this is a very personal and individual decision that a BD professional must make for himself.

The best alternative to getting a traditional MBA is to do a part-time program. Many universities that offer MBAs also offer executive MBAs or night courses. These can be optimal because they allow the individual to obtain the formal training and education on topics that she might need in her career while balancing a job and remaining in touch with trends in the industry.

CHAPTER **10**

Digital Identity

It is obvious to say that BD at startups takes place mostly by using technology: for example, emails, tweets, and LinkedIn messages. As a result, it is critical that you as a partnerships professional have a robust, yet curated digital identity. Whether it's getting a job in BD, closing a deal, working with a partner, or networking, the first course of action anyone takes when meeting another person is to look him up online. A simple Google search turns into browsing social media and other public forums for tidbits and a leg up on understanding the other person.

Maintaining a digital identity is well within your control, and should be an enjoyable task. There are several aspects of a digital identity, but generally this refers to anything about an individual that is available online. Here are best practices for creating, cultivating, and maintaining a digital presence.

Twitter

Be active on Twitter. No excuses. The majority of the world's trailblazers and thought leaders are on this social platform and maintain an active presence there. Twitter is a great forum for expressing opinions, sharing interesting articles and news sources, or showcasing products. It can also be used in reciprocation; indeed, many prominent BD professionals use it to learn about what other prominent people in the industry are discussing.

As a BD person, however, it is important that you ensure that your conduct on Twitter is professional. It is easiest to find and follow individuals whose handles in some way reflect their name. It is always recommended that you maintain a professional profile with a handle that is @firstname+last name or @initials, so that followers know whom they are following.

It is also important to ensure that your profile page has a short and appropriate bio. The site allows bios of up to 160 characters, and they should be thoughtful, concise, and relevant. Unless you are Hillary Clinton, being witty doesn't always work. Punchy and apt bios on Twitter are helpful in many scenarios: they provide a brief and easy way to understand a person's core essence for writing introductory biographies or making introductions. Because Twitter is an interest network, it can also make it easier to find other relevant and interesting people to follow.

The most critical element of maintaining a Twitter presence is to stay current and be active. No one likes a profile with an egg as the avatar and no bio. Tweets go stale quickly, so be sure to publish something on the site at least once a day. Get involved in the conversation: the platform is best for engaging in dialogue, even with complete strangers. Activity means that it is easier for you to be discovered or noteworthy and can even provide the foundation for professional relationships offline.

Acquire and Maintain Websites

Regardless of the end result, it is critical that you to own a few domain names for protection and posterity. Many people even create a brand around their identity. It would be difficult to do damage control if someone else controlled a relevant domain name and created inappropriate or slanderous content and, if necessary, it is better to have nothing at all associated with your name than to have negative content. Be sure to purchase or acquire the following websites:

FullName.com
AlternativeFullName.com
YourFullName.tumblr.com (this can be acquired from tumblr.com)
YourFullName.anybloghost.com

Domains are sold or brokered by domain managers like GoDaddy and Namecheap. Often these sites give better deals on longer-term sales of two to five years rather than the up-front cost for just one year. If those web addresses are not available, consider alternative domains like .co, .me, and the like.

Blog

The most open mechanism for asserting an opinion or maintaining a digital presence is to create and keep a blog. Blogs are ubiquitous, and it can be difficult to stand out, but maintaining a blog ensures that you are cultivating an online identity, defining your interests, and staying current on those topics.

Blogs should have a purpose and a theme. No one is policing the blog, and it is normal to include tangentially related content, but to keep the blog relevant and on-brand, and to maintain a steady user base, it makes sense for it to revolve around one theme.

Deciding how frequently to blog is a daunting first task, but once you have set a cadence, users can expect you to stick to your schedule (whether you post daily, biweekly, monthly, or at some other interval). Don't let users down; the purpose of having a blog is to cultivate a following of interested parties. As mentioned in Chapter 5, "Networking," a blog's comment section is a valuable piece of real estate where readers can engage and even network with the author. This means that posts must be drafted, well reasoned, and somewhat relevant.

Create an About.Me Page

About.me is a service that aids or augments the 160-character Twitter bio. It serves as a repository for individual biography pages that allow for hyperpersonalization and can range from including only a name and background image to links to various forms of social media. It is a simple, one-stop portal that can link to other parts of a digital identity.

To use the About.me page effectively, the first course of action is to claim the appropriately named page (similar to what we mentioned earlier). It is important that you grab about.com/firstname+lastname. This is not a platform for nicknames or quirky screen names, since it is an easy place for networkers and others to obtain information. Next, it is critical to link all accounts, including Twitter, LinkedIn, Facebook, and other relevant sites. This increases accessibility to other parts of a digital identity. Be sure to include a photo and a short bio, especially one that can be used if someone is giving a presentation and would like to provide information.

Finally, master the Google search. Ensure that you own the first page of results when someone searches your name on Google. Your Twitter page, LinkedIn bio, website, and other sites that show up on the first screen should all be about *you*. If you have a common name, doing this can require extra effort, but it is nonetheless important so that people who search for you can find accurate facts about you easily.

For maximum publicity and effectiveness, BD professionals often add the link to their email signatures. This can replace links to various social platforms, which make an email signature clunky and cumbersome.

PART 2

INTRODUCTION TO PARTNERSHIPS

CHAPTER 11

UNDERSTANDING OTHER COMPANIES

IN THIS SECTION, we will focus on the process of mastering partnerships and coordinating with other companies through preparing pitches and determining the best partnerships for your company. The best way to do this is to start by understanding the ins and outs of other companies: What is another company's business model? What is important to its business? What is its focus? Answers to these and a host of other questions are critical before you should consider partnering with a company.

What to Know About Other Companies

There is no such thing as knowing too much about another company, but for the sake of maximizing efficiency and minimizing the resources required, there are a few key points that all business development professionals should learn about a company in order to assess whether a potential partnership with that company would be viable.

First, it is important to understand a company's background and history. Notable information includes the company's founding date (or its approximate age), its fund-raising, and its key employees. Other fundamental details include team size, location, and employee breakdown, especially how many engineers and how many nontechnical employees work there. The best places to find this information are sites like CrunchBase, TechCrunch's database warehouse for information about startups in all industries, AngelList, and a general Google search. In addition, you can read articles in major publications such as the *New York Times*'s DealBook section, VentureBeat, *Fast Company*, and Mashable, among others.

Second, you need to understand how the company views itself and tells its own story. While the company may be seen by the public as focusing on one particular sector or demographic, find out how it pitches itself. Learn any underlying stories that might be critical to the company's identity, including the story of the company's founding. Once you figure out how the company pitches itself, make sure you understand how the media, press, or users think of the company and its products and if this differs from the company's own view. This will help you balance your game plan by allowing you to understand both sides of the equation.

Next, learn about the company's growth trajectory and what areas of growth opportunity it is emphasizing. It might be easy to assume that all companies want to expand their user numbers, but user growth is probably not the entire story. If you can understand what drives the company's growth or how the company wants to grow, you have a better chance of understanding what kind of partnerships may be appealing. Again, these numbers may be found in databases like CrunchBase or articles on company blogs that detail their publicly disclosed user numbers (sometimes the information is not in either, and you might just have to ask the company for a ballpark number in person). In addition, the company's growth trajectory can tell a story about where it acquires users or what types of users frequently access its product.

Learning about the company's growth provides an interesting window into its business model as well. Consider how the company is monetizing its product or intends to make money. How long has it been making money, and what order of magnitude is the revenue? Understand how it partners with other companies to make money, if applicable. PrivCo, a paid service, has financial information on privately held companies that can reveal this information. If the company is not monetizing, try to evaluate what it is doing with the funding it has raised during its seed and series rounds. Does it have a long-term run rate, or is it living from fund-raising round to fund-raising round?

In addition to understanding the actual company structure, become a user of the product and learn about the ins and outs of the platform. By using the product, you will have a sense of where the company's strengths and weaknesses lie, and you may even have insight into the company's road map.

Finally, read everything you can get your hands on about this company. Chances are that if it is relatively small, there will be a limited online profile of its service. If you are able to obtain a holistic perspective on the company, you will be able to speak knowledgeably during a pitch about why your two entities pair nicely together.

CHAPTER 12

Four Golden Rules
of Partnerships

The nuances of partnerships are highly dependent on the two companies involved, the stage of both companies, and the reasons for the deal. There are, however, four golden rules that are broadly applicable when you are soliciting a partnership, regardless of the details of each specific pairing. These four rules are standards that are implemented in different ways depending on the companies involved, but that generally provide a benefit to both sides of the deal. These rules apply to situations in which you are soliciting a partnership with another company.

Partnerships That Emphasize Revenue or Profit

Rule 1: Companies will want to partner with you if you make money for them.

Money, money, money: making money is at the heart of every business venture, and therefore, revenue generation is the key metric for a large number of partnerships. The most common type of partnership is one that provides potential (or immediate) revenue opportunities to one or both sides of the deal, with revenue as the reason for or central theme of the partnership.

In most cases, the types of companies that emphasize revenue or profit in their partnerships are those that can offer a product or feature that will help another company make money. This could be anything from a subscription children's toy service partnering with a mommy blog (and sharing revenue on new leads that follow) to a clothing brand partnering with a popular TV show to get more awareness (and subsequently more sales or revenue). The truth is, with rare exceptions, almost every partnership comes back to revenue or profit at some point. It is the bottom line.

For example, American Express has a team that specializes in partnering with startup companies, and monetization has been a driving force behind many of these partnerships. A prime example of this type of partnership was American Express's deal with Clickable, an online advertising solutions company that provided search capabilities via the American Express portal to small and medium-size businesses using the service. Former business development lead Kristal Bergfield told us that the partnership with Clickable started because American Express was seeking alternative revenue streams during the recession. This partnership enabled the company to diversify its offerings and enter the business of software distribution. Not only did the deal prove to be profitable, but it ended up improving American Express's overall product.

Where you are in your company life cycle will affect how quickly you move when a revenue-generating partnership comes your way. If you are a small company that is focused on completing and building out your product, even a good-looking deal that will bring in a significant amount of revenue might not be feasible. The idea is that if you stay focused on building the product that you believe your company should build, then you won't have problems getting revenue-generating partnerships when you are ready for them.

The same is true for medium- and large-sized companies: each entity has different priorities. Revenue-generating partnerships are obviously very important, but the amount of revenue generated, the magnitude of the deal, and the opportunity cost of not partnering can vary depending on the deal. For example, if there is a substantial amount of revenue projected, but it will take 100 percent of your team's focus for the rest of the year, and your pipeline includes building features that will generate alternative sources of revenue, the deal might not look quite as compelling. If a deal promises less cash but is also less labor-intensive, you will probably dig in to see how you can execute on both what you need to do internally and what is needed to make the partnership happen. The cost/benefit analysis of doing a revenue partnership is much like a similar kind of assessment for any corporate deal.

Anyone who is pitching another company on a revenue-generating partnership will do his or her best to make the partnership worth the time and effort of the company he or she is pitching. This means making sure that the partner will potentially make enough money to justify agreeing to the partnership. This should not be just enough money, as a successful partnership will make more money than originally anticipated. A deal can also be structured in such a way that one of the partners (usually the one that is getting pitched) initially makes more money than the other, so that the prospective partner has an incentive to make the deal happen. Once the partnership has proved successful, the profit arrangement reverts to an equal split.

The deals that actually get done are the ones that can prove their worth. Companies often have a minimum monetary threshold, but if you can prove that a lucrative alliance can be made, then you should be able to persuade any company that a deal is doable. But more important, proving your worth in advance of a deal is what makes the deal actually happen. The best way to prove your worth is by doing a good job of showing your value proposition to a prospective partner. Proving your worth also entails showing a company that you have already done with others what you are proposing to do with it, rather than just telling the company that what you are proposing is possible. In other words, showing is better than telling. In the case of creating revenue for a partner, you'll want to show the company you are pitching where you've created revenue for other companies before. Seems pretty straightforward, doesn't it?

The size of the opportunity will determine how a company will react to the proposal of a partnership. As mentioned previously, many companies have a minimum monetary threshold that must be guaranteed if the investment is to be worth the time and effort required. For example, during Alex's time at Aviary, he was hoping to work with a big-name comic book publisher on a partnership. The comic book publisher was interested in the cross-corporation efforts, but could seek only opportunities that would *guarantee* a minimum revenue stream of $250,000 per year. Some companies have an explicit minimum, while others just go with what they feel is best worth their time and prospective upside.

Partnerships That Cut Costs

Rule 2: Companies will partner with you if you can help them save money.

All companies, even established ones, like to save money. When big companies assess their overall strategies and the future of their business, they must assess whether they will grow a business from scratch, acquire talent or products, or partner with other companies. As with the classic business case, companies that determine that it is not financially or strategically sound to build the product and grow revenue will seek external solutions to get the job done. Most often, these deals are done as cost-saving measures to advance the business.

For example, Julie Vaughn Ruef, who is the head of business development for MessageMe, once worked on a deal in which a media company wanted to partner with a wireless carrier. The company wanted to revamp its on-device web portal, and the media company wanted to help service the business. The wireless company would save money by not hiring an in-house team to develop proprietary software, but instead leveraging the expertise of another company to do so. In return, the media company received the exposure and distribution.

If starting from scratch does not make financial sense, a big company will look to acquire the best company in the space. If neither of these options is feasible, the company will look for partnerships in order to save time and investment in R&D. These kinds of partnerships are done with cost cutting as the primary reason for working together.

There is no limit to the kind of expenses that companies may be seeking to reduce or eliminate. Cost savings can come into play anywhere, from payment processing to healthcare to salaries. These partnerships help reduce the difference between the top line and the bottom line.

Even though it isn't the obvious choice, Facebook is one of the strongest examples of engaging in partnerships that save money in order to allow its team to focus on its core product. Developers and companies that have already invested the time and money to generate products can leverage Facebook's platform, saving Facebook the cost of app development. After all, Facebook's mission is not to create games and tools; instead, it is focused on giving people the power to share and stay connected. That being said, these partnerships maximize user experience. Facebook has had deep integrations with companies such as Zynga, Spotify, and Skype. The alternative route would be to build out this functionality on its own. By partnering, Facebook gets the best of both worlds.

Partnerships That Grow a User Base

Rule 3: Companies will want to partner with you if you can help them grow their user base.

Another motivation in strategic partnerships is the potential to leverage an existing company's user base and access to consumers. As with the first type of partnership, the company should be able to prove that an alliance will be mutually beneficial and will grow something for each side; for example, one partner grows its user base, and the other grows revenue.

There are two types of user base partnerships: those for companies that are looking to partner with other companies with similar user bases (if they are looking for more of the same type of users), and those for companies that are looking to partner with other companies that have a different or specific type of user that they are hoping to attract. In either type of partnership, the best way to attract the user base is to do a basic email swap, allowing one company to target the other company's users. One company will let another company contact its users, on behalf of the company that owns the contact information, to promote the partnership company. Sometimes a swap means that both sides benefit from each other's lists; other times it is a one-way deal.

To enhance the offer, companies usually set a partnership in motion around a promotion or a deal. In some cases, it's a discount code that can be found only in a specific promotion in conjunction with another partner. A great example of this is a promoted tweet on Twitter that contains a discount code that can be found only in that tweet. A company needs to figure out what the lifetime value (LTV) of a user is and then make sure that it spends less than that to attract each user in order to reap a lucrative partnership outcome.

Two great examples of partnerships to grow user bases are the Amazon/LivingSocial and Uber/Savored partnerships.

In 2011, Amazon and LivingSocial launched a partnership in the form of a deal on LivingSocial. Buyers who subscribed to LivingSocial were able to purchase a $20 Amazon gift card for just $10, meaning that Amazon was essentially giving away money that it could have earned. At the peak of the offering period, LivingSocial reported that it was selling 2,000 coupons every minute—85 per second. Originally, this wildly successful partnership was merely a follow-up to a $175 million Amazon investment in LivingSocial, but it ended up benefiting users of both sites. Not only did this generate revenue for each party involved, but it mobilized LivingSocial's smaller user base, propelling it into a clear second place in the deal space, behind Groupon. Additionally, it drew customers to Amazon's site who might not necessarily have been patrons. While the specific promotion was considered successful at the time, at the end of 2012, Amazon wrote off LivingSocial at a $169 million loss. This clearly signaled that Amazon believed it paid too much for LivingSocial.

Uber, an app that connects you with a driver at the tap of a button, and Savored, a members-only service for deals at some of the most popular restaurants around the country (and was purchased by Groupon in 2012), entered into a partnership in 2011/2012. According to Ben McKean, CEO of Savored, the deal with Uber was a cross-promotion to drive users. "The idea was to inform our users about Uber and vice versa," said McKean. By signing up, registrants were entered to win a $100 Savored dinner with round-trip transportation provided by Uber. This very simple partnership proved to be extremely valuable; both Savored and Uber reached their high-end customer user bases and leveraged their well-known brands to increase the number of clients of each service.

Partnerships That Will Improve a Product

Rule 4: Companies will want to partner with you if you can help them improve their product.

The final golden rule of partnerships is that companies will want to do a deal that will improve an already existing product. This occurs when one company offers a product solution and prospective partners would rather integrate that solution than build a similar one themselves. The product will probably improve the user experience or the efficiency of the business, as well as the relationship between the two companies.

One of the best examples of this kind of partnership involves a New York–based company called SinglePlatform, bought by Constant Contact in 2012, which helps local businesses get discovered and provides publishers with the enhanced experience of bringing local storefronts online. SinglePlatform's product is the largest provider of real-time menus of products and services sourced directly from local businesses. The company has closed deals with partners ranging from YP.com and Foursquare to the *New York Times* and Metromix. Kenny Herman, who was the executive vice president of business development at Single-Platform, points to significant boosts as evidence of the company's success; for instance, "YP.com (AT&T's local search app, which reaches more than 30 million users) experienced a more than 3000 percent increase in search traffic in its number one category, a 200 percent increase in mapping/direction requests, and a more than 200 percent increase in phone call volume."

Finally, there are plenty of examples in which strategic partnerships are forged to take advantage of more than one of these four golden rules. One that made headlines in startup and mainstream outlets alike was the Foursquare/American Express deal.

Tristan Walker, who led the deal on Foursquare's behalf, said that the partnership actually hit on all four of the golden rules: it grew user bases, saved users' money, made the product better, and was financially beneficial to both sides.

According to Walker, "When we approach partnerships, we do it as users of the company's products, rather than employees. If we would enjoy the experience as a user of our own product, then we know the deal will work."

These four rules are the basic rules of partnerships. They don't cover how partnerships get started, but rather how one company will work with another company. If you are working on a partnership and it doesn't fit one of these rules, it will probably not be a very good partnership. The actual deal may begin because of a friendship, a need, an obligation, or something else. But be wary of a deal that you can't put into one of these quadrants. It's better to walk away than to spend your time on bad deals!

13

THREE TYPES OF PARTNERSHIPS

PARTNERSHIPS ALMOST always begin when one company is looking to gain from another company something that it cannot or will not build or achieve by itself. There are always at least two parties involved, but occasionally more parties are affected. One company is often spearheading the partnership, and this is usually the partner that feels it has more to gain from the pairing. Ordinarily, the company that is taking charge of initiating the partnership has a list of companies that it would like to pair with, and is seeking a partnership to accomplish a set of goals. If the desired companies are unable to partner or to accomplish these goals, the original company has the options of trying to engineer a solution on its own or approaching the solution from a different perspective.

In the previous chapter, we established some of the key reasons for engaging in strategic alignments or partnerships. While every individual partnership opportunity has a different manifestation, there are three main types of partnerships into which almost every deal can be categorized.

1. *Product partnership (integration partnership):* a partnership in which one company integrates another company's technology into its own product
2. *Brand partnership (cobranded partnership):* a partnership in which one company leverages another company's brand or two companies leverage each other's brands

3. *Distribution partnership (network partnership):* a partnership in which one company uses the distribution system of a second company to grow its own user base

Product Partnerships

Product partnerships, sometimes known as integration partnerships, are ones in which two companies work together for the sake of enhancing their products. The basic structure behind a product/integration partnership is one company building an offering or feature that another company (or several other companies) would benefit from using in its product. The offering typically consists of a product or feature that a company needs but finds prohibitive to build or develop on its own; either the product would cost too much to produce or the team at the company feels that it doesn't have the appropriate skills to build the product. For most companies, the strategy is to do one thing and do it well, so partnering with other companies whose products can fill a void while allowing the company to focus on its core product to provide a stellar offering is the key to building a great company around product partnerships.

Some great examples of product partnerships, and ones that might surprise you, are the variety of product partnerships involving Walgreens. Walgreens is mostly known for being a Fortune 50 company specializing in pharmacy and retail stores in the United States. But you might not know that Walgreens also has a billion-dollar photo-printing business. In 2012, Walgreens released a printing API to allow photo-related apps to have the ability to print photos that were sent directly to stores nearby. This was a pretty innovative way to get people into the store, which is one of the most valuable metrics that Walgreens tracks. Then in 2013, Walgreens released a pharmacy prescription refill API (also known as Rx API) to allow third-party mobile app developers to integrate the drugstore chain's prescription refill technology. Even big companies can be innovative in product partnerships.

Brand Partnerships

The second type of partnership is known as a brand partnership or a cobranded partnership. These types of partnerships happen when two companies want to leverage each other's brands. This usually leads to more exposure for one or both companies and can help establish a company or put it on the map. Branded partnerships can require technology or involve major product changes, but usually they require only complementary user bases, and the companies going into partnership can leverage each other's key abilities. Often, the partnerships can be executed by the marketing and communication team. The thing you need to focus on with branded partnerships is whether the partnership will be good for your brand, especially in terms of the time it takes to do the deal and the potential upside.

Foursquare is a champion of branded partnerships. In January 2010, Foursquare was one of the hottest startups in the tech world. One of its earliest partners was the TV channel Bravo. The partnership sought to engage viewers after they turned off the television, and it did so by offering Foursquare players "badges" and special prizes when viewers visited one of the more than 500 locations that were featured on Bravo Channel shows. The locations were picked by Bravo to correspond with shows such as *The Real Housewives*, *The Millionaire Matchmaker*, and *Top Chef*, among others. Part of the partnership was that Foursquare received airtime and had its logo on the screen during some of the most heavily watched shows on Bravo.

This is a perfect example of a mutually beneficial brand partnership that actually had third-party vendors happy as well. Both sides won: Bravo was able to promote its image as an innovator in digital platforms and was able to engage with its audience via social media, while Foursquare got plenty of publicity, prime airtime, and brand awareness. Foursquare was able to tap into Bravo's "user base," its viewers, and Bravo was able to engage its audience and acquire data about its viewers' whereabouts, a valuable proposition for advertisers.

Another example of a branded partnership is the one between Uber and the NFL. In September 2013, Uber and the NFL partnered to promote safe rides for pro footballers to and from games. The NFL has had a history of players receiving DUIs and wanted a better way to get pro footballers home safely. Uber promoted itself as a "safe" alternative for transport, and the NFL promoted an easy means of getting to the game. The partnership allowed the NFL to work with an up-and-coming technology company while creating a positive PR story for the NFL.

The NFL has notoriously been very guarded about its brand and its partnering. It is interested in working only with the best of breed when doing any deal, so this means quality over quantity. So when the NFL does a deal with a company, it really means something. As a result, this was a big win for Uber.

Both sides benefited from cobranding. Uber was lucky enough to partner with an extremely popular and high-profile organization, and to associate with the most popular sport in the United States. The NFL also won: it came out in favor of promoting the right values concerning the safety and security to its fans.

Distribution Partnership

The final type of partnership is a distribution partnership, also known as a network partnership. In this type of partnership, one company uses the distribution network of a second company to grow its own user base. Some distribution partnerships help small companies with a deep value proposition get distribution to acquire new users. In most distribution partnerships, the company providing the distribution will make money from the partnership: it uses the value of its distribution mechanism or population of users as a selling point to partner with other companies in return for monetary compensation. Other times, you'll see two big companies partner, with each offering distribution for the other. This happens when both companies have their own users who will benefit from the partnership. Usually one company is good at one thing and the other is good at something else, so both sides get the benefit of "distribution" from the partnership.

The first example of a distribution partnership is the marriage of Square and Starbucks. Square is a merchant services aggregator and mobile payments company, and Starbucks needs no explanation or introduction. In November 2012, Square and Starbucks announced that they would be teaming up and that Square would begin processing all credit and debit card transactions at Starbucks stores in the United States. Along with the partnership, Starbucks invested $25 million in the round of funding that Square was conducting at that time.

Until that partnership, Square had coordinated largely with small and medium-sized businesses. Starbucks was its first big partnership, and the news came out in a press blitz. It is assumed that Starbucks pays less in processing fees by using Square than it paid to its previous credit card processors, and in return Square gets the benefits of a branding partnership and a high volume of transactions.

Another example of a distribution partnership is that between Apple and Yahoo!. Since the release of the original iPhone, Yahoo! and Apple have had a deep relationship on certain applications, including the weather application. Every iPhone comes with a weather application powered by Yahoo!. This gives Apple a great product for users and Yahoo! massive distribution.

Apple is very selective with its preloaded app distribution partnerships, but the success that Apple found with Yahoo! was not replicated in its distribution partnership with Google. Famously, Google was one of the other big partners for the first iPhone: it provided predownloaded apps like Google Maps, which powered most geolocation services on iOS products. When Apple released iOS6, Google Maps was noticeably absent and had been replaced by Apple's proprietary version, known as Apple Maps. This new software was met with a significant backlash about its low quality and poor usability. Apple had to fall on its sword, and this proved that distribution partnerships are truly beneficial for both parties.

The Skinny on Partnerships

Successful partnerships are not easy and take time, preparation, and finesse to work correctly. There are usually two scenarios when partnering. The first is when a company already needs what you are peddling. It could be a service or an offering (for example, an email delivery service), and yours is one of a few options that a company is evaluating. Whether or not the partnership will happen depends on how your company fares compared to similar companies in the space, and the product and user aspects on which the company chooses to focus. For example, if you have a payment offering and the company that is looking for a company to facilitate payments on its website needs superb customer support and a great mobile experience, then that company will probably go with the payment solution that best caters to those needs.

The other type of partnership is one in which the other company is not particularly interested in what you have to offer. This is not to say that what you have isn't spectacular or unique. It's simply that the company you want to work with wasn't going out to look for your solution (or any solution). This is obviously a much harder sell, as you need to take the partnership from "zero to hero." You will be competing with other company priorities, the things the company *is* going after. Don't get discouraged: while these deals are more difficult, they do happen all the time. You just need to point out a problem that the company has and help it solve that problem.

14

Identifying the Right Person at the Partner Company

In the abstract, partnerships occur between two companies, products, or user bases. But the logistics of a partnership boil down to a relationship between two individuals who actually get the deal done. In order for these partnerships to take place, it is critical that the two individuals on the two sides of the table be able to come together and agree on an actual partnership.

This inevitably means that when you are dealing with other companies, identifying the correct person at the other company will enable you to initiate conversations to make the right kind of deal. As we noted in Chapter 3, "BD Team Structure," there are many possible combinations of BD people at other companies who can make deals happen. In addition, of course, other professionals at the company are able to make the right connections to do a deal, so identifying the "correct person" can be a bigger challenge than you originally expected.

One of the biggest issues in partnerships is failing to get in front of the right person. The ideal counterpart at a company you are looking to partner with is usually a mix of someone who understands your offering and someone who is a necessary part of the partnership or integration. But these relationships also depend on your role at your company. If you are a technical person, you will usually liaise with other technical people. If you work in BD and partnerships, you will try to connect with your deal counterpart on the other side. The number one thing to think about when it comes to your counterpart on the other side is to trace the other side's steps and thought processes. What we like to do is map out what an integration would look like. Who is needed to make the integration happen?

The Right Person for the Three Types of Partnerships

The first type of partnership is a product partnership or integration partnership. For this type of partnership, you *can* start with the BD or partnership lead, but sometimes it is better to bypass her and go directly to the lead engineer or the head of product to sell your vision and integration idea. We've learned the hard way that when you are attempting to do a product partnership with another company, it is sometimes best to avoid people in BD roles (as they can slow down the selling process).

The second kind of partnership is a brand partnership. This type of collaboration is done between two people who are business-focused or, occasionally, two marketing or brand employees. This makes sense given the branding and marketing aspects of the deal and the need to ensure that the correct message is disseminated by both sides. At some point, you'll want to loop in and connect with someone from product, marketing, and branding, as they are key decision makers.

Distribution partnerships, the third kind, can also be conducted between two BD or partnership professionals. Before launching, you most likely will need to connect with someone technical on the other firm's team in addition to including someone technical from your end. However, the BD professionals should have a strong understanding of the types of users and channels the distribution partnership needs to reach.

The Right Person for the Four Golden Rules of Partnerships

Identifying the right person can be tied to the four golden rules of partnerships, discussed in Chapter 12. All the deals begin with someone who is focused on business, but other decision makers will need to be involved as well. The job of the business-focused person is to figure out who needs to be in the room (or to sign off) if the partnership is to be most effective. Let's go through each of the four types.

Making Money

Identifying the right person when the deal is going to make money for another company is usually is done by a business-focused person, who might be either someone from the management team (the CEO, COO, CFO, or founder) or one of the people who will execute the deal (the product lead, engineering lead, marketing lead, or someone similar). This depends on whether or not the money-making deal requires technical or product work, but in either case, the CFO and the revenue and finance teams ordinarily get involved with matters of monetization.

For example, Eric Friedman, who leads sales and revenue operations at Foursquare, has had extensive experience working on partnerships with other companies that either involve a revenue-sharing component or lead to a sales relationship. His role as a partnerships professional who is intimately involved in the company's revenue operations is needed for deals that involve making money.

Saving Money

Like partnerships that enable companies to profit as a result, those that reduce costs are most likely to begin with a business-focused person. They will quickly include the director of operations, COO, or CFO to determine whether the savings are worthwhile or insignificant. Once the team decides that it will continue with the deal, depending on the nature of the deal, you may need to include the product and technical teams. Most likely, the same type of professional as in the previous example would be the person to lead this kind of deal.

Growing the User Base

When a partnership helps a business grow its user base, the deal originates with the business team. As with the other rules, who has to be involved depends on what type of deal is associated with growing the user base. If the partnership is a basic email swap, then you will probably need the marketing and communications teams. If the partnership is some sort of product integration to grow a company's user base, then you will probably need people from the product and engineering areas. Seldom do financially inclined people at these companies get involved in deals that focus on growing the number of users, unless growing the number of users has an immediate direct tie to growing revenue, which isn't often the case.

Improving the Product

A partnership that will save a company money can be sourced by someone from the business side, but most times it is the product team that identifies other companies' products or features that can improve the product. When the deal comes in through the BD or partnerships team, bringing in the product team as soon as possible is paramount so as to not waste any time. If the product team doesn't like the deal, the conversation should not go any further. If the product team welcomes the opportunity, then the engineering and marketing teams will eventually be brought in, as the deal touches on their business as well.

Tanuj Parikh, for example, worked on the business development and business operations teams at the group messaging platform GroupMe. In his time there, he created mockups for pitches of how the integration would look. "It empowered us to be really product-centric in our pitch. We made pixel-perfect mockups (in PowerPoint and Photoshop) of how GroupMe would look inside certain apps. Visually demonstrating exactly how the flow would work and be additive to the user experience was instrumental in convincing developers to use our application programming interface (API), particularly early on. Making wireframes and mockups part of your sales and partnership pitch process makes you a much more dangerous business-focused person."

In addition, the product team within a company can enable and contribute to the evolution of a partnership that improves a product. According to Itai Ram, director of product management at Vidyo, "The product team also plays an important role in evaluating the implication on technological development and feasibility in an event of a successful deal or partnership. Timeline of the product delivery is also key for BD to understand when negotiating terms of a deal."

Talking to the Wrong Party

There is no quicker way to mess up a deal than by starting the deal conversation with the wrong party. Non-decision makers can help you get to the right person to make the decision, but sometimes such a person will claim to be the decision maker, even when he is not, and it will be very hard to get around that. While it can be difficult to discern who the decision maker is, you can ask probing questions such as, "Who at your company is responsible for making decisions on X?"

Occasionally, BD professionals feel that the best way to have an "in" with a company is to speak to anyone who will listen about a partnership idea at that company. But this can often be disastrous when you are trying to close a deal if the person you are talking to cannot make the decision. In this scenario, the person will always say no because she can't get in trouble for saying no—only for saying yes. In our experience, once you make contact with a company, you should be transparent with your counterpart by asking her if she is the decision maker, and if not, who is. Wait to give your full pitch to that person. The most you should give your contact is enough to get her excited and make her want to put you in touch with the decision maker.

Finding a champion in a company can be similar to finding the right person at a company, but there are some subtle differences. There are fortunate times when your biggest fan at a company is also the decision maker. In that scenario, deals move fast, and the process feels efficient, effective, and streamlined. But sometimes the "wrong" person is the one who is championing you the most. That's still okay; the goal is for that person to facilitate getting the right person to become a fan and champion of your offering. So if someone is championing your company to his team, but it is clear that he is not the decision maker, don't fret. Simply make sure that you express the need to get in front of the right person or decision maker and continue to leverage your close relationship with the champion.

If All Else Fails

Regardless of the type of partnership, having a combination of product and engineering team members is always critical to facilitating and implementing a partnership. If you have a strong offering that directly helps your prospective partner, you will go from zero to integration much faster by going directly through these people. The bottom line is: in terms of product integrations, it's a lot better for the product and the engineering teams to recommend something to the business side of the company than the other way around.

Given their proximity to the meat of the product, the product and engineering teams are often savvy about what deficiencies the company's product might have and what needs for a partnership the company might have. If you keep a direct line of communication to the people who are building the actual product and solicit their feedback, you will find useful partnership ideas that a business professional may never have previously considered.

CHAPTER 15

PARTNER FEEDBACK

ALL STRATEGIC PARTNERSHIPS have an underlying ulterior motive. Some partnerships are done for the sake of generating revenue, others for growing a user base. But all cross-company collaborations should be done with the intention of getting product feedback.

Feedback is a gift, as they say, and users supply feedback to companies implicitly by utilizing some features and backing away from others. It is important, however, beyond A/B testing or focus groups, to receive product feedback from a partner or prospective partner. It is the job of the BD team, in conjunction with the developer advocate and other technical members of the partnership, to solicit and collect this feedback and then work to incorporate it into the product.

In BD and partnerships, you will hear some of the same feedback repeatedly. The most commonly heard phrases in prospective partnership discussions include, "If only your product did X, we'd be interested in integrating or partnering." This type of feedback can drive a young company into a frenzy and cause the team that is working on the core product to lose its focus. The more diverse the feedback from potential partners and the more directions the engineering team gets pulled in, the more likely it is that the company will fail. The most dangerous act for a new company is to go from being a startup to being a custom product development shop while still operating under startup conditions.

Eli Portnoy, cofounder of Thinknear and former senior product manager for digital video at Amazon, speaks of the importance of partner feedback in his business development experience:

During the early days of Thinknear, I met with a very large company in our space that had heard about what we were doing and wanted to talk about a potential channel partnership (we would white-label our solution and they would sell it for us). We pitched them multiple times across different levels of the organization, but it felt as if we were moving sideways.

After four or five meetings, I had an informal chat with one of the people that I had developed a closer relationship with and asked why we kept getting meetings, but couldn't make progress toward closing a deal. He told me that everyone at the company who met with us was fascinated by our model, and they all wanted to find a way to make it work, but that whenever they internally discussed how to actually execute on a deal, they were worried that our product was too complicated for them to sell. Here I was trying to pitch them on all the functionality and incredible options that we had built, and all they wanted was something that was easier and simpler to sell.

The next meeting I had with them went very differently. I simplified my pitch and focused only on the essence of our product, and we quickly sealed a deal. They ended up becoming a massive partner for us and teaching me a valuable lesson about simplicity in a pitch.

There are, however, a curated set of reasons why you would spend time and effort building something into your product that a potential partner hopes to see. These reasons apply in ordinary circumstances, but should your company need the partnership as a lifeline, these reasons can apply more broadly.

Many Companies Have Asked for the Same Thing

Seeking a range of diverse opinions before building a product or making major product overhauls is the key to developing a successful product. Although this seems intuitive, it guarantees that you will have a market for something before you build it and that you will not alienate a currently existing user base. Since users of a product can be easily disturbed by changes within it, large product overhauls can often do more damage than they prevent, which is why it is important to both collect user feedback and carefully consider any changes you make.

If you talk to a certain number of prospective partners, building the right product will leave you with a fraction of those initial parties as launch partners.

When the feedback *consistently* involves the phrase "If only your product did X," *and* that criterion is exactly the same across different types of companies, then that requested feature becomes something that your product should provide because there are many companies that want it. In addition, adding that feature or making that product change could be the difference between launching an initiative with several launch partners and having no launch partners. Setting sail alone is a dangerous game, and it means that you have ignored the crowds.

For example, Facebook has played with its home page and news feed for several years. Its profile pages, however, remained largely unchanged from the initial renderings in 2005–2006 until 2011. In 2011, the company overhauled the individual profile pages and separated the content into two columns. Users were up in arms, designers were confused, and the personal profile experience as a whole was diminished. Facebook took user feedback into account and reformatted the feed to use just one column, which in turn put in place an easier structure for monetization.

A Big Company Has Asked for It (and You Have a Contract)

This is where things get tricky. You really want to work with that big fish, but it will work with you only if you build the thing that it wants. And building that thing is going to take you a month or two. On the one hand, the partnership is with a big, splashy brand name, but on the other hand, building the product change may slow down progress in other areas, or even change the nature of the product in a substantial way.

While it may seem as if partnering with a large company is succumbing to the desires of the mass media, the truth of the matter is that when partnering with a large company, the small company often gets more out of the splash that the deal makes than the larger company does from integrating the product. Given the major benefits to both sides of the deal, unless there is a technological hurdle that is insurmountable, you should accept a partnership with a large company.

There are a few caveats about making changes for larger companies, however. First, the deal, including the desired product changes, should be in writing. If the larger company signs a contract that says that it will integrate your product once a particular feature has been built or integrated, then it is worth diverting engineering time and resources toward building the product. In addition, that individualized tweak may work to the advantage of the smaller company, which can use that new technology to work with similar companies to use the same features in a less-customized fashion.

For example, at Aviary, there were several early potential partners asking for specific custom builds of the photo-editing product. Avi Muchnick, the founder, smartly decided that at that point the company wasn't going to build one-offs for each interested party. Instead, it devised a partnership threshold at which it would agree to create custom integrations for companies, and it made that rule known to potential partners. The strategy worked, and eventually those bigger companies used the product the way it was built because it had become the standard in the space.

Keep in mind that a wasted month or two preparing for and building a one-off can derail an entire company. It is critical that you stay focused, ship great products, and build for scale.

CHAPTER 16

Doing a Deal Versus Doing the Best Deal

THERE IS A BIG difference between doing just any deal and doing the best deal. If you have a great product, a passionate team, and a relevant group of potential partners, you should have your pick of partners and deal terms. The deals should make an impact on your business, whether it is growing your user base, making money, improving your product, or something else.

Not All Deals Are Created Equal

This may sound obvious, but not all deals are equally valuable. Understanding the worth of a deal has several components, including the actual monetary value of the deal, the potential earnings, and metrics that you have deemed important for valuing the deal (like user growth, customer base, client size, and so on). There are also intrinsic ways to value a deal, especially revolving around the publicity it might afford (being connected to a leader in an industry) and the flashiness of the partner name to help bring on more partners.

Each of these elements should be weighed differently depending on the desired outcome of the deal. Each side of the partnership should clearly outline its expectations for what it wants to accomplish, and should have a set of internal metrics against which to benchmark. If this is a branding partnership, the value of having a partnership with a household name can be just as powerful as an infusion of cash. If the partnership is for user base growth, working with a partner that has 100 times as many users as you do can be more effective than working with a name-brand company.

Doing the best deal also means ensuring that the deal terms, whatever they may be, are favorable for your business. This seems logical; however, in the heat of the moment, you might want to just do the deal rather than do the best deal.

Wasting Time on Deals

The worst thing a BD professional can do is to spend time on deals that aren't going to do anything for the business in the long run. This isn't to say that partnerships with small companies early on are not worth your time. As we mentioned before, you need to build a repertoire of companies that are willing to work with you so that when the time comes to prove your worth to larger companies, you have a tangible way of doing so. But when you set out to develop a catalog of experiences, you should be able to see beyond the deal to future results. Don't waste time on deals that are unrelated to what you need to get done.

For example, if you are seeking distribution partnerships to ramp up monetization, but you come across an opportunity to partner with a well-known brand simply for its brand name, the efforts seem misaligned (unless there is some implicit benefit to monetizing from partnering with that brand). The partnership will help with exposure, but is likely to fall short of expectations on the monetization front. A good BD or partnership lead will pass on spending time on deals like this.

Pursuing the Best Deals

So how do you figure out which deals to spend time on? Look at the metric or benchmark that your company defines as the most important. Emphasize that number or value in your pitches and focus on deals that can enhance that metric. Usually the metric has something to do with the population of users or the amount of money generated, but it can be as wide-ranging as unique site visitors, monthly active users, transactions, or photo uploads. If the deal you are about to embark on is one that will improve the key metric, then it's the correct deal to do and is worth spending time on. If the deal is not going to move the needle substantially, then it is probably not one that is worth pursuing.

CHAPTER 17

SINCERE SELLING

HALF THE BATTLE with partnerships is getting the other side to agree to a deal. Although we will delve into the mechanics of deal making in Part 3 of this book, part of understanding strategic alignments is recognizing that you have to believe in the partnership in order for it to work. Sincere selling is one of the most genuine business tactics, and it can serve you well in any situation, not just those that involve negotiating a partnership.

The best way to sell something is to truly believe that what you are selling will benefit the buyer. This sincerity is rooted in several beliefs. First, you must genuinely believe in the product, which is probably a prerequisite for working in BD at a company in the first place. Belief in the product stems from understanding the product and its mechanics, and understanding the applications of its capabilities. Next, you must believe that the integration of the two products, companies, or user bases will be beneficial to both sides.

If you are bringing users to another company and they are giving you money, the deal needs to be fruitful for both sides in order to continue. Conversely, the fastest way for a deal to fall apart or be discontinued is if one side doesn't live up to the hype provided during the pitch or the courting process. This, of course, depends on the type of partnership, but setting expectations properly is very important.

For instance, if your user base is simply a subset of another company's, then a distribution partnership will probably be beneficial for one of the parties. If you will realistically add only a handful of new users over a few months, be honest and up front with the people on the other side of the deal so that when the results are examined, neither party is surprised. If their expectations are that the partnership will bring in tons of users, you might not make it to month 3 to actually prove your worth. Communicate, communicate, communicate.

Sincere selling is another way of saying, "Believe in what you are offering." If you don't believe in your offering, then who else will? There is a very slim chance that you will be able to convince another individual, let alone another company, that what you have to offer really matters. You have to believe it, deep down, and your sincerity needs to shine through. On top of that, you need to go out of your way to help the other side that you are courting. This could mean helping it with unrelated items (hiring, introductions to investors, the press, and so on). Be ready to help the other company in any way possible.

For those who adhere to the expression, "Fake it 'til you make it," this is a huge challenge in the pitching process. BD professionals may have difficulty pretending to believe in a product, since these deals often involve either the fates of both companies or large sums of money. The other side can see through insincerity, just as you should when you are the recipient of a pitch. And, if you don't believe in what you are currently peddling, it might be time to find a new kind of job or even a new industry.

Sincere Selling Versus BD

Sincere selling is a bit different when you're looking at sales versus BD, as discussed in Chapter 4. To jolt your memory, BD is a precursor for sales, and partnerships are a big piece of BD. When you are thinking about sincere selling, there is a lot more emphasis on selling sincerely in BD than in sales. The reason is that BD takes place much earlier in the process and is more of a question mark for the person you are pitching. You *need* to be as sincere as possible to convince people of the value of a new product or an innovative solution, since these things are relatively untested. In sales, on the other hand, the deals and processes are more structured and a product pitch formula is in place, so sincerity is not critical (although the best salespeople are sincere).

Why does sincere selling even matter? Sincere selling can be a sales tactic in and of itself. Once those on the other side see that you are genuinely willing to help them, they are more receptive to whatever you are pitching to them. This tends to be true regardless of the nature of the partnership or the size of the other party, and it usually foreshadows success for future partnerships as well.

Sincere selling is really an extension of networking and having a good rapport with others with no immediate and personal gratification in the pipeline (doing a favor, for example). People want to work with other people who have their best interest in mind. If you are sincere in your pitch, while it may not work out, the other side will be more inclined to work with you on the next opportunity, whether at your existing company or a few years in the future when you are both in different places.

When Sincere Selling Falls Short

While we are on the topic of having a failed pitch, sometimes you can be the most sincere person in the world, but your timing is off. Maybe the other party sees the value of your offering but has higher priorities at the moment. We guarantee that if sincere selling tactics are implemented, you are likely to have the opportunity to pitch your product again when the timing is better, to find a way to work with the individual you are pitching in the future, or to be referred to other people that the person you pitched is connected to (and don't be afraid to ask this person for introductions). There is absolutely no way you can go wrong if you sell sincerely.

Conversely, if you don't try the sincere selling tactic, there are several possible outcomes. It is possible to put on a fake smile and hope for the best. Most people would feel guilty about such a partnership, especially if they knew it was doomed to fail. Another tactic is to try to force products and offerings that don't make sense. This is a strategy that also meets with limited success. People can cut through the fat and see the lack of genuine fit for the partnership. Once they probe beyond the surface, it will be hard for you to make a strong case in favor of the partnership, and you will be spinning your wheels for no reason. Both strategies ultimately yield a loss of personal credibility, as you are overpromising and underperforming; indeed, it is not likely that the same partner will take a chance on you twice.

CHAPTER 18

Vapor Sales

As we described in Chapter 4, "Business Development Versus Sales," BD involves "selling" a product or a partnership idea to another entity. But sometimes that process necessarily involves a smoke-and-mirrors show. It is very common in BD to pitch a product or a partnership idea to a willing participant while the product is in the process of being built or finalized.

There are a few circumstances in which vapor sales are necessary, the first of which is the ideas stage. Hypothetically, you are working on a new startup or a new product at an existing company. You would like to get some market feedback on your idea before spending resources and time building it. While this scenario ordinarily takes place in the partner feedback process, the "sell" involves pitching the idea and then asking the obvious question: "If we built this, would you use, buy, or integrate it?" That kind of direct feedback can motivate a team or even create deadlines and a road map for the company that wants to build it.

The second is the development stage. Continuing that same example, you've justified spending resources and time on the product, and it is in development, but now you would like the potential users, buyers, or integrators to help shape it. In the beginning of the development stage, you should talk to as many companies as you can about the features that they would like to see in the product. In later stages of development, you should be in dialogue with companies of varying sizes about potentially being involved with the launch of the product.

This can be tricky, because most potential partners want to see performance data or metrics to extrapolate what a successful partnership might entail. Mike Dudas, mobile BD at PayPal (via Braintree and Venmo) and formerly BD at

Google Wallet, MTV Networks, and Disney, talks about the need for metrics. "The bottom line is that even in a 'promise-driven' sales approach for new products, the long-term viability of the product depends on performance data. Sell on market data and trends and product demos initially, but structure initial customer relationships to gather product performance data. Customers of new technology products will demand performance data in very short order."

The third is the launch stage. Now you are putting the finishing touches on an amazing product, and you want to get the most awareness of your launch. The best way to do this is by having a handful of companies use, buy, or integrate your new product offering. Furthermore, you should announce the launch of a product with "product partners," companies that are using the product and are willing to comment publicly on their experience with it. This way, when other companies look at your new product and wonder about its utility, they can go directly to one of your launch partners to test it out or ask about it.

When Do Vapor Sales Occur?

The question of when to begin selling a product or a vision is a delicate balancing act that any company that is seeking to monetize or partner must ask itself. The answer, of course, depends on who is the recipient of the pitch and the nature and complexity of the partnership. Generally speaking, it is best to approach other companies as your product is nearing completion.

Building a relationship early is important, but trying to do so too early makes it difficult for you to convince another company of your product's power or to time the launch. Often, you want to launch your product with a series of partners, and therefore you must connect with other companies before the product is completed. Sometimes these other companies will want to launch something of their own in conjunction with your product, so timing is critical, and sticking to a schedule becomes of the utmost importance. Either way you choose to go, any time the answer to the question includes a time frame before the existence of an actual product, some element of vapor sales is involved.

The Art of Vapor Sales

Mastering the art of vapor sales consists of taking the feedback you receive, integrating it into your future pitches, and actually getting it built into your product. If you can continue to vapor-sell your product until you are satisfied with the final version, defined as one that a handful of companies will commit to using, buying, or integrating once it is built, then you are putting yourself and your company in a position for great success.

The main difference between vapor sales and the sale of an actual product is that you can be creative in your delivery. But don't stray too far from the truth. If other companies want what you are peddling, you need to deliver, or forever be known as a bullshitter (well, maybe not forever, but it's hard to get rid of that label). If you feel confident that you can get your product and engineering teams to build or add something that you have vapor-sold, then go for it. And don't forget, vapor sales do not preclude sincere selling

For example, if you are in BD and partnerships, at some point you'll have to sell something that isn't fully built yet. This typically happens in the earliest stages of a company, as well as in new product cycles.

We've seen the most success in selling something that isn't ready when the pitch focuses less on selling and more on gathering information. Instead of pitching an actual product, you should phrase the pitch to imply that your company is considering building a product or feature, but you are trying to get feedback from clients and prospective partners. You can be explicit by stating that if there is enough interest, you expect to build the product. As companies give you feedback, you continue to take note and roll it into your ongoing selling process.

Scott Britton is a master of vapor sales, which he learned by working with the masters of vapor sales: Kenny Herman, executive vice president at SinglePlatform, and Wiley Cerilli, the founder of SinglePlatform and former head of sales for Seamless. While Britton was at SinglePlatform, he was able to close several partnerships based on these principles. He says that the key to preselling is to understand the needs of the other company by asking a lot of questions. Once you have all the answers you need, craft a story that makes it as easy as possible for the other side to say yes. And, as he says, the most important aspect of vapor sales is never to move forward with just a soft verbal commitment. If you are going to build something that doesn't yet exist, you need to have a firm deal in place.

Tirath Kamdar mastered the art of selling a product that doesn't yet exist during his time in partnerships and loyalty marketing at Fab.com, an online retailer, and Pawngo.com, an online pawnshop. His strategy was to rely heavily on publicity that the company had already received. "The way we pitched this was through heavy use of PR, and getting key publications and media to write about us as a clean and seamless way of getting short-term loans for your assets at better prices. Once we gained some PR from personal financial publications and the like, we built landing pages that incorporated this messaging and used this messaging across the site experience. We noticed people applying for loans and mailing us their watches and valuable assets to get the loans. It took us upwards of six months to actually gain credibility, but we ensured a consistent message from day one with PR driving credibility, and by sticking to this, we started to create a brand."

The bottom line: selling something that isn't ready isn't easy, but if you strike the proper balance, you can garner some early interest to capitalize on once your product is ready.

PART 3

PITCHING AND CLOSING

CHAPTER 19

PIPELINES AND PREPITCH EXECUTION

WE HAVE COVERED what it takes to perform in business development roles and introduced you to partnerships in the abstract. But pitching a business and closing a deal are not small efforts; a great deal of strategy, planning and, most important, organization are required before the deal is inked. In addition, the first deal you go after is not necessarily the one that gets done, nor is it necessarily the best deal, so having a pipeline of potential partners gives you options.

As a BD professional, you must build and manage a pipeline. This will help you decide your partnership direction and allow you to focus on which meetings to set up. Your pipeline, which contains information about the companies, products, and people you are pitching, will therefore house the information you need in order to prepare for partnership meetings.

Building a Pipeline

A partnership pipeline is simply a list of all of the partnership candidates for your team and the stage of progress of each deal. This should be an abridged list of the people in your personal network, those contacts that are relevant to your industry and in the networks of the people on your team. In addition to the people in your existing network, it should also include partners that you'd like to work with. Your pipeline should always be current and should be constantly updated and maintained. To make sharing easier and to avoid duplication, most professionals use some kind of cloud-based Excel file, like a Google spreadsheet.

Scott Britton says that this file is the only object that is open on his computer at all times. "I house all my prospects in a Google doc which I call [initiative] + hitlist. It's the first thing and the last thing I look at every day. It's literally always open to make sure I'm maintaining it properly. I also have weekly meetings with my team where we review it, which keeps me accountable for keeping it tight."

At larger companies, the pipeline can be maintained by a more junior BD professional. Managing the pipeline means keeping it current and reflective of the deal trajectory, constantly updating information about contacts. The person maintaining the pipeline should also utilize a system that gives easy access to other members of the team. You can use Salesforce, Trello, Highrise, or a similar customer relationship management (CRM) tool, but a simple spreadsheet with several columns will also work well.

Column 1: Company name.

Column 2: Name of contact at company.

Column 3: Email address and/or phone number for that contact.

Column 4: How big is the opportunity? Find a common metric that you can use across all companies. This might be user numbers, revenue numbers, market cap, or any other creative way of evaluating a company's size and the opportunity at hand.

Column 5: How likely is it that the company will work with you? Again, find a common metric. We like to use a 10-point scale, with 1 being least likely and 10 being most likely. Things to take into account: how close you are to the other company, what it is focused on, and your personal gut feeling.

Column 6: Status of the deal. Usually this is denoted by percent complete (for example, a deal is in the contract phase, so it is at 60 percent complete). You can make up what the percent levels represent, but remember that getting a meeting with a company doesn't mean that the deal is at 80 percent. It is more likely to be at 20 percent.

Column 7: Notes. Include any additional notes that may be relevant. These can be updated or overwritten as status changes.

	A	B	C	D	E	F	G
1	Company	Name	Title	Size	Probability	Stage- %	Notes
2	ABC Entertainment	Jeffrey Chang	Director of Business Development	Big	Low	40	Post-Meeting-- responded with a request for more info and questions for tech team.
3		Meghan Sweet	President (Sales & Marketing)				
4		Bob Benson	Executive Vice President (Marketing)				
5		Jason Pepper	Marketing				EMAILED THURS
6	ABC News	Leslie Cosette	Sales	Medium	Medium	60	
7	A&E TV	Shane Olson	Original Content	Small	Medium	60	Post Meeting-- wants too do something once they get content online
8		Peter Konti		Small	High	80	Wants to do pilot with DD
9	Fox Interactive	George Espinoza	SVP	Big	Medium	60	Interested in testing tech
10		Stephanie Siskel					
11	HBO	Jessica Ido	VP of Emerging Tech	Medium	Low	40	Post Meeting--- Went very well. Wants follow up in May-- will distribute info throughout the company
12	Lionsgate	Kathryn Elgin		Medium	Low	40	WAITING FOR A&E pilot stats
13	MPAA	Winston Wright		-	-		Need to follow up
14	MTV	Allison Stanley	VP of Business Development	Big	Low	20	Maternity Leave
15		David Rodman					Spoke briefly and then no correspondence-- Will follow up
16	NBC/Universal	Liz Nelson	New Media and Marketing	Big	Low	40	Not now, keep updating
17	Paramount	Duncan Smith	VP of Digital Distribution	Big	Low	20	Conf call tomorrow-- then trying to get meeting in LA

Sample Pipeline

Overall, this document should be the guiding light on the status of your partnerships and the relationships that you can leverage should a new partnership opportunity or need come your way. Pipelines are also used in other non-technical situations, including managing press relationships (known as the press pipeline), raising money (the fund-raising pipeline), and other such areas.

Mike Ghaffary, vice president of business development for Yelp, believes that all partnerships should be rooted in an investment thesis or a strategic vision:

The first phase of building a partnership pipeline is to establish a strategic vision of what you're trying to accomplish. Phase 2 is building a pipeline. It can be as simple as Excel or Google docs or go all the way to using Salesforce or another CRM tool to build. If you are one person alone at a startup managing the pipeline, a spreadsheet is sufficient. But the more people there are on the team, the more you should move toward using CRMs like Salesforce.

Managing a Pipeline

Categorize your potential partnerships by how big the companies are and the probability that you will close the deals. Rank the size as small, medium, or large and the probability as low, medium, or high.

When looking at your pipeline, focus on the deals that fall into the medium and high categories in the probability column and the medium and large categories on the size column. This should be fairly obvious, but you would be surprised how often such a simple concept gets overlooked.

Ghaffary says, "Phase 3 is thinking about 'whom should I be calling?' This is where a strategic road map comes into play. Here you should also be thinking about the distinction between sales and business development."

Use the relationship between probability and size to determine the likelihood and influence of the partnership. If you have no partners for your product but your strategy is partnership-driven, focusing some attention on getting a few high-probability but smaller-sized partnerships should be the first step. Once you have a few notches on your belt, you can shift your focus to the high or medium probability and large or medium-size deals.

Managing your team pipeline is important. After you have ranked the size of the company and the probability of the deal taking place, it's time to start working on these partnerships and making some pitches.

Strategies for Getting Meetings

To learn how to pitch effectively, you must build upon the knowledge that you have gained from previous chapters about types of partnerships, identifying the right person, and refining and perfecting the product for a partner. Then, reach out to potential partner companies with a short but effective introduction. Finally, make your pitch and hopefully find a deal that works for both parties.

Andy Ellwood, founder of BOND, says that as a partnerships professional, he was often given the task of finding companies to target for meetings. "When we were making a game plan for our product road map, I would 'take requests' from our teams, and we'd pick companies that we thought would be the ideal partner for the new feature or release that was coming out. I would then 'go hunt' and see what we could come back with in time for that release."

To actually get a partnership meeting, you first need to identify all methods of getting in front of the company. The first thing is to look online, usually at sites like LinkedIn, to see if you can find a common denominator between you and the company. If you have a mutual connection to a strong starting person, ask that connection for an introduction. If your contact is the wrong person, still ask him for an introduction, but with the caveat that you are looking to talk to the right person (it is best if you have that person's name already) and are hoping that he can facilitate.

While all the phases of the partnership cycle are important, pitching is critical. If you don't do a good job of getting the other side excited about what you are offering, you will probably be out of luck when it comes to BD.

Identifying Targets

Part of managing a pipeline is identifying key deal targets. As we discussed previously in Chapter 14, "Identifying the Right Person at the Partner Company," locating the target company or person for a strategic partnership is the first step toward completing a deal. Once you have a robust pipeline that lists all the companies that you might work with, you should narrow down the list to those companies that might actually do deals with a company like yours in terms of size, stage, vertical segment, or even product. This list of companies ultimately becomes your short list and is where you focus first.

Connecting with Companies

After you have mapped out the appropriate vertical segments and determined the relevant companies, it is time to get in front of those companies. You may already have existing connections at several of them, including people you have met through networking events. Get in touch with these people first. If you are close to them, you can test out the pitch on them before going to anyone that you do not already know.

The absolute last option is the blind reach-out: introducing yourself to strangers. Getting in touch with people you don't know is a learned art, and the best way to meet strangers is to get a warm introduction. If you know someone who knows the person (and knows her well), and he can vouch for you and is willing to make an introduction, you have a higher likelihood of getting in front of her. If you have been introduced by a mutual acquaintance, your prospect is likely to respond favorably to your correspondence, but setting up a meeting with her is not necessarily guaranteed.

When you are asking for an introduction, a simple email to the mutual connection will suffice. Ordinarily, you can send a quick note with the subject "Introduction to [Person's Name] at [Company]?" Within the body of the email, explain the reason you are asking for the introduction and give as much context as possible. You can also provide a brief overview of the work you are doing (a sentence or two) and the reason for the pitch. If what you are asking is clear, concise, and not phrased as an imposition, your mutual connection will probably be happy to make the introduction if he is close to the person you are trying to meet.

The optimal way to obtain a warm introduction is by using services like LinkedIn, which can show you how you are connected to a person or a company. *Be wary of asking for the introduction on the platform itself; it can be clunky*—use regular email to ask for it and mention that you saw the person's connection on LinkedIn. If you know exactly whom you need to speak to, find that person's profile and see if you are directly or indirectly connected with her.

The trickier part is when you want to reach a company and don't necessarily know the correct person to contact. Using the principles outlined in Chapter 14, "Identifying the Right Person at the Partner Company," you can use services like Google and LinkedIn to search for the company to see if you are connected to anyone. If not, look for a strong secondary connection, even if it is to someone in an unrelated role. If you have multiple mutual connections with someone at the company, it is bound to generate a warm introduction, albeit by a roundabout route.

If both these strategies fail, a short blind reach-out is your best option. These seldom lead to either conversations or pitches, but you don't get what you don't ask for.

For the blind reach-out, the nature of the correspondence is slightly different. Email is still the preferred method of contact, although messages through other social media platforms can work if an email address is not available. The subject of the email should be self-explanatory: "Reach Out—Company X to Company Y" (for example, "Reach Out—NewCo to Facebook"). The body of the email should be limited to no more than five sentences. Provide a brief introduction of yourself and your company, and use the remaining word allotment to explain why the person should talk to you. *Keep in mind that the purpose of the blind reach-out is not to get the other party to say yes or close a deal, but merely to get him to respond to you.* Give him enough to intrigue him and make him want to find out more, and he is likely to follow up with an email or request a phone call.

Preparing for a Meeting

Doing Research and Understanding Other Companies

When you are getting ready for a call or meeting with another company, regardless of the nature of the conversation, there are a few things that you should do ahead of time to prepare yourself. Even if the other company is not expecting a pitch at the time of the phone call or if the premise of the interaction is to have an exploratory conversation, it is critical that you first do some research on the other company. As we described in Chapter 11, "Understanding Other Companies," having a basic working knowledge of the other company before you speak on the phone is a must. Using strategies similar to those recommended for networking in Chapter 5, "Networking," read about the history of the company, its product, its monetization efforts, and its fund-raising history.

This exercise should not be just memorization of a fact sheet, although you should commit to memory basic facts about the company. To understand another company holistically, there are a few things you can do. First, you can read its blog and read any press it has received in the past few months. If it isn't a publicly traded company, you can try talking to its investors. If it is publicly held, you should talk to any of its partners and read its published financial statements (in the form of 10-Ks, or annual financial reports, and 10-Qs, or quarterly financial reports), and any investment analysts' reports. If you do the proper research, you should be able to position your offering to match what the company finds important or what is at the core of its business.

Preparing for the Actual Meeting

Most meetings involve some kind of implicit pitch, even if it's informal. Always come prepared with an online presentation about your company and what you are asking for, even if you don't ultimately use it. Always be ready to make the pitch in case you have to give an impromptu presentation.

In addition, do some research about the people you will be meeting. Try to find their professional histories on LinkedIn, or learn something about them via their online presence on Twitter or other social media sites. This way, you can utilize some of the tools from Chapter 5, "Networking," to connect with these individuals.

Managing Your Team's Expectations

As the old business adage says, you should always underpromise and overdeliver.

If you have five deals that you think will close in the same week, don't promise anything until you have the contracts signed and in your inbox (and the money in the bank, if it applies). Deals are always falling apart, and getting your team members' expectations up when you don't know which way a deal will go is just bad practice. They won't know the difference, for the most part, so don't overpromise.

If you need to talk to your team members about a deal, tell them the truth about the status: things look good, there's lots of interest, but there are still obstacles along the path to success, and you will let them know when this is done.

20

MAKING THE PITCH AND CLOSING THE DEAL

HERE WE GO. This is the heart of our book. BD, partnerships, and everything in between are ultimately about pitching and closing. Our hope is that after you read and internalize this chapter, you will have more than enough information to go out there and make a good impression on the people you want to work with.

Pitching

The standard business pitch has not changed in decades. The process usually entails face-to-face interaction at one of the companies' offices. The company that is seeking a partnership will create a pitch deck (that is, a presentation) that contains relevant and concise information about the business. During the presentation, the person making it will be peppered with questions from the listeners, who are looking for holes in the arguments. Most presenters will steer the conversation back to the deck, and will conclude with a specific request to the company.

Over time and with more confidence, you can begin to deviate from the classic slide-by-slide method. Indeed, in the technology space, most classic pitches seem outdated and can be met with a tepid response. But in this chapter, we'll show you the proper way to approach pitching in a more modern environment.

Pitching Materials

There are a few schools of thought about using materials when pitching. Some professionals prefer to have a short deck that they use to guide them through the discussion of the product, the offering, and, finally, the request. Other people opt for longer, more extensive presentations with handouts. And some people don't use any materials at all, opting to just converse (ask questions, talk, and listen) with the other side.

Most companies, no matter how small, have some form of canned deck. Even if you are the founder of a company, it is your responsibility to put together a concise yet comprehensive deck that includes information about your product, your business plan (or strategy), your team, and anything else that is noteworthy. The first deck may help you secure an initial round of funding, but when it comes to seeking partnerships, your deck must be tweaked to focus on the partnership itself.

Making the Pitch

Anyone can pitch. Pitching is just the act of attempting to convince other people to do something that you want them to do. We all pitch frequently, whether we realize it or not. You've pitched to your spouse to see the movie that you want to see rather than the one that she wants to see. You've pitched to your parents for gifts around the holidays. You've pitched to your friends about what to do on a Saturday night. Pitching your business, product, or offering is not much different. The means to the end is the same: your pitch needs to convince the other side to do what *you* want them to do rather than sticking with what *they think* they need or want to do.

The template pitch deck has a standard flow and a similar series of slides no matter which company you are pitching. Your pitch deck needs slides on your product or service offering, the basic features, the benefits of working together, a screen shot of the product or service offering, a screen shot of what a potential partnership looks like, a slide listing all the companies that are working with you already (if applicable), and a slide listing the next steps. Each slide is important and helps tell a great story to the person you are pitching.

Product/service/offering slide. This slide includes a high-level overview of what your product does, usually one or two sentences at most, in big, bold type.

Features slide. This slide describes and elaborates on the capabilities of your product. You can *either* give each feature its own slide with explanation bullet points under each one *or* include all the features on one slide, giving all bullet points, and then expound on each feature when you are presenting. Either way is perfectly professional. This is a matter of personal preference.

Benefits slide. This slide is where you jump into why your offering is going to help the company you are pitching. Go back to the four golden rules of partnerships and use them as a guiding light when filling out this slide. Pinpoint the specific benefits you offer, and set proper expectations.

Screen shot of your product or service offering. To fully explain your product or offering, include a screen shot of what you have created. People respond favorably to visuals, and showing is always better than simply telling. If applicable, you may want to jump into a demonstration of your offering at this stage of the pitch. The downside to this is that you probably will never get back to the rest of the pitch if you go off on a tangent with the demonstration. Once you jump into a demo, it is next to impossible to go back to a static slide deck.

Do a demonstration only if you have a viable product that looks impressive and is ready to be shown to a captivated audience. Showing is better than telling, so if you can demonstrate (even briefly), it's always preferable. If the product is not ready, or if it is still susceptible to massive bugs, do not demonstrate the product, since you are likely to lose credibility if you show a faulty product.

Screen shot of what a potential partnership looks like. If you don't sidestep into a product demonstration, the next logical slide is a screen shot of what a partnership could potentially look like. This usually makes most sense for product partnerships (particularly if there is a product or feature integration to look at). When dealing with other types of partnerships, sometimes you put your logo and the other firm's logo on the same page with some other graphics.

Partners slide. This slide helps to validate your operation. It usually includes the logos of all the other companies that are already partnering with you or using your product. If you are an enterprise company, this should include your major paying customers. Displaying known entities and their logos that patronize your product or service offering adds

credibility to your pitch. For example, if you
are pitching to an e-commerce company and you have Amazon as a
partner on your partner slide, the e-commerce company will view you
in a better light and will be more likely to want to partner with you
as well.

Next steps slide. Always end your pitch deck with a next steps slide. You've
done a killer job of pitching your offering, and the company is interested
in working with you; now what? What you list here could be the next
steps from a business perspective, a technology vantage point, or even a
legal or logistical point of view. The next steps slide brings that discussion
to light and also leaves the audience with a taste of the future. It makes
you and your team seem forward-thinking, organized, and committed to
the partnership. It also is the next step to actually closing the deal.

The pitch to potential partners will depend on the nature of the partnership
you are seeking and how your two companies will work together. A distribution
partnership pitch to a business-to-consumer (B2C) company will probably be
led slightly differently from a pitch for a monetization partnership to a business-
to-business-to-consumer (B2B2C) company.

If the pitch is being made in an office setting, make sure to bring your own
collateral and technology, including printouts of the pitch deck, your own laptop or tablets, and so on. You will probably want to connect your computer to
one of the other company's projectors if you are in its office space. If you are in
your own space, you will have more time to set up, but if you are not, be sure to
ask about cords and compatibility before you enter the company's office. There
is nothing more embarrassing than showing up and not being able to make the
pitch because of technological constraints.

There are two ways to go into your pitch. The first is to project a presentation deck in a conference room (PowerPoint and Keynote are the most popular
software services) and go through it slide by slide. This pitch tactic is more traditional and often expected.

The second is to jump right into your product or offering and demonstrate it
to the audience. This works best if you have a web or mobile product with functionality; even a minimally viable product is sufficient, and you want to introduce the product very quickly. As mentioned previously, it is usually important
that you provide some context and set the stage for a product demonstration,
even if you plan to let it serve as the pitch itself. You can do this by giving a quick

background on yourself and the company, and setting up what the product is and what it does. Then, jump straight into the product.

Truly, there is no better way to pitch a product then to show it! Regardless of the type of partnership you are proposing, you should be able to show how your product works. Show what it does. Show how the other company can use it. If your demonstration hits on something that the company cares about, you should be on track to closing a deal. If possible, try to give a hands-on copy of the product to everyone in the room so that they can try it for themselves.

Pitching for the Three Types of Partnerships

Depending on the type of deal you are trying to close, there are some nuances to keep in mind. Remember the three types of partnerships: product partnerships, brand partnerships, and distribution partnerships.

Product Partnership Pitch Nuances

For a product or integration partnership pitch, you want to make sure that you show what the product will look like once it is integrated with the other company's product. You are trying to get this company to spend the development time to integrate your offering. Come prepared to show what that will end up looking like, how long it will take, and how much the company can benefit (whether your product offering brings it more users, brings it more money, saves money, or improves its product). Use screen shots to show how your product will look once it is integrated or, even better, bring a working prototype of the integration. This effort takes time, but it can be the silver bullet that pushes a company over the edge to work with you.

Eric Friedman of Foursquare says that he "always tries to understand what motivates someone and the company he works for. Knowing this can sometimes cut through all the clutter that can cloud a deal." He also advocates setting expectations internally, especially among the people who touch the product, so that they understand what they are getting into at every stage of the deal.

Brand Partnership Pitch Nuances

For a brand partnership pitch, make sure to include what that cobranded experience will entail. This is mostly done with highly polished screen shots and mockups of the cobrand. Everything else is the same in terms of the pitch and method of attacking the partnership opportunity. The idea here is to show the other company what the cobranded product will look like and to spell out what each side will bring to the table in order to make it happen. For example, one side might have the user base of customers, while the other side has something new and exciting.

Maxine Friedman, former vice president of business development at Contently, has extensive experience with branding partnerships and went above and beyond the framework of the partnership to maximize the effect:

> I worked on a brand partnership with a large social media network. As a startup, we were very interested in the "halo" effect that its brand could have for us in gaining credibility and mindshare. Essentially, and in addition to integrating on its application programming interface (API), we cohosted a few events together, developed cobranded collateral, and worked on some cobranded pitches.
>
> The requirement for these partnerships is that each party believes the partnership is mutually beneficial; focuses on creativity and ideation, which are essential in developing the go-to-market strategy; and trusts the other (also an imperative, as these kinds of deals are often developed through an initial personal relationship and therefore are not on paper but given through verbal agreements). The way I've seen these play out typically is that one more traditional (larger) company is trying to gain access to new technology either to advance its offering or to provide an increased perception of its being on the "cutting edge," while the smaller startup entity is trying to gain access to a user base or garner stature as a player in the market.

Whenever you are conducting a branding partnership, you need to spell out what each side is bringing and show what the partnership will look like if you are looking to close this deal.

Distribution Partnership Pitch Nuances

When what you are after is a network partnership, you will find yourself in one of two positions. One is that you are looking for distribution, and the other is that you have distribution and are looking for people to leverage that distribution (we should all be so lucky!).

When you are looking for a distribution deal, let's assume that you have found the right company to work with. When pitching that company, remember that it has the distribution and most of the time is looking for money or for

104 · PITCHING & CLOSING

even more distribution for itself, as you can never have too much distribution. There are some network deals in which each side is in need of more distribution and each side has distribution to offer, like the mobile partnerships that Lars Fjeldsoe-Nielsen, formerly at Dropbox and now at Uber, oversees. In all distribution scenarios, one side, usually the side with the distribution capabilities, needs to show or share numbers on how much distribution it really has. The company that is pitching, usually the one without distribution, unless you are doing a codistribution deal, needs to explain what it brings to the table if it wants to do this deal without money. If it doesn't have something to bring to the company it is pitching, then the conversation usually goes straight to money, and at that point it is less of a pitch and more of a negotiation.

In the unlikely case that your preliminary research was inconclusive or incorrect and your offering is not relevant to the company, it's best to cut your losses and move on. This usually means either that you didn't do your research and the other company didn't do its due diligence on who you are, or that the other company was just taking an exploratory meeting. You can use the opportunity to tell the firm about your company and say candidly that you think the prospects for a partnership might not be good at the time of the meeting. It's better to end on good terms than to offer false promises.

Making Your Pitch Better

The best pitchers find a way to ask the company two questions (or get answers to the two questions) even before the pitch begins. The first question is: what is the other company focused on now, and the second is: what is most important to that company at this time? By beginning your pitch meeting with these questions, you get information that you could not possibly learn by doing research. It also shows that you have done your research up to those questions, and are thinking about pitching the company in the right way. Once you hear the answers, you will know immediately whether your offering is relevant to the other firm's business. *This is probably the most important part of the pitch, and it shouldn't be overlooked.* Make sure that the asking is done naturally and not as an interview of the business that you are trying to work with. If you do it right, you will get the valuable information that you need and be able to be a more effective pitcher.

Regardless of whether you choose a more traditional style or the free-form demo pitch, a big part of your success will depend on your being able to tell a good story. Sometimes you have something exciting for the company right now (or will be imminently releasing it), and other times you are still trying to figure out what that killer offering will be. Whichever it is, craft a good story and make a supporting case for why this company should want to partner with you.

Understanding Why Someone Would Want to Work with You

If you want to work with another company, you'd better bring something to the table. We've written before about the four golden rules of partnerships, and this is where they apply. Figure out what the company's focus area is, and use the rules to determine how a partnership with your company can be of help. After you identify what it is that your company can do to benefit the other company, you should focus on that company's road map and try to understand its priorities.

There are three stages in the business cycle of startups: product development, scaling, and monetization. If you want to work with another company and the partnership would help its monetization efforts, but it is still focused on building the product, this would probably be a wrong fit at the wrong time. If you can help with scaling when the other company is focused on making money, then you probably won't partner.

Let's take Tumblr, for example. In 2012, Tumblr was in the monetization phase. It had scaled its user base to more than 170 million users worldwide and was looking to monetize those users and turn itself into a business. If you had come to Tumblr with a user acquisition or product improvement partnership proposal (unless the integration of your product made the firm money), it would most likely not have been interested in partnering with you. But if you had had a way for Tumblr to earn money from its existing user base, it would probably have been interested in a potential partnership. Yahoo! came to Tumblr with the ultimate deal, and eventually acquired the service for more than $1.1 billion in 2013.

How Much Can You Help Them?

After you have identified what you have to offer and understand where the other company is on its road map, the next big question is how deeply you can affect that company. Take a company like AOL. If you want to work with AOL, and you offer a way to grow its user base, the question will be, "Well, how many new users will you bring?" If that number is five users, then you definitely don't have anything to talk about. But if that number is 50,000 new users a day, then maybe that's interesting enough for AOL to explore further.

Have You Done It with Anyone Else Before?

After all is said and done, the big question is, "Can you prove it?" You can talk a good game, but all the company really cares about is whether you will be able to do what you say you are capable of doing. Prove your case with examples of other companies you have worked with.

Refreshing Your Pitch

The arc of your story can stay consistent if you are making several pitches in a short period of time, but every few months, you must refresh your pitch. Ordinarily, this becomes relevant when you have new products on the horizon. In your pitch and with any marketing materials you use, including the pitch deck, the takeaway deck, or linked articles, you need to ensure that you include the most up-to-date and forward-looking company offerings. For materials, you always need to be updating and refreshing the information on upcoming products. With every meeting, you will receive more and more feedback. That feedback will continue to drive changes in the offering, which will, in turn, continue to drive changes in the pitch.

Timing and Motivators for Partnerships

One of the major elements of any partnership is that timing is everything. Sometimes your timing may be off when you first connect, but keeping in touch with the other side could lead to something down the road. It's good to remember that it is not always you who holds the other side back; it may be your timing. If you get rejected and you sense that it is because of timing, continue dialogue with other companies and circle back to your earlier prospects periodically. If you have a strong fit between two companies, timing usually aligns at some point.

Learning by Witnessing

The best way to get good at pitching is to find a great pitcher and shadow him. Every company that gets to a decent size has at least one solid pitcher on the team. Find that person and work closely with him. If you don't have such a person in-house, go out and find someone whose public presentation skills you admire. Spend as much time with that person as possible and learn to do as she does.

Prove It

There is no particular formula for how a deal is generated or completed, but there are a few critical elements that must occur when you are in a conversation with another company. As we outlined in Part 1, deals are made partially through networking or connections, partly out of financial or product necessity, and finally out of the desire to take a risk with a great potential payoff. But these deals do not get completed through luck; you must prove what you can do in order to get the deal done. You can have the nicest slides and the coolest demo, but if you can't back it up with numbers, you will have a hard time closing the deal.

One of the most important factors in developing partnerships is being able to prove your value. This means not only being able to demonstrate what your company offers or speak about the benefit of the products, but also knowing who else gets value from your company. In essence, which other companies are using your service or product? In the infancy of your offering, the answer will be not many, and you should be honest about that. Most players in your space will understand that as a new company, you must begin to gain traction from a starting point.

As you add small- and medium-sized companies to the list of those that use the product, your answer will become stronger and more robust, and you should ultimately have some big-name partners that will help convince prospective partners that they should commit to partnering or integrating with you (otherwise known as *validation*). Being able to "prove it" to potential partners by showing how others have found value in your company and how this particular company could benefit is based on perception and your pitch.

If you have various clients who are already using your product or who are able to speak of the value that your product or offering provides, but you are still having difficulty closing deals, it is probably because the other side is having a hard time justifying the benefits. It's likely that the other side is hesitant to take a risk on the product either because it hasn't seen tangible results or because the tangible results are not what its team is looking for.

The best way to go about proving your value to another company is to show raw data that tell a positive and, more important, cohesive story that will compel this company to want to work with you. In Chapter 36, we will talk about turning a "nice to have" into a "need to have," and this is most frequently done by substantiating claims with actual data. If you can show a company direct results from another similar partnership that has performed well and resulted in a benefit for both sides, you can all but guarantee the success of a partnership.

The nature of the data depends on the type of company you work for and the metrics against which the company benchmarks itself and its success. This could include providing data about user numbers and proving that a distribution partnership with another company grew the number of users on both sides. Alternatively, if you are a later-stage company or you are partnered with a company that is focused on monetization, you can use data to demonstrate how you grew a company's user base or how you helped a company monetize really well. Whatever the metrics you have that will help you close the deal, use them to your advantage. The flip side is that you need to go out and get those tangible results, usually via your stand-alone business, before you approach a third party about working together. It will save you the time of trying to sell the other side on something that is probably not ready.

Some businesses are able to pull off the smoke-and-mirrors show, selling a product that does not exist without metrics or results to demonstrate. We spoke about this in Chapter 18, "Vapor Sales." Generally speaking, this is a daunting task that only the most skilled pitchers can carry out successfully. More often than not, the other party will be able to tear the arguments apart and recognize the lack of anything tangible behind the curtain.

The minimum that is needed to "prove it" can vary depending on the type of company. In an example that we will touch upon later, one savvy CEO was able to go far with some wireframes, a robust PowerPoint, and a persuasive pitch. This isn't common and should not be attempted lightly. Most partnerships between companies are predicated on the pitching company's having at least the start of a working product, and perhaps even a small core user group that has provided feedback.

Keep in mind that perception is key, especially the attitude of other partners who are currently working with you. A positive product recommendation speaks even louder than data-driven results at the early stages of partnerships, and you can leverage such recommendations to your advantage when cultivating a base of partners. As with most things in the partnership world, creating a powerful and positive network of professionals in your space can contribute substantially to the success of your business.

There is a difference between "proving it" at early-stage companies and at later-stage companies. At later-stage companies, or at least for mature products at later-stage companies, you should have data to support your proposals. At early-stage companies, you might not have this information handy. You may have very few or no partners, and those that you have are probably very small companies and not behemoths. Be wary of a startup company that has major name-brand partners way too early without having tested the waters with smaller companies. Something is usually amiss; for example, the company may not have a "full" deal with the bigger company.

So what do you do when you are in the early stages of a company or product's existence? How do you prove it? Well, you don't, but you do your best to position question marks in a favorable light. You need to try to get as many smaller and medium-sized companies as you can to take the leap of faith with you (this can be accelerated if you pay them to do it) and help you acquire these much-sought-after and absolutely essential data that will enable you to prove your theories. You will often be rejected in this phase, but if you are a decent presenter, you should get one or a few people to work with you. It also helps if you start off by going to friends and friends of friends. Strangers usually want to help less; they don't like to be guinea pigs.

Closing

You can be a natural-born pitchman, but there is no such thing as a natural-born closer. By far, the best way to learn to close is to work with or for someone who has done it many times and can teach you the craft. If you are a junior employee and you have the opportunity to either jump to the majors and run the show or work under a founder or a vice president of BD and partnerships to learn the fundamentals, work under the seasoned pro.

As soon as you've identified the right person, had the meeting, and made the pitch, it's time for the hard sell and, finally, the close. Sometimes the process of closing a deal can be as fast as a first meeting pitch and agreeing on deal terms all in one. Those are the most ideal, yet most uncommon, circumstances. Usually, the close cycle starts with the first pitch meeting, then continues through follow-up meetings and discussions with key stakeholders, conveying final decisions, and finally closing the deal.

The Four Most Important Things to Think About When Closing a Deal

Create a Sense of Urgency

A sense of urgency is the first thing to think about when closing a deal, because it is the most important. Closing deals means having the ability to put yourself on top of the other firm's priority list. If there is no urgency to do so, you will be out of luck in closing the deal. There are many ways to create a sense of urgency, such as offering an exclusivity, being part of a launch of special discounts or deals, or being featured in press and promotion. Make sure the urgency is authentic so that the prospective partner actually cares to prioritize your deal.

Pitching Is 80 Percent of the Close

The description of pitching in this chapter is much longer than the section on closing for a reason. Pitching represents the lion's share of the work in closing. The best pitching will lead to closing. If you pitch correctly, you'll get to the stage where the closing is high probability. The deals whose timing isn't right or that are not at the right life-cycle stage for the company will appropriately fall by the wayside, freeing up time to focus on doing deals that matter.

Use Competition to Motivate Partners

If you have worked with a company that competes with the company you are pitching, playing up the competition angle sometimes works. Companies can, at times, be motivated by fear. If they are behind one of their competitors, this creates a sense of urgency for them and makes them give priority to a deal with you.

Overcommunicate and Get Things in Writing

Once you've pitched and the company is interested in taking the next steps, make sure that both sides are communicating about what you are working on, how the deal might be structured from your available collateral, and what barriers you might face. Make sure to put this information in an email and go through terms before you get sucked into a contract. If you can agree on the terms via email, then you'll save yourself considerable time that would otherwise be spent on contract negotiation. You should get to the contract stage only after all the big nuggets have been agreed upon, as we will discuss in the next chapter.

The dirty secret of closing deals is that it has, for the most part, more to do with timing and your offering than it has to do with your ability to sell a vision. While you have the ability to define what the time horizon is, especially by creating a sense of urgency around the deal closing, and you can influence how the offering is executed by pitching and positioning the product and the deal, *at the end of the day, either you have something that the other side wants or you don't.* Your goal in selling is to understand what the other side wants (or what it should want) and then give that to it. That's all. If you don't have what the other side wants or you don't have something that it currently cares about, you'll receive either an immediate decline or a simple "please come back later when we do have the capacity to work with your product," which translates as "not no, but not now."

The logistics behind closing a deal are simple. Once all terms have been agreed upon, which is ordinarily the most complicated and labor-intensive part, both sides need to sign a legally binding contract. The contract usually includes your terms of service, which the other party needs to agree to. Once you have the agreement inked, it is up to you, your team, your counterpart on the deal, and the other company's team to get to work on implementing the terms.

Simply putting ink on a paper is not fully closing a deal. Closing a deal is inking the paper *and* implementing the integration, promotion, and offering. As a BD or partnership professional, it is your responsibility to continue to work on this deal after the pitch, through the close, and until the deal is announced. Once the announcement is made, that is when the deal is finally closed. Go celebrate, but don't party too long. Any deal that is worth getting is one that someone else wants, regardless of whether or not an exclusivity clause is involved.

Walking Away

One of the scariest things to do in life is to walk away. This could be from a BD deal, a job opportunity, a new apartment lease, or a relationship. But we're here to say, don't be afraid to walk away (from a BD deal). Sometimes walking away is the right thing to do.

We used to be terrified of saying no to deals. But walking away from a deal or offering because the terms don't make sense for you is not only the smart thing to do but the right move. Most of the time you have nothing to lose. It's easier said than done, but one of the obvious ways to cultivate the ability to walk away is to give yourself many options. If you are trying to close a deal in a certain vertical segment, speaking with many competitors in the space will help. This way, you can be fine with saying no to an inappropriate deal as long as you have a robust pipeline that includes other great potential partners. Trust your gut; if the partnership doesn't seem like the right idea and you feel that you have more to lose than to gain from closing the deal, walk away.

It's difficult to walk away. Sometimes the downside seems infinite. But that's not the reality, and you shouldn't be afraid to walk away when something isn't right for you.

CHAPTER 21

THE LEGALITY OF DEAL MAKING: CONTRACTS AND BEYOND

ONCE YOU KNOW the basics of pitching and closing, you need to get into the more complex details of contracts, letters of intent, revenue sharing, forecasting, terms of service, negotiating, and so on. This chapter describes the formalities of deal making.

Contracts

In creating a partnership between two entities, each side is largely focused on how it can accomplish what it wants to do, get deal terms that are favorable to it, and define a metric that will determine success. But the meat of the partnership is the actual contract that is signed between the two parties. It can be easy to lose sight of the binding agreement that details the arrangement when you are bogged down in pitching and closing, but it is important to remember that the deal is not finalized until the contract is signed.

Five Insider Tips for BD Contracts

Phillip Eubanks, a lawyer-turned-BD analyst at Spotify, has five tips for understanding and crafting partnership contracts. These suggestions are broadly applicable regardless of the nature of the partnership or the two entities involved:

1. *The simpler, the better.* "Keep it simple, stupid" is the KISS design princi-
    ple. Partnership contracts are no exception to this rule. Remember that
    the contract is supposed to spell out the terms of agreement and not much
    more. It should be clear and precise concerning what is expected from
    both sides. Occasionally, there will be complexities within the contract that
    must be explained, but in general, the more concise it is, the better.
2. *Lose the legalese.* Legal jargon can be intimidating, and one side of the deal
    might try to use it to intimidate the other. Don't be overwhelmed, and
    do your best to stay away from this language if possible. As Eubanks says,
    "Include technical terms only where necessary and don't overuse connec-
    tors, such as 'furthermore,' 'aforementioned,' and the like."
3. *Standardize.* As your company grows, you will need to become more
    efficient at executing these contracts so that you do not lose momentum
    or create a bottleneck when demand is high. Standardize the contracts as
    much as possible so that you can spend more time focusing on the terms of
    the deal. As your company grows and increases its partnerships, standard-
    ization allows you to compare deals and pinpoint areas for negotiation.
4. *Consider the tech.* Partnership professionals are inclined to include only
    details about the economics and the financial arrangements in the terms.
    Instead, be sure to include the terms of the technical integration as well.
    According to Eubanks, "This does not mean that the contract includes every
    little detail of the technical integration. Rather, to the extent that there are
    technical issues requiring both parties to work together, the parameters of
    how that process will take place should be outlined in the contract. Com-
    mon examples include API integrations, sharing of email lists for removing
    duplicates, and development and ownership of marketable assets."
5. *Renewal.* The goal of a partnership is not to create a one-time deal. Any
    BD professional knows that the deal is about the long game, with the goal
    of renewing the contract if the deal is successful. You want to consider
    having an autorenewal clause in the contract so that high-performing
    partnerships can be extended without renegotiation. "The key is to peg the
    performance of the partnership in some way so that you can dissolve or
    renegotiate the deal if it is not advantageous for both parties, but can also
    extend the partnership where it is clearly performing well," says Eubanks.

Rob Weiss, a lawyer and director of BD at RentHop, also cautions that both
sides of the deal should be aware of (and up-front about) who can actually sign

on behalf of the company. He says, "*Don't* assume that you are authorized to sign for the company. If you sign for the company, and the other side reasonably believes that you're authorized to sign for the company, the company will have great difficulty later getting out of the contract on the grounds that you weren't the right signatory."

Jeremy Schwartz, business development manager at Squarespace and a lawyer, reminds us that the lawyers can nitpick the contract, but ultimately the BD professional is the one who has to execute and uphold the terms of the contract. "It is your responsibility as a businessperson to read and understand the entire contract. Remember, you're the one who has to live with its repercussions. If there's a section you don't understand, ask."

Letters of Intent and Nondisclosure Agreements

Letters of intent (LOIs) and nondisclosure agreements (NDAs) are two standard forms signed by each side of a deal at various stages of the cycle.

Anyone who has ever entered the offices of a big tech startup has probably had the experience of being asked to sign an NDA. In its most basic form, an NDA is a binding agreement by the signatory that she will not disclose anything that she sees. According to Eubanks, "A nondisclosure agreement protects your nonpublic business information from unauthorized use by a potential partner who may gain access to such information during the exploratory process."

Letters of intent are more specific to the execution and discussion of deals. When two companies are beginning conversations regarding deals, letters of intent become important. Eubanks defines a letter of intent as "An agreement describing in detail a negotiating party's intention to complete an action prior to the execution of a formal contract. LOI's can be used for a variety of reasons, such as protecting you from a partner that has no intention of pursuing a partnership in good faith (i.e., it protects you from wasting your time)."

When to Sign an NDA or an LOI

The timing of signing these two documents can depend on how adamant your company is about protecting its product. If you approach a pitch meeting with an NDA or an LOI, your potential partner could be put off by the aggressive nature of the gesture. On the other hand, it is critical that you protect your proprietary information.

Eubanks recommends that you consider signing both LOIs and NDAs when you move beyond discussing a partnership in the abstract and begin detailed discussions about the development of your product, your corporation's long-term objectives, and the competitive advantages you've been able to maintain in the marketplace. After the initial pitch, further conversations will follow. Ordinarily, those conversations will involve the disclosure of nonpublic material, so having an NDA in place can protect company information. The NDA should clearly state all material, knowledge, or information that the parties wish to share. The LOI should clearly state what corporate actions each party will take to pursue the partnership in good faith.

If a partnership does not require divulging a great deal of information, there will be instances in which an NDA or even an LOI is not necessary. But it is better to err on the side of caution when it comes to protecting company knowledge.

Timing

Letters of intent, especially when related to BD, should be signed relatively early in the partnership cycle. In general, an LOI should be agreed upon prior to the drafting of the formal contract and prior to making a significant investment in the potential partnership. Many partnerships will require a significant up-front investment: increasing personal capital, divulging confidential information, and analyzing the feasibility of integrating across multiple platforms. It is important to reach an understanding of both parties' intention to actually pursue a partnership in good faith before investing significant resources. This is where an LOI can help. These documents are used most often to express intent to a partner and signify that the party is serious about its negotiation.

The timing of supplying the other side of the deal with an NDA varies. Ordinarily, you will ask your potential partners to sign the NDA before you disclose any important nonpublic information. Most companies that have legal counsel will have an NDA or a template ready to go.

Caveats

One major caveat about LOIs in particular is that, with certain exceptions, they are not legally binding in their entirety on both parties. Intending to do a deal and agreeing on the actual final terms of the contract are two distinct things. Taking this into consideration, Eubanks reminds us that, keeping in mind the nonfinality of the LOI, "It is not necessary to include deal terms (for example, revenue sharing) that will be negotiated between the time you sign the LOI and the time you sign the final contract."

Another caveat is to be very cautious about whom you tell about having signed the LOI. According to Weiss, many LOIs have confidentiality clauses baked into them. As a result, it could jeopardize the deal's exemption from registration under the securities laws if third parties become aware of the arrangement. Second, if the other side of the deal thinks that you are using the LOI to get a more favorable deal elsewhere, you will probably lose the deal altogether.

Terms of Service

A partnership's terms of service are ordinarily outlined in the main contract and spell out the exact terms on which the deal is to be conducted. They include not only the economics and the technology, but also the actual logistics of how the contract will be executed. The terms of service that are in the contract can still be changed after execution of the contract, but doing so will involve the legal team and will require adding an addendum to the original document. Eubanks notes, "The addendum should state what, if any, terms in the original contract will be affected by the addendum as well as any new terms that were not previously considered. The addendum will generally mirror the original contract but add or amend specific terms within the original agreement."

The contract and the terms of service of the partnership should also include a clause in which both sides acknowledge that the terms are to be executed assuming that all necessary approvals are received. If the appropriate approvals are not obtained, the contract should state, the deal can be dissolved.

Finally, most terms of service include a clause about terminating the partnership. Despite the good intentions of both sides, there may come a time when the partnership is no longer mutually beneficial. According to Eubanks, this is where the sunset clause comes into play. "The sunset clause should contemplate how assets will be distributed in the event of the dissolution of a partnership and, perhaps more important, how customers will be able to continue as customers of yours without any interruption in service."

Revenue Sharing

In the early days of partnerships and in a handful of classic situations today, there were barriers to entry when it came to partnering with some big brand names. These brands would require a type of deal that would eliminate some of the smaller, more innovative companies from pursuing partnerships with them. The agreements would involve some kind of up-front payment for working with the partner with the big brand name, with the idea being that the smaller entity could earn back what it had paid once it had the brand name. It used to be the case that big companies could partner only with other large companies because they were the only ones who could afford to do so.

While this still happens as in certain partnerships with the NFL and other sports leagues, there are industries in which smaller companies can partner with larger entities without facing that major barrier. Instead of requiring an up-front payment, the two sides agree to share revenue as it comes in.

Eric Friedman from Foursquare has a great deal of experience with revenue-sharing partnerships from his time at the company:

> Typically, when setting up revenue sharing, there is a flat fee for referring a customer. For example, if you are working with a partner and you end up sending a customer to that partner, you should have an agreed-upon fee per new customer.
>
> The most extreme cases I have seen are 70/30 splits, with 70 percent going to the partner bringing the platform and doing the bulk of the deal and 30 percent going to the partner who is leveraging the assets and perhaps bringing in the customer. For BD professionals who are going into a negotiation for a revenue-sharing partnership, 70/30 gives you a starting point to negotiate. I have worked on deals that have been started by me for 70/30 and started by others for 70/30.

Revenue-Sharing Arrangements

For a small company, your ability and need to share revenue will change over time as your company grows and expands. The larger company may have extensive leverage over you at the time the contract is signed, but a year later, the tables may be turned. According to Eubanks, you should allow for renegotiation of the revenue-sharing agreement after predetermined time intervals in order to ensure favorability as the company changes. On the other hand, if you think your position will worsen, lock in a longer-term agreement up front.

You should also try to partner with a company when you both have equal strengths and value to bring to the table. The symbiosis and needs of the two partners should flow both ways, and each partner should be able to benefit from the other. As a result, try to make the revenue-sharing arrangement as equitable as possible. A 50/50 split is always preferable.

In addition, revenue sharing should be tied to performance. When the deal is closed and signed, both partners should bring equal value to the partnership, but as time passes, it could be that one side will be providing more value than the other. Revenue-sharing agreements should have a clause that ties results to profits, thereby giving each side of the deal an incentive to do its part. This can be structured in the contract by detailing certain benchmarks. Once these benchmarks are attained, the terms are available for renegotiation.

Friedman says that tracking the chosen performance metric is crucial, especially since it has been scrutinized and vetted by both sides of the deal. According to Friedman, tracking can happen in several different ways. "First, you can URL track referrals. Second, you can employ API tracking, using actions that happen through a specific key. Third, monthly or quarter-end tracking can be done by one designated partner. And finally, you can track the total percentage of revenue for a specific product that is only available through this means so that you know it's part of the deal."

The terms of the revenue-sharing agreement should be airtight, with no room for interpretation. According to Weiss, you need to ensure that the price terms and the duration of the agreement are clear about the calculations and the length of time. In addition, you need to understand the governance arrangements of the revenue sharing.

Finally, the actual payout structure and the mechanics of the payment should be explicitly detailed in the contract. "Although each deal will have nuances to consider," says Eubanks, "generally speaking, there should be designated metrics for measuring the performance of the partnership, such performance should be measured at regular intervals, and there should be designated periods for making payment."

Forecasting

When you are beginning to discuss a partnership, the counterparty will often want to understand your financials and have a sense of where your company is headed. This is fair for the other side to ask, so you should be prepared to offer forward-looking statements about how your finances might look, even if you are a brand-new company. As a result, forecasting becomes an important skill to have. We won't delve into the mechanics of financial forecasting, but Weiss has five recommendations when it comes to forecasting:

1. *Understand your audience.* "Before you make a forecast for any purpose (be it sales projections, unit financials, or otherwise), consider *who will receive the forecast* and *for what purpose(s) they will use it.* In particular, if the forecast is to be provided to *current or potential investors*, you should be scrupulous about (a) the reasonableness of the projections and (b) the methodology you used to create them. If you intentionally or carelessly falsify information that is presented to investors, you risk securities law liability both for yourself and for the company."

2. *Ensure confidentiality.* Forecasts should be confidential. The other side of the deal should be required to sign an NDA before seeing the forecasts, since this inevitably entails material nonpublic information.

3. *Understand your company's accounting system.* Although you don't have to understand complex accounting, it is critical that you have a basic understanding of some of the standards that your company chooses to adopt. This way, you can remain compliant when inking a deal.

4. *Be realistic.* It's easy to be optimistic when projecting. We hope for the best, and we seldom expect the worst. But Weiss cautions that, as with anything, being too optimistic can mean a loss of credibility down the line.

5. *The real thing happens after the forecasts are made.* Forecasts are just forecasts. There are potential risks involved and roadblocks to be hit. Be up front about the fact that these are just forward-looking statements and are not to be taken as gospel.

Negotiation

Negotiation, like pitching, is a give-and-take that happens all the time in your day-to-day life. In the context of BD, negotiation comes up at every step of the deal, starting with setting a date and time for the pitch and continuing through the deal negotiation and through contract negotiation. These are some principles that we always follow, especially when negotiating deal terms for a partnership.

First, don't negotiate unless you are okay with losing the deal. The minute you open the door to negotiating deal terms, you run the risk of the partner's running away. As with anything else, when you express dissatisfaction with the deal terms, the other team could be unwilling to negotiate. Similarly, don't be afraid to walk away. In your mind or on paper, map out a list of terms that are nonnegotiable for your side of the deal. As we discussed in Chapter 20, "Making the Pitch and Closing the Deal," if the deal does not meet your targets or if your gut tells you that it is not the right deal to do, walk away. You will know if the deal is right for your company by thinking about the potential outcome six months or a year down the line. As Eubanks says, "A deal's success is not measured at the date of signing, it is measured several months or years later as the deal matures and its impact on the organization is clear. Don't sign a bad deal that you won't feel proud of down the road."

Second, play the long game and think about what the deal means for your company in the long term. Negotiate terms that are going to be beneficial both for now and for the future. For example, negotiating a deal that is good for you and your company but less favorable for your partner may work for a short time, but people talk, careers are long, and you want to be the one who both negotiates well for your side and also does a great deal for the other side. In addition, if you negotiate a deal that is less favorable for your partner, that partner may have less incentive to uphold his end of the bargain. The other side needs to believe that it is getting 110 percent of both you and the deal.

Third, ask for a combination of what you need, what you want, and what you think you can get. Being realistic in negotiation shows a level of humility that will be endearing to the other side. Couple that sentiment with requests that might be slightly more aggressive than what you think you can get, recognizing that you may have to settle.

Weiss advises that both sides should look for "win-win" scenarios. Of course, in order to do a deal, it should be beneficial to both sides, but Weiss reminds us that "connecting on [points of mutual interest] will help build goodwill and momentum between the parties, which will come in handy when the negotiations get to more contentious points where one side needs to make a painful concession."

Schwartz corroborates that sentiment. "Understand that a successful negotiation doesn't require an outcome in which you 'win' and your counterparty 'loses.' If you understand the logic of the deal in connection with your own business and strategy, then a successful negotiation can be defined as one that is consistent with your logic; it's not necessary that you extract the most money or concessions from your counterparty."

Jared Cohen, former vice president of operations and general counsel for Kickstarter, and current COO and general counsel of See.me, advocates that you always keep your attorneys involved. Sometimes the legal team can be perceived as a barrier to success or even to deal making, but the contrary is true. "A good legal team helps the deal along, a bad one can be a barrier. I think the best results are when the deal team and legal team work closely together and communicate well."

As Eubanks points out, the worst possible situation occurs when the deal has been negotiated and both sides have made compromises, but the terms of the deal are not legally possible. This can make both sides look as though they haven't done their due diligence. Keeping compliant throughout the negotiation to ensure protection on both ends will lead to success.

Things can and do go awry if you don't inform your lawyers early enough. Andrew Ferenci, a three-time dorm room entrepreneur, had this happen to him. "We had fantastic collaboration, and we made a ton of progress on all aspects of the deal: revenue sharing, product vision, prototype, go-to-market strategy, and brand partners for launch. The deal was about six months in the works and everyone was on board, but the last sign-off was legal, and we found out that our product was in a legal 'gray area' for some recently established terms of service for the social network's developer API. Our product for this partnership was deeply dependent on the social network's API. Once a public company's lawyer suspects anything of this nature . . . they tend to be more risk averse. The deal ended up being scrapped."

Finally, don't be a jerk. You will find yourself on both sides of the table, so treat your counterparts with respect.

CHAPTER 22

LAUNCHING DEALS AND COMPOUNDING EFFECTS

ONCE YOU'VE INKED a deal, it is time to launch the partnership. This means finalizing your launch strategies and logistics and getting the most out of the partnership. This chapter covers all that and more.

Prelaunch

How do you know when it's time to launch a partnership? There is usually a sweet spot at which the partnership is ready for public disclosure.

When launching a partnership, you ordinarily set a date or time when the deal will go into effect, and that ticking clock helps you and your partner work backward to determine the timeline for what needs to be accomplished. When you are subject to this deadline pressure, partners often respond quickly and have an incentive to work around the clock on launching the partnership.

Convincing Partners to Do Pilots

When you don't have enough data or enough partners to showcase when you're trying to close a deal, convincing partners to try a pilot is the next best thing. A pilot is like a trial run before closing a full deal. When you have an unproven product, you sometimes need to convince prospective partners to do a series of tests before closing the full deal. Pilot partnerships are very common, especially among larger or more sophisticated entities that cannot take as many product or partnership risks. Doing a pilot in a limited fashion lets them test without fully committing.

One pilot partnership that took place before a larger partnership launch is one that Mike Ghaffary of Yelp orchestrated during his time at TrialPay. The e-commerce payment site was the leader in transactional advertising payments just as Facebook was beginning to need payments for commerce on its site. In exchange for Facebook credits, TrialPay would arrange for Facebook users to see advertiser content on the site. A practical example would be that a user would sign up for Netflix (via placement from TrialPay) and get Facebook credits as a result. This yielded a customer acquisition for Netflix and engagement for Facebook, and TrialPay provided the solution:

> The partnership between TrialPay and Facebook was first a pilot of a distribution partnership. Facebook had more than 100 million users, and the people there didn't want to show to everyone immediately. They wanted to make sure that TrialPay's conversion metrics were what they were hoping for. They ended up very happy and rolled it out. It's pretty common for transaction-based deals to start in a pilot period of making sure that things work and scale.

Another example of a pilot partnership is the deal that was done in 2012 between Square and Starbucks. As we described in Chapter 13, "Three Types of Partnerships," the major coffee retailer piloted the partnership by accepting payment using Square in only a few locations, and once that proved to be successful, it expanded the program.

The one thing that must be ironed out before agreeing to do a pilot is a metric of success. What is a metric of success? Usually pilots are carefully measured and scrutinized during the process, and the two parties agree on a certain benchmark that, once hit, would pivot the relationship into a full-scale partnership. Ordinarily the metric of success, which could range from the number of users gained to the amount of money generated, is the number that needs to be hit in order for both sides to say, "We are on to something." It usually boils down to one of two things: how many users the deal brings or how much money the deal made or saved us. Putting a number on what success means is your metric of success.

The last thought about convincing partners to do pilots is assessing how to eliminate as many barriers as possible to get the trial deal closed. This could mean everything from cutting down the integration time to covering costs to make the deal happen. The more you cut out barriers, the greater the chance you have of closing the deal. And who knows, if you cut out enough barriers, you may even end up with a full deal on your hands without needing to have a pilot slow you down.

Launching and Announcing a Partnership

Partnership discussions are ordinarily conducted behind closed doors, but when the deal is inked and the time is appropriate, an unveiling of the partnership should take place. There are a few ways you can go about launching partnerships.

Product Partnership Launches

If you are releasing new features and you have a few third-party integrations for the launch, the best way of disseminating the news is to send the announcement to a few outlets. Sometimes bigger outlets like major world newspapers or publications lead the charge, and then smaller outlets (such as tech blogs) follow on. For example, Yelp launched a new food-ordering platform in partnership with Eat24 and Delivery.com. The news broke on sites like *Business Insider*, the *Next Web*, and *VentureBeat*.

If you are launching a feature with several launch partners, one of the best strategies is to give each publisher a slightly different angle on the story. As described in Chapter 34, "Working with the Press," giving out variations of the story while keeping the facts and the story line consistent will enable various outlets to cater to their own demographics and provide slightly different insights to avoid redundancy.

Brand and Distribution Partnership Launches

If you don't have a major feature announcement, but instead are announcing a branding partnership or a distribution partnership with one major partner, then depending on the size and goals of the partnership, it is more beneficial to go to one outlet and give it an exclusive. This way, you can be certain that it will be covered.

As a result, in these scenarios, it is worthwhile to provide information about the partnership through an exclusive interview with one major outlet, and if other outlets want to follow, they will. If you don't have a major feature announcement and the partner isn't a big one (which isn't a bad thing, just a fact), you should write a blog post, include it in the next blast to your users, and share it on Facebook, Twitter, and other social outlets. You should always promote the integration of your product by helping to expose partners to your user base.

Compounding Effects of Launching Partnerships

Earlier in this book, we spoke about the compounding effect of networking. If you get an introduction to the right person, that introduction can lead to multiple introductions and have a positive, compounding effect.

The same concept applies to partnerships. Typically, when you have someone integrate your API, if it is done well, other people will take notice. If it is relevant and helpful to them, they will also want to integrate it. And on and on.

This is why we like launching new products *with* companies rather than just releasing the product solo. While this may delay the launch of a product by a month or so, when people see the integrations it has a compounding effect. Launching the product alone, with no integrations (especially if your business is partnerships- and integration-driven), can indicate a weakness in the product, since companies ordinarily want to see whom you are already working with and how current applications of the product are built or used. In addition, when you are asked, there are no good excuses for why you don't have any partners at launch.

The bottom line is: launch integrations with partners. These partners will help compound your integrations and validate your business even more.

We've Launched; Now What?

Assuming that you were able to launch successfully and your partner is very happy with the outcome, the partnership must be monitored, and your partner must continue to stay happy. Make sure your partner support is outstanding! Listen to your partner's feedback. If you have something worthwhile, there will probably be a competitor with a product similar to yours vying for the same deal.

In addition, you could also end up with companies similar to your partner that want to partner with you. As Tristan Walker, founder of Walker & Co., says, for every Coca-Cola, there is a Pepsi. If you can get one of them to partner with you, the other one will not be far behind.

Turn your partner's feedback into an improved solution for other companies, since this will help you get and keep their business for the long run. This kind of relationship, with one side truly listening, ensures that the other side won't switch to a competitor. In addition, specifically with regard to the product, don't be afraid to give your partner some feedback on the integration. However, tread carefully if the integration looks a bit off. At Aviary, for example, a partner began using the API to enable photo editing on its site, but hid it under a difficult-to-reach drop-down menu on the site. All the functionality was there, but the user experience for users on that site suffered. The business development team at Aviary took the responsibility for trying to show the partner how the integration could be improved. It was fixed, and conversion skyrocketed for that partnership.

CHAPTER 23

KEEPING THE DEAL

WHEN PEOPLE TALK about pitching and closing deals, they focus first on making the pitch and then on closing the deal. But once the deal is closed, they assume that all the work on that deal is complete. Quite the contrary! Closing the deal is just the end of the beginning; keeping the deal and maintaining the partnership are just as critical to ensuring the success of the arrangement and its benefits to your company.

Keeping the deal can be loosely defined as ensuring that the product integration, launch partnership, or monetization strategy is actually implemented in the manner that the deal closing specified. As we described in Chapter 8, "APIs and BD," this ordinarily involves heavy lifting on the part of a developer evangelist or a product specialist at your company who is working closely to oversee whatever integration work needs to be completed. In addition, BD professionals must keep in constant contact with the partner during the partnership development process to ensure proper implementation.

We've said this a few times already, but it is worth repeating: if you have something worthwhile, there will probably be a competitor vying for the same deal. Maintaining the partnership means not only working to have a smooth integration, but also preventing the competition from stealing your partners. As we mentioned in Chapter 21, "The Legality of Deal Making: Contracts and Beyond," exclusivity clauses are not necessarily a given in partnerships, so you want to ensure that you do a great job of maintaining your partnership so that your partner does not abandon you for a competitor and take all its knowledge of your product with it.

As a result, keeping the deal means building up loyalty on both sides of the deal so that you can trust that you and your partner will continue to work together and build a symbiotic rapport. It should be unfathomable to your partner that he would work with one of your competitors if approached, even on better deal terms. As we discussed in Chapter 17, "Sincere Selling," ensuring that loyalty is more important than getting the deal done. Mike Ghaffary mentions that it is more important to him, and to his colleagues at Yelp, to protect the relationship with the individual and remain loyal to her rather than have her work with Yelp if the deal is not best for her.

The question of exclusivity sometimes comes up with partnership deals. Occasionally, an exclusive deal that prohibits both sides from doing a similar deal with another partner is necessary. But more often than not, the goal of a BD professional is to make the other side comfortable and so satisfied with the working relationship that an exclusivity clause becomes unnecessary.

If exclusivity is necessary, however, it does not need to last throughout the entire duration of the partnership. It is common to see a contract in which there is exclusivity for a certain period of time, but it then fades after a few months or a few years. This is one way to ensure that your deal will be upheld in the short term, while giving both parties flexibility in the long run.

If you are working hand-in-hand with the partner, you will probably receive small pieces of feedback along the way, especially where the integration is concerned. But just as you might look for peer feedback during a professional review cycle, solicit professional feedback from your partners to understand what you might be able to do to better service their needs.

As we discussed in Chapter 15, "Partner Feedback," don't be afraid to give your partner feedback on what it is doing. Again, this will probably happen naturally in the course of working with that partner, but it is not unacceptable to provide high-level feedback for the partner. But tread carefully.

For example, if you see the integration of your product being implemented in a way that, given prior experience, you know will not succeed, bring this up with the partner. Don't be afraid to say that if the partner doesn't fix whatever is causing the problem, the integration is not likely to perform well and will be a waste of everyone's time. But when you are providing feedback about making changes, get consensus from your own team before pushing back on your partner.

Remember to provide feedback tactfully, without insulting the partner. On the other hand, withholding feedback from your partner could result in a deal that wastes time and effort.

Success in Keeping the Deal

What does success look like when you are able to "keep the deal"? Success can be best described with a scenario. Imagine that another company releases a competitive product that is deemed to be a step above what you currently offer. Scared for your business, you call your partners to assure them that your business is sound and that you are planning to add these additional features to keep them happy. In this example, if your partners are willing to give you a grace period to get your offering up to par or even close to par, you've done a killer job of keeping the deal. Reaching out to your partners proactively with a positive outlook will reassure them and encourage them to think with their hearts instead of their minds.

Ultimately, what happens if you are able to keep the deal for long enough? As your company matures and grows, you will most likely bring on account managers to take the responsibility for maintaining the partnership and continuing to make your partners happy. These account managers are able to help keep the deal by listening to what the partner wants or needs, sharing these desires with the team, and working on delivering solutions, which ultimately keeps the partners happy. If the company is large enough or needs a large deal team, you might see BD teams with one account manager for each large partnership.

Failure to Keep the Deal

Failing to keep the deal boils down to loyalty. Of course, failure can manifest itself in several ways, but being unsuccessful in achieving a metric or completing the task at hand is not necessarily failing to keep the deal. Failing to sustain the relationship or build it for longevity, so that the partner becomes frustrated and no longer wants to work with you, means that the deal has truly failed.

In addition, if you unfortunately do lose the deal, don't freak out. Always be gracious. Apologize for not being able to live up to your partner's expectations. Never bad-mouth the other side of the deal. If the deal is with a small partner, try not to sweat too much. If it is with a big partner (and potentially newsworthy), try to get ahead of the news and explain the story on your own terms.

Remember, you've lost a partner for a reason. There is something wrong, either with the product or with your support of the product. Internally, rally the team. Tell people what went wrong and how it happened. More important, have a game plan for fixing the problem. Externally, if you know that the failure will be picked up by a news outlet, pick one you are close to and tell your story first.

This allows you to control the message, instead of having to perform damage control or, worse, look defensive. But primarily, be sure never to speak ill of the partner. If you aren't sure whether the word will get out, you need to make a judgment call on whether to lead the story or not. Usually, it is better to tell the story on your own terms than to have it surface at an inopportune time.

You can discount your pricing, wine and dine the partner, and use a slew of other tricks of the trade to keep the deal, but at the end of the day, it all comes down to making sure that your product or service offering continues to meet your partner's needs. That's it. If you keep that up, you should have no problem keeping the deal.

PART 4

BEST PRACTICES: PREPARATION AND EXECUTION

CHAPTER 24

INTRODUCTIONS: BEST PRACTICES

WITHOUT INTRODUCTIONS, partnerships between companies wouldn't exist. In the world of business, it is impossible to subsist solely on the network that you have or cultivate, and introductions are very often reciprocated.

Making a business introduction is very different from developing a personal relationship, and it should be executed with some thought and care. Remember that an introduction reflects as much on the person making the introduction as it does on the two parties that are introduced.

Introduction: Context and Progression

Introductions are usually requested by one party and only rarely by both. As a result, you usually know only whether one of the two people to be introduced is interested in meeting the other. Often, there is an imbalance between the two parties in either seniority, experience, knowledge base, or expertise.

First, ask both parties if they are open to being introduced. If one of the parties to the introduction is caught unaware, he is less likely to respond. Sending a blind introduction is not always appreciated and can cause confusion, depending on how well you know both of the people involved. The only reasonable situation in which it is not necessary to ask one of the sides if she would like to be the recipient of an introduction is if you are personal friends with that person or if you work with her every day. If she is not someone you would feel comfortable texting (or if she would say, "Who is this?"), you probably should wait until you have her approval to go through with the introduction.

There are two types of introductions:

1. Asking someone to *introduce* you to someone that he knows
2. *Suggesting* an introduction between two people that you know

In the first type, make it as clear as possible why the person you are asking should actually make the introduction. This means that you should provide context for the connection you are looking for by telling the person you are asking what you need from the connection and why speaking with her contact will help. If you are asking for an introduction over email, make your email forwardable or add a piece of information on the bottom that she can copy and paste into her "ask for intro" email.

An example of this email is as follows:

Asking for an Introduction to Someone

Subject: Intro to Y at Z?

Hey X,

I hope all is well! [Keep this to *one sentence.*]

Quick question: I see on LinkedIn that you know Y from Z. Do you know her well enough to make an intro?

(Insert your company name) is working on A, and we think this would be interesting to (insert person or other company name) because of B.

Let me know if you can make an intro. No pressure. Just trying to get in front of her.

Thanks!

W

The second kind of introduction is one in which you are offering to introduce two people that you think would benefit from knowing each other. For this kind of introduction, make sure you provide all the relevant information that both parties would need in order to make a decision on whether they would like to be introduced. Important information for you to include would be why you want to make the introduction and how the person you are introducing her to would be helpful to her, and vice versa. Spell it all out.

Once both sides agree, it's time to make the introduction. The email should be short and concise, especially since both sides are expecting it. The introduction should include the formalities: an actual mention of both names. Write one or two sentences about each side and explain why you are making the connection, even though both sides know what to expect.

Here's how to do the actual introduction:

Making the Introduction

Subject: Intro (X/Company A and Y/Company B)

You two should meet.

X, meet Y.

Y, meet X.

You are both working on projects that would benefit from each other's expertise.

I'll let the two of you take it from here.

Best,

Z

Getting in Front of People You Don't Know

As we discussed in Chapter 19, business development is the art of working with other people at different companies to convince them that you and they should partner. In many cases, however, you have to liaise with people that you do not know. Networking can help you expand your connections, but there will always be circumstances in which you have to engage in person with someone that you don't know.

There are a variety of methods and strategies available for getting in touch with someone. In the end, it's all about personal preference. Building upon what we discussed in Chapter 5, "Networking," here are five of the many methods you can use to reach out to someone.

1. Get a Warm Introduction

Look on your social networks to see which of your friends or colleagues are connected to the person you'd like to meet. Reach out to one of your friends and explain why you want to speak with this person. If there is any merit to your request (and if your friend is close enough to the person), he will typically make a warm introduction.

2. Attend the Same Event

As discussed in Chapter 5, "Networking," try to find events that this person will attend or host. You can do this by seeking guest lists or hosts of BD or regular industry events. Very often, the individual you want to meet will serve on a panel at least once a year. If that person is a guest of the event and the list of attendees is public information, find her and introduce yourself, using the techniques we outlined in Chapter 5. On the other hand, if this individual is serving on a panel, listen to what she has to say and wait until after the panel is over to introduce yourself. This way, you have a point of connection and a topic of conversation.

3. Send an Email

Most email addresses can easily be found online. If you can't find the email address, look for how the email structure works for other people in the company (for example, FirstName@xxxx.com, FirstInitial+LastName@xxxx.com, First-Name.LastName@xxxx.com, and so on). Once you obtain the email address, put together a rough draft of what you want to say and send it. Most people won't read more than a few sentences (even if they know you), so be sure to make every word count (keep it to five sentences or less)!

4. Tweet at Him

You have 140 characters. Grab the person's attention. Make sure you give him a way to follow up with you and get him to want to email or message you to find out more.

5. Call Her

Get on the phone and call her. Every company has a telephone number. Ask for the person you want to speak with, and give it your best shot.

When you are speaking to a person that you do not know that well or have never met before, be sure to have succinct goals for your interaction. Come prepared to talk not only about what you are specifically asking for, but also about yourself and your company. Since you are a representative of your entire organization, be sure to provide context and background about your position and your company's goals.

Pitfalls to Avoid

A potential misstep to watch out for when making introductions is getting in the way of the two parties. If you follow best practices and get approval from both sides, you should have everyone on the same page. If that is the case, the introduction should be short and sweet. Anything more is intrusive.

One of the worst pitfalls when it comes to introductions is to make the introduction without one or both sides knowing that it is coming. There is no quicker way to lose social credibility and impose on your network than by blindly introducing people. The best way to avoid this is by overcommunicating with both parties to ensure that they both know that the introduction is coming. If this happens to you, you might be put off by the abrupt nature of the email, to which you can respond with a request that you be consulted before being introduced.

CHAPTER 25

REACHING OUT AND CORRESPONDING

BD PROFESSIONALS ARE only as good as their networks, as we described in Chapter 5, "Networking." But when your network falls short, you need to perfect the art of reaching out so that you can expand that network. Getting in touch with someone with whom you were not previously connected is an art form that depends on what indirect connections you find you have to that person.

As we discussed in Chapter 14, "Identifying the Right Person at the Partner Company," after you identify the right person, you should also think about the most strategic approach to actually getting in touch with that person. Here are some tips for successfully reaching out to a third party who doesn't necessarily know who you are or what your company does.

The Person Won't Come to You

Unless you are a big-time entrepreneur with a proven track record or a hot commodity that's on the rise, there is only a slim chance that anyone, let alone the right kind of person, will reach out to you inquiring about your project or your startup. Even if you have a fantastic product idea that has already soft launched, you probably will not receive inquiries or help from the person with whom you need to get in front of.

The Cold Reach-Out

When reaching out to anyone, regardless of how well you know her, your goal is to get enough of the other person's time to properly pitch to her or sell her your idea. As discussed in Chapter 19, "Pipeline and Prepitch Execution," a "cold reach-out" is an email, a self-made introduction, or an inquiry to someone whom you have never previously met. Often, the cold reach-out is done because you have few (if any) mutual connections, and none of them are strong enough to make a warm introduction.

The cold reach-out isn't the sell, it's the tease to get to the sell. Keeping your email short and intriguing will get the person to ask for more. Because the cold reach-out was not backed by any introduction, the initial point of contact needs to be catchy and convincing. The goal is ultimately to get the other party to respond, not for her to buy whatever you are selling. A simple response is enough to get the dialogue going or to establish yourself as a contact.

The bottom line is: next time you are thinking about blindly reaching out to someone, remember that less is more. Your only goal is to get the person to respond. Take the process one step at a time.

An example of a cold reach-out email is as follows:

Subject: (Company 1)/(Company 2)—Reach Out

Hey X,

We have never met, but I wanted to introduce myself to you. I'm W, and I work in (lead) Y for Z.

I saw that you run the A app, and I was hoping that we could connect.

Company 1 launched B (link). I thought it would be great to do C with you. This would allow for D.

Are you still doing any development on E? If so, I would love to chat.

I look forward to hearing from you soon.

Best,

W

What Not to Do

At startups and bigger companies alike, there comes a time in the BD life cycle when potential partners solicit partnership interest by reaching out using the "spray and pray" method. With this method, an individual, sometimes from a legitimate organization and other times just a self-promoter, will email the same message to a plethora of people across various divisions of a company (the spray), hoping that one of them will respond (the pray). While you might think that contacting several people at a company would lead to a higher rate of response, the message comes across as disingenuous. The spray and pray reach-out strategy will most likely label you as being either spammy, annoying, or someone who does not conduct research properly before reaching out.

The professional universe can be small, and people talk. They forward each other emails and tell stories. Usually, the fact that someone sent a similar email to multiple people surfaces quickly. If a spray and pray email gets sent to a lot of people at a company, it will be forwarded to the correct person multiple times, and that person will probably recognize that the initial offender used this spammy mechanism for getting his foot in the door. As a result, the intended recipient is likely to either ignore the email altogether or respond with a predisposition of negative feelings toward the sender.

If you are thinking of spraying and praying, forget about it. Do some research to find out whom you really need to be connecting with, write a creative and concise email, and send it to one person! If you don't hear back in a week or so, try that person again with a nice and concise follow-up. If you don't hear back a week later, approach someone else. One at a time.

Email Correspondence

Whether you are initially reaching out to someone you don't know or communicating with a team member about a deal, your email correspondence speaks volumes about your demeanor and work habits.

People inevitably have different habits when it comes to email. Understanding what type of person you are dealing with helps tremendously with correspondence and expectations.

The Fast Responder

The fast responder is the type of person who responds to every email within a two-hour period. The responses are not necessarily lengthy or comprehensive, but the individual is probably tied to her mobile phone and can get back to you quickly. In most cases, this is exemplary behavior. Whether the response is favorable or not, receiving an answer is better than silence.

There are several types of individuals that fall into the fast responder category. One type will respond to your requests quickly only if he knows you. Another type will get back to you quickly even if he does not know you. These people are benevolent and generous with their time, and are willing to respond to everything that comes their way. The only downside for that type of responder is that being "on" so frequently does not give these people time for anything else besides work. Also, in their haste, they do not necessarily give the most thorough responses.

The Once-a-Day Responder

This individual usually responds to all emails in the morning or at night, but only once or twice a day and all in one bunch. During the day, she skims through her inbox and responds only to time-sensitive emails (changes in meetings that day, family, and the like). Depending on the individual, this person can be a morning or a night person. For a professional who needs to multitask, this is the most manageable and common type of email communicator.

The Organized One

This archetype usually has a plethora of inbox filters, including color coding and an exact strategy for dealing with and prioritizing emails. This respondent's MO can be seen as a hybrid. Some filters get the fast responder, others get once-a-day, and a bunch go into the empty abyss. Organization and prioritization of email is an enviable talent, and one that may take years of discipline to perfect.

Inbox Blow-Upper

This aptly named individual waits until she has received a critical mass of emails (sometimes hundreds or even thousands) before responding en masse. You may wait weeks or even months before hearing from her, and then she will respond to all your emails at once, causing your own inbox to flood.

If you're lucky enough to catch this person at the right moment (when she is finally responding to emails), you will get a fast-responder response and hear from her within a short period of time. Most often, however, your emails get lost in an inbox black hole.

This is not the fault of this type of individual: she is probably the founder of a company or an executive who does not have assistance and has too much inbound email to react quickly. It's not necessarily fair to expect people like this to respond to a large majority of their emails. They probably have meetings day and night and have internal things to do (presentations, board meetings, and so on), and spending a few hours answering their email is not their top priority. For responders of this type, it is best to have other avenues to contact them (gchat, text messages, the phone) and know that if someone truly needs to get in front of them, they will find a way.

If you email someone who frequently blows up his inbox and starts over or responds to noncore things once a week, you need to make sure that you follow up periodically with a nice note, so that you can get back on the person's radar. It's not you, it's him. If you just happen to hit this person at the wrong time, which could happen for a myriad of reasons, a follow-up and note could get everything back on track.

Content of Correspondence

There is an unofficial correlation between the length of an email and its response rate. In our experience, the shorter the email, the higher the probability of receiving an answer within 24 hours. Many longer emails, classified as any email longer than a few sentences, often go unanswered, especially in a cold reach-out situation.

A common misconception among professionals entering the working world or taking on a new leadership responsibility is that they must write lengthy emails with long explanations. Especially in an initial correspondence situation, short and punchy is substantially better than long-winded or verbose. The goal of most emails, regardless of whether the recipient knows you or not, is to receive a response. Make it as easy as possible for the other person to respond to your email by making it short.

After an introduction or a cold reach-out, BD professionals often face the conundrum of whether to begin a new email thread, either leaving off some of the initial connectors or removing old, stale content from the thread. Most of the time, it is considered best practice to continue the thread if correspondence has been regular or if there is an important history in the previous emails that should remain easily obtainable. Even if the follow-up is months later, continuing the email thread makes it easy for the other side to remember the context of the interaction.

The time to begin a new thread is if you are trying to discuss an entirely new topic or subject with the other party. The new thread allows for a fresh conversation. Another reason to start a new thread is if you have responded within an old thread and received no attention from it. In most email clients, a new thread can garner slightly more attention than one that has many layers of correspondence. This can be a successful way to revive a waning conversation.

CHAPTER 26

FOLLOWING UP AND OTHER BEST PRACTICES FOR CORRESPONDENCE

ONCE YOU HAVE perfected the art of reaching out, you are likely to receive positive responses from your newfound connections. Following up after reaching out is a separate skill that necessitates building and maintaining a relationship while keeping the other party interested and on her toes.

Best Practices for Following Up

After sending an email and receiving a response, make sure you follow up in a timely manner. A response ordinarily means that the recipient saw enough merit in your reach-out email to look into your background and your company's information; be courteous enough to keep the dialogue flowing at a professional pace.

Even if the response is a respectful decline, it is important that you acknowledge the receipt of such an email in order to maintain the relationship for future ties. These responses should be concise; even a one-sentence "Thanks, I'd love to keep in touch" is sufficient for those circumstances.

If the response is positive, maintain the tactic that you used during the initial reach-out. Answer any questions this person may have, and perhaps try to leverage the communication for an in-person meeting or pitch. Remember, the first follow-up email is more about getting the other party hooked on an idea or interested in the concept of partnering with you than about simply getting him to respond. While doing so, make sure to be concise. Lengthier conversations can be held in person or on the phone. In addition, make your follow-up actionable. Ask for something from your counterpart in order to ensure that there is another level of follow-up. By doing so, you will find yourself corresponding with this person on a frequent basis, which inherently cultivates a relationship and keeps it warm.

After Sending an Email and Receiving No Response

The initial reaction in this scenario might be to do nothing. But, as we mentioned in Chapter 5, "Networking," being persistent is important for BD professionals. Companies and products can move quickly, and occasionally a lack of response is due to another person's busy schedule. If you do not receive a response after three or four days, it is acceptable to send another note within the same thread to the original recipient, nudging it to the top of her inbox.

An example of an email to send when you haven't received a response:

Hey X,

Don't mean to bother you; just checking in to see if you got this email.

I would love to find time to tell you more about Y.

Let me know if we can find a time this week.

Thanks,

Z

This also goes for a long line of communication, not just an initial reach-out. If you are in the middle of a contract negotiation and the other side of the deal does not respond, it is acceptable to follow up with another email after a few days, reminding him that he owes you a response. Keep the nudges short, just like any other reach-out or correspondence.

After Meeting in Person

If you have met someone at a networking event or even just for coffee, it is your responsibility to follow up. The follow-up should take place via email and can be a short acknowledgment that you enjoyed meeting that person. This correspondence should take place immediately (at the latest before the end of the next business day) after the meeting, especially if there were action items from that meeting that require further attention. This keeps the ideas fresh and serves as a reminder that you met this person, so that in future interactions, you both can cite the correspondence as a reminder of what you discussed.

After Speaking on the Phone

For one-on-one communication regarding an introduction, a potential deal, or product advice, the same rules apply as if you had met in person. If you have a conference call with someone regarding a deal, it can be easy to forget to follow up because of the group setting. Do not fall into this pattern! Conference calls are just as important as individual phone calls and can actually establish credibility and rapport more quickly than in one-on-one settings.

People appreciate it when others follow up, so make sure that you do.

What to Expect When Receiving Follow-Ups

The truth about following up is that people are busy. They get emails all the time. Sometimes they are in front of their computer, but more often they are on the go. They will respond to legitimate things (for the most part), but if they forget to attend to a follow-up email, they usually don't spend time searching for what they missed. As we previously mentioned, if you don't receive a response, send a quick follow-up email and you will get back on their radar.

There is no harm in reaching out to someone after any type of interaction, and it is better to err on the side of too much communication rather than too little.

Standing Out to Get a Response

How to Make Yourself Stand Out

Once you learn how to think and take BD vision into account, putting it to work to show that you can stand out from the pack is a useful skill. Distinguishing yourself from other BD professionals can yield great professional results and have ripple effects. To be the most valuable professional you can be, in addition to having a stellar job performance, you need to make yourself inextricably linked to the revenue and knowledge stream. The way to achieve individuation boils down to four core principles: make yourself valuable, make yourself publicly visible, get involved with events, and finally, blog.

1. Make Yourself Valuable

This is easier said than done, but you should spend the first few months in any job making yourself valuable to the team by becoming an expert on some aspect of the job or by being known for one specific asset or quality. If you are in a BD role and you can become the go-to person to help make the pitches or structure a deal, then you will stand out among your peers.

Having a great network can also help you make yourself valuable. If you are expected to generate partnerships that will grow the business and enhance the product, you can be valuable by having a broad network of people, among whom could be your potential counterpart deal maker. In addition, your network can help you carry out small tasks that seem like big wins to potential partners. Knowing someone at a company whose product everyone uses means that you can help win over a partner by obtaining product support or resolving issues for him without his having to go through a user service team. In addition, you can woo him by using your network to help him do something that is beyond the scope of both your and his job descriptions, earning major brownie points and also helping to close deals.

In addition, make yourself valuable by keeping an ear to the ground and staying attuned to trends in the business. Obtaining a piece of knowledge before the rest of the industry, or even just your competitors, can give you a business advantage that could, in the most drastic circumstances, save your company. At the very least, knowing something before the rest of your industry does means that you can react appropriately when the news breaks. If you can be the one who makes your company look good, especially in the face of adversity, you will stand out and be rewarded for doing so.

2. Make Yourself Publicly Visible

Being externally visible as a representative of the company means that you should be someone who other people think of immediately when they think of your company. We all have iconic images of founders and can recall the names of company CEOs, but when it comes to the day-to-day work of building a product and growing a business, it is critical that you make yourself a public-facing figure so that you, too, are outwardly associated with the company's success. While it is easier to obtain this reputation when you are an engineer who is building the product, a business professional who is able to achieve the same success will be associated with strategically growing the company.

How can you make yourself externally visible? Maintaining a network and discussing your work (where applicable and appropriate) will mean that everyone in your community has a general sense of the company you work for and what you do. Provide some level of value to these people and you will remain top of mind when they discuss your company. When they are being solicited for introductions to people at your company, you will be the first person they turn to, instilling in others the idea that you are a valid representative of the company. The cycle perpetuates, as described later, and eventually you will become the person that people associate with that particular brand.

3. Get Involved with Events

As we described in Chapter 5, "Networking," attending events is a great way to expand your network. But keep in mind what we discussed earlier: simply attending is not enough to make you stand out in a crowd. Associate yourself with these events: become a coordinator or, if you have the honor, a panelist. Speak at conferences (at some conferences, you need to be invited to speak; others have breakaway sessions where everyone can speak). Invite friends and combine your existing network with the new network. The importance of doing this is to be known for something outside of your job that allows you to be a connector of like-minded individuals in your field.

In addition, the cycle of networking continues when you take a prominent role at externally facing events. If you speak on a panel relating to a certain topic, members of the audience will associate you with expertise in that area, which could potentially lead to deal-making discussions. This, in turn, can make you stand out at your job and link you to revenue generation for the company.

4. Blog

As we discussed in Chapter 10, "Digital Identity," it may sound incongruous, but blogging is at the center of the perpetual cycle that keeps these traits linked. Blogging can make you stand out because it can attract the attention of distinguished people in your field. If they know that you have valuable insights to share, then they know that you exist before you even meet them. They might be interested enough in your content to reach out to you, as opposed to the other way around. In addition, blogging helps you establish and solidify an online presence that can ultimately make you respected and well known in your field.

Additional Distinguishing Factors

Finally, be great at your job. When you are trying to be a superstar in many different facets of your professional and personal life, it can be easy to forget about doing an outstanding job in your current role. This means anticipating problems before they happen. Think about all the ways a deal can go awry and come up with solutions to a problem before it happens. Focus on your attention to detail and anticipate partnership needs before they arise. Close deals and help grow the company in many appropriate areas, and you will stand out above and beyond other BD professionals.

This can also mean setting expectations early and sticking to them. Rick Armbrust, who worked in business development at Facebook and Microsoft before becoming an angel investor, cites setting clear guidelines as one of the most important things to do to stand out from the pack. "Set expectations early. This includes your objectives, culturally how your company works, things that could go wrong, and so on. This both prevents bad partnerships from being formed and prevents or softens events during a partnership. I can't count how many times this has been helpful."

Conference Calls Versus In-Person Meetings

The disruption of the telecommunications technology industry means that you have many options for interacting with other professionals, especially during deal making. Strategic partnerships necessitate many in-person or telephone conversations, especially since the vast majority of deals are not accomplished solely via email.

Most companies do not limit employees to one particular service, so partnership discussions can happen via Skype, join.me, GoToMeeting, Blue Jeans, Google Hangouts, or an old-fashioned phone call. Indeed, for an initial meeting, it is easy to hop onto one of these systems and have a preliminary conversation about what a partnership might entail.

But there is no possible replacement for the in-person meeting. There are many reasons why meeting in person might not be feasible; if you work in different cities or countries, or with time zone differences, you may be forced to speak only by conference call. But if you can meet in person, you will have a substantially higher chance of closing the deal and making a sustainable connection. There is something about the ability to use voice, body language, facial expressions, and the like that does not translate to web calls and can often make a deal fall flat.

The bottom line is: if you are presented with both options, and you'd really like to close the deal, choose to take the in-person meeting.

CHAPTER 27

PERSISTENCE

ONE OF THE most salient qualities of a BD professional is the ability to be proactive. At a fast-moving company, you may have a sense of what your job entails, but it will be your responsibility to actually execute these tasks, and those who succeed at these companies are self-starters. These proactive go-getters are, at their core, persistent.

What Is Persistence?

Persistence is a sacred virtue in the world of fast-moving companies. This quality is what enables many self-starters to drive deals forward and make action happen, even when the other people involved in the process are not necessarily as proactive.

Persistence comes in many incarnations depending on your personality type and audacity, but it always involves pushing deals forward. Sometimes persistence means not resting until you have an answer from someone else; in other instances, it means reminding someone that she owes you something (an email, an introduction, or something else).

Maxine Friedman, former head of business development at Contently, says that she finds that there is a fine balance between persistence and pushiness, and that crossing that line can be annoying:

> When you are overly persistent as a BD professional, you come across as either inexperienced, anxious, or callous. I tend to be more conservative

and keep my tonality continually positive. . . . [I assume] the answer is "yes" if I'm not hearing back from my target partner and he or she actually says "no." When deal making, we tend to think only of what is in front of us: what we want and are hoping to achieve through a close.

The reality is, the deal may be the most important thing to you, but you have to remember that life is happening in the background. Companies go through restructuring; new initiatives or fire drills come up; kids get sick.

Lesson 1: Your agenda is not your target partner's agenda. I recall a time when I was working on a deal and there was a ton of momentum behind it for several months, and then suddenly things stalled. I couldn't get a response from my target for the life of me. I was getting all worked up thinking it was something I did—or didn't do!—and very frustrated that it was out of my control.

Lesson 2: It's always out of your control (for the most part). There are factors you can control and those you cannot. I have finally learned this and give myself much more grace than I did when I was less experienced.

Lesson 3: Assume the best. Rather than go negative, which can affect your overall professional performance and your attitude at the office, and even turn your personal life sour, assume the best about the situation and remain steadfast. For example, when Alex was working at Aviary, he found out that the person with whom he was coordinating a deal was dealing with a family emergency and was off the grid for almost a month. He ended up finalizing the deal at a later time, but had he been overly aggressive, he could have come across as rude.

Proactivity, Pushiness, and Persistence

Early-stage companies, and many jobs held by people there, tend to veer toward being reactive, meaning that they reach out to other companies only once their product is in the market. Instead, they should begin soliciting partnerships proactively, before the product has been released. They need to respond to challenges that the market or the product throws their way. But regardless of the company's maturity, a BD professional must be proactive in her role in order to accomplish anything. Being proactive means actively reaching out to potential partners and aggressively seeking deals (if appropriate). Proactivity is the first step, whereas persistence is about the art of following up and providing gentle nudges and reminders until what you require is complete.

On the other hand, there is a fine line between being persistent and being annoying, pushy, or generally too aggressive. If you are looking to do a deal and the contact on the other side has explicitly given you instructions not to contact her until a certain date or until a certain set of circumstances has arisen, persistence in contacting her will not benefit you. In this case, and other similar ones, persistence can turn into pushiness.

The objective is to continue to achieve your team's goals and create effective partnerships while remaining timely and organized. Persistence is one of the traits that can help you achieve, but every situation calls for a different level of engagement. You should always trek forward, especially in spite of opposition.

The major difference between successful BD professionals and those who struggle is that successful people were persistent at the appropriate level of interaction; they never gave up—but they were never intrusive or belligerent, either.

Conflating Persistence and Confidence

When we think about the qualities we admire in founders and business development professionals, one thing that comes to mind is confidence. When you speak, no matter how much you actually know about the topic, there should be an assurance in your voice that makes those on the other side believe what they are hearing.

Persistence, or sometimes pushiness, can often be conflated with confidence. But if it is done correctly, being self-assured in what you are asking for can help augment the level of persistence necessary, and can indeed push the other side over the edge of wanting to help.

Having confidence helps in all aspects of startups, ranging from convincing investors to give you money, to pitching a story to a reporter, and even to getting the best talent to join your team. If there was one thing we would recommend to prospective founders and BD professionals, it would be to have confidence both in yourself and in your product and get good at convincing other people. It will go a long way.

CHAPTER 28

REJECTION

VERY FEW PEOPLE enjoy hearing the word *no*, especially in a professional setting. We cringe and feel ourselves sink into the ground under our feet. Rejection stings, and we have an innate tendency to take it personally. We feel inclined to dislike the person who is saying no. But hearing the word *no* is an integral part of BD and partnerships, and it's not all bad.

The Rejection

The rejection itself can be subtle or overt, depending on whom you are pitching. Most often it will come after the meeting via email after (hopefully) some careful thought and deliberation. "Sorry, but you aren't a priority," and, "This isn't the type of partnership we are pursuing at this moment," are some of the most frequently used rejection responses after pitching, but they can come in many shapes and sizes. Occasionally, you may receive a flat-out "no" on the spot, and this should be met with grace and dignity.

What does that mean? Grace and dignity means thanking the other side for taking the time, then asking why it isn't right for them. Those on the other side may ignore your question about understanding, so be careful not to bother them or be pushy in trying to find out why (ask only once). Be very appreciative and respectful of their time. Alex Guttler, partner manager at AppNexus and former account executive–enterprise sales at Apple and business development account manager at Dell, lives by that principle. "Life is short, and the world is a very small place. Odds are, you'll cross paths with someone you worked on a deal with in the future. Even and especially when a deal falls apart, always treat the other person and company with respect, and never say something you'll regret. You could soon find yourself on the same side of the table or needing a hand from the other party."

When (and Why) You Might Receive a Rejection

Stuff happens. In BD, deals fall apart or never come to life in the first place. You try to move on. Most often, rejection comes about because of a misalignment of company interests or product offerings rather than a personal dislike of the person pitching or the company.

As we discussed in Chapter 11, "Understanding Other Companies," it is critical that you understand the priorities of the other company before pitching and that you learn about what is important to that company at that time. If your pitch does not touch upon or aid one of the other company's priorities, you should go into the meeting expecting a rejection. For example, if the other company cares about entering into a distribution partnership to bring in more users, to avoid rejection, your pitch should focus on this specific goal. If you can point to specific figures and pitch the company on exactly what numbers you can help generate, you will surely avoid a rejection.

If you let rejection immobilize you, then you will continue to fail. The best thing you can do is go out and keep pitching. Make the company that rejected your pitch come back begging to work together.

But You Thought You Had It in the Bag

Everyone gets rejected, and rejections come in many different forms in our lives. Perhaps you were rejected for a date or a job. Most go-getters do everything in their power to prepare for job interviews or even dates, and the preparations follow a similar pattern to those for preparing for a pitch.

But rejections still come. Why? Most of the time, we get turned down because we are in the wrong place at the wrong time or have the wrong product, not because we are underprepared. Don't get us wrong; you'll definitely be rejected if you are underprepared or if someone doesn't like you. Just remember, even if they like you and you come prepared, you can still get rejected.

Nam Nguyen, director of business development at Giphy and former head of partnerships at Aviary, recommends that if you are interested in getting involved with partnerships, you must get accustomed to getting rejected often:

> Getting rejected is part of the partnership game, and the sooner you accept that, the better off you'll be.
>
> There are too many variables and emotions involved in a partnership that you can't foresee. For example, a five-minute meeting with decision makers can easily overturn the six months of hard work you've put in to convince a potential partner that he should work with you. An internal hackathon can be the birthplace of a few developers building a proof of concept to replace your product (I've had this happen to me a handful of times at Aviary).

What to Do with a Rejection

Any time you get a "no," the absolute best thing you can do is find out why. Most people, in our experience, will tell you why a deal doesn't make sense for them. But you need to ask and actively solicit information; they are probably not going to just tell you.

The reason could be anything from your pricing being out of their range to their not being focused on your product or the type of partnership that you are offering. There are sometimes extraneous circumstances, like the company that doesn't do a deal because the founder's girlfriend works at a competing company. You just don't know until you ask.

In addition, asking shows that you care enough about the partnership to probe. This is likely to impress the team members on the other side of the pitch, and they will remember you for future business endeavors.

Nguyen says that you must learn from the experience of getting rejected lest the entire experience of interacting with that partner in the first place go to waste.

> I've had contracts signed, products integrated, and PR lined up, only to receive a cancellation email 15 minutes before the launch.
>
> How do you deal with this? Simple. Set yourself up for success with backup partnerships. If you need 5 launch partners, talk to 20. If you

need 20, talk to 50. Things are going to slip here and there, and the only way to succeed is to overestimate the number of partners you need and to secure twice as many.

Learn from the rejection. Ask questions to understand why. Was it a product-related issue? If so, what was it? Bring it back to the team and reevaluate your product. Was it a legal issue? If so, what can you do to prevent it from happening again?

With that "dream" partnership that turned you down, don't stress about it. Lock in its competitors. Combine it with some PR. Keep the "dream" partner informed about the companies you're working with. Fast-forward a year and that "dream" partner will be knocking on your door to learn more.

Turning a "No" into a Positive

Getting a "no" can actually be a positive: it's an opportunity to ask why and understand the deal's shortcomings. Sometimes they are problems that you can control, while other times they are out of your purview. But whatever the reasons, don't hate it when someone tells you no. This isn't the time to lose focus on what's important: improving your offering so that you can turn those noes into yeses.

If you are truly not a priority for enough companies, it might make sense to go back to the drawing board and build a product that more companies find to be a priority. If your offering is too expensive or doesn't provide something that is exciting enough to the other company, you will probably receive similar feedback at the next partnership meeting. Lower your prices; dream bigger. Getting a "Sorry, but you aren't a priority" is exhausting, but if you really understand other companies and are honest with yourself about your offering, you will spend your time focusing on opportunities in which you are a priority and can be a clear winner.

Rejections and negative feedback are not personal (unless you have truly offended someone). Get used to them and thrive on the rejection. Make it feed your hunger to succeed. Every time you get a no, strive to get two yeses. Arianna Huffington has written about this topic, saying, "Fearlessness is like a muscle. I know from my own life that the more I exercise it the more natural it becomes to not let my fears run me." This statement received the following comment from Michael Galpert, cofounder of Aviary: "Recently I've been trying to push myself daily to get rejected to help destroy my fear of being rejected. It's a great exercise; I recommend that everyone try it."

We love this. Getting rejected every day is tough. However, going after something that is realistically unattainable and getting a big, fat *no* once a week seems plausible and will thicken your skin. We should celebrate our rejections. It will take the fear out of the equation and push us to greater heights.

Sometimes getting a no is actually *better* than receiving a thumbs up. Not only is it a place for personal and professional growth, but it can also be a wake-up call for a piece of your product or a direction that your company plans to take. Sometimes, a no with a follow-up explanation can actually save you from throwing the company behind efforts that could be detrimental or undesirable.

In addition, getting a hasty yes can set you up for a partnership that can ultimately be more trouble than it is worth. Getting an initial yes is a great feeling, but if you don't take the proper steps to vet the partnership, you could end up in a bureaucratic nightmare or a situation in which you have to divert company resources to produce something that you did not initially anticipate.

In fact, once a company says yes (or, better yet, before the pitch), you should map out the proper next steps needed to complete the partnership. If they are too burdensome or expensive, it may not be worth it. Usually, this comes down to three major questions:

1. What do we need to do?
2. What do they need to do?
3. What is the time frame for both sides?

Sometimes, a rejection can save you from the headache of misalignment of the answers to any of these questions.

CHAPTER 29

Being Helpful and Adding Value

Networking, reaching out, and following up all lead to the art of being helpful, adding value, and asking for help, and in the BD world, favors can go a long way. The BD and deal-making professions usually straddle the divide between asking for and giving out both personal and professional favors, both of which rely on maintaining a large network of colleagues and friends.

Professional favors can range from asking someone to spread the word about a job opening at your company, for a Like for your company on Facebook when you are starting out, or for someone to help out a friend or family member. Asking for favors goes hand-in-hand with doing favors for others. If someone asks you for a retweet on Twitter or to spread the word about something she wants to get out there, it is your responsibility to help her in any way possible. Remember to treat people the way you would want to be treated. On top of that, perhaps one day you might ask for the same thing in return. Favors consist of everything in the realm of helping out both people you know and people you don't know. Plus, this generates good karma for you and your business endeavors. You never know when it will come back to benefit you!

Gary Vaynerchuk, founder of VaynerMedia, underscores the importance not only of favors in partnership dealings, but also of not keeping score on who owes what. "I really don't keep score on this exact thing. I'm so much more into paying it forward. I really can't even think of a specific time when I did a favor because I believe it happens behind the scenes every day."

As anyone who has ever asked for even a small favor knows, currying favor with others is similar to a form of currency. We often feel that if we are asked to do something on behalf of someone else, we can ask that person for a favor in return. Indeed, professionally speaking, we are asked to help our colleagues, bosses, or direct reports with tasks all the time. It is a tacit agreement among professionals that if you help someone with an assignment or cover for him for a shift, you can ask for something from that individual.

In partnership generation, a similar cadence applies. BD professionals constantly reach out to their contacts to ask for introductions or connections to particular individuals, and in return those people are likely to ask the same of you.

CHAPTER 30

FEELING THE PULSE
OF THE MARKET

ONE OF THE easiest ways to be successful in the world of partnerships is to stay current on the market in which your company exists. This means not only understanding your direct competitors but also staying abreast of entire industries or types of companies as a basis for comparison. You can often extrapolate from your understanding of the industry to determine patterns and forecast trends.

Different pieces of news are noteworthy depending on the industry, but some market information is relevant across the board. Reading about current events and industry-specific news reports is critical for staying up-to-date and learning about what other companies in the space are doing. For startups, you should know what types of companies are being started, who is getting funding, what the press is thinking or writing about, and the feedback or fallout from the stories that are being written.

For example, we like to read specific tech-related blogs like TechCrunch and Mashable in addition to classic news sources like the *New York Times* and the *Wall Street Journal*. But we recommend that BD professionals get more niched than that. Find blogs that are specific to your tech area of interest or even your location.

Jeremy Lermitte of Uber says that feeling the pulse of the market is driven just as much by networking as it is by reading articles and following trends. "Always be in the scene. It can be difficult to manage in our fast-paced work environments, but the more coffees and beers you can schedule, the better you'll have the pulse of the industry. Reading tech articles is one thing, but having a presence at local events is also important. I'd always recommend getting involved in local charities and education programs where your expertise can be an asset. It's a great place to meet like-minded people while also making a difference."

Everyone in your company will have a slightly different opinion about the way she understands the market or industry. Each of them will have a different understanding or reading of the angle of the articles, or perhaps someone will have missed something that you have read about. As a result, to get maximum benefit from keeping your finger on the pulse of the market, be sure to share your findings with your team members. If you are able to have a routine dialogue about it, the pulse you feel will remain more accurate.

CHAPTER 31

THE "SHINY THINGS" DISEASE

The Disease

Everyone is intrigued by the literal, and sometimes the figurative, shiny new object in the room. In partnerships, this manifests itself when a hot new deal opportunity comes on your radar and you consider dropping important things to work on it. This is known as the "shiny things" disease, and it occurs when your BD team can't focus, but continues to follow the newest and shiniest thing whenever it arises.

In the case of partnerships, that shiny object could be a big company that wants to work with you or a brand-new company that has garnered a great deal of notoriety. Even the best BD professionals fall for this constantly. It's shiny! It's alluring! And really, it's hard not to. The intrigue of a new thing is difficult to fight. But if you don't fight it and continue to jump from thing to thing, you will accomplish little, and you will have no one to blame but yourself.

The shiny things disease happens at companies of all sizes, but it is an especially profound feeling when a big company you want to work with reaches out to you. This happens with digital agencies and the brands they represent frequently. You feel special, and you want to make time for that company because it noticed you. But making time for that company means taking time away from something you *need* to do. This can kill a startup very easily.

As an example of the shiny things disease (although not in the partnership space, but rather a company operation example), Fab.com began its life in 2010 as a social network. The founders then noticed the rapid growth of daily deal and discount companies like Groupon and Gilt Groupe, and pivoted the company's service to incorporate the latest trend, flash sales. They chased the shiny thing for a time, but unfortunately, the bet didn't pay off. They are, as of the beginning of 2014, pivoting to sell design-focused furniture online.

When you're dealing with a startup, once you figure out what path you want to take, you need to stay hyperfocused. If you decide that you are going after a specific type of deal, then stick with that focus until either it works out or you decide that you need to change up your strategy. Chasing one-offs never ends well.

The Cure

There are two ways to cure yourself of the shiny things disease.

The first is to ignore shiny things. It will take time, but you should work on training yourself to ignore random one-off requests or emails that come your way that don't seem promising. This means ignoring emails and calls making a specific type of request (for example, please build this or that because we want to use it). You should log the request, but you can't do everything, and you need to respond with: "We are focused on X for the next few months," which will help keep these companies at bay. You need to try your best to stay focused on the uglier, duller things that will actually make your business more successful. This is obviously easier said than done.

The second cure is to put a major stumbling block in front of shiny things. This allows you to see which ones are really serious about working with you and which ones are going to waste your time. A stumbling block could be that you need the other company to sign some sort of binding letter of intent saying that if you do what it is asking for, it will definitely use or integrate your product. Some people are of the opinion that the only way to cure yourself fully is the first way. But I've seen some success with the major stumbling block strategy.

Either way you go, if you don't cure the shiny things disease, it can have a major negative effect on your BD team, which will subsequently hurt your company. Make sure that you try to identify shiny things opportunities and make a conscious effort not to fall into that trap.

CHAPTER 32

INTERNAL COMMUNICATION

It may not seem like it, but internal presentations and meetings are as important as, if not more important than, communication outside of your company or team. Selling your partnership ideas, product suggestions, or strategic focus to an internal audience is crucial. If you don't do a serious job of preparing, your ideas might not be heard on their own merit or, even worse, might be deemed not valuable or even counterproductive.

As a partnership professional, it is your job to liaise with various other people around the company. You want to ensure that the product team is onboard with any product integration, or that the financial team is eager to see potential monetization efforts from the partnership. At the end of the day, how you pitch your idea internally is just as important as how you pitch it to other companies.

So What Can You Do?

Take internal meetings seriously. Come with research and ideas. Be prepared. Talk! But do not speak to hear your own voice; add value to the conversation. It might seem as though when you are among your peers, it is acceptable to speak casually about your intentions. The worst possible scenario for an internal meeting, however, is to show up and hope to ad lib. It shows a lack of commitment to the assignment or the deal, and it means that your colleagues will probably not believe that the company's efforts or resources should be dedicated to this endeavor.

Effective communication takes the form of either writing or persuasive public speaking. If you learn how to express yourself and your thoughts properly, you have a powerful tool at your disposal. For the purpose of internally communicating a strategy or partnership idea, try to utilize one of these two methods to disseminate your message. The first step is to express it in writing to the relevant stakeholders. Persuading them to be interested enough to take a meeting on your desired topic can require finesse.

Once you have a stage for expressing your ideas to your colleagues, be sure to pitch it in a way that benefits them. Highlight the areas through which your partnership will benefit their work or the company as a whole. Pandering to their personal interests will make it easier for your colleagues to understand the benefits of your idea in the context of what matters to them.

The second method is to speak publicly as often as you can. It is the only way to get better at public speaking. Challenge yourself in a small conference setting or at a companywide all-hands meetings. Speaking persuasively and with authority will lend you the credibility necessary when it comes time to pitch internally.

Lars Fjeldsoe-Nielsen comments on his time at Dropbox and his frequent communication style:

Companywide communication is more about telling people what we are up to, why we are doing it, and what the goal is. For example, three years back (2010–2011), when I first presented the mobile goals for Dropbox, nobody understood what the goals meant, or even if we could achieve them. The primary goal was simply to ship the product deeply embedded on 100 million phones. When we later met that target, I presented new overall targets, but I also spent some time getting people excited about the potential and challenges we had from the users we had got from the 100 million units shipped. The basic objective was to get the company excited about supporting the deals, as they were having a real impact.

As far as the deal team is concerned, I communicate often and in as much detail as possible. People want to know what is going on, basically status and next steps, any risks that are present, and opportunities.

I play the role of a coordinator between teams, as many units are working on deal-related items, but in isolation. This includes the engineering, product, analytics, accounting, comms, marketing, and business teams. So getting people in a room once a month is useful, especially as the team is growing so fast that people often have never met.

Then there is communication with the CEO and other such people. They get regular updates—sometimes daily, depending on what is going on, or weekly. These are done in person or by email and are brief and easy to digest.

Finally, there are board meetings, where I present one or at most two slides that give an overview of the results, the risks, and the future.

Looking Forward

When a deal requires more of your employees to move forward, you should include the right people. Always have ongoing honest and open conversations with your internal team members or direct reports, but only when you need to have other people included should you start including them. Once a contract is signed and multiple people in the company are needed to take the deal to the next level, it would be best to update every employee at whatever companywide gathering occurs. Continue to temper expectations, since deals fall apart or get delayed all the time. But give everyone the details, the timeline, and the game plan. Remember, if you are going after a big enough industry, there are always more deals to close, but losing the confidence of your team members can be demoralizing.

What Should You Share with the Full Team Versus the BD Team?

Expectations at small companies can be quirky. Given the limited number of people or even the physical space in which your company operates, information can get disseminated similar to a game of telephone. As a result, you want to be careful about what gets spread to the entire company, or even shared within your team, while balancing the culture of open dialogue often associated with small companies.

Working on a team that handles partnerships in a deal-related fashion means that you have the knowledge to drive everyone forward and keep employees optimistic about the company's growth. On the other hand, that opportunity and excitement can be distracting or simply confidential. You want everyone to be optimistic about your business and to always keep the excitement and energy, but how can you strike a balance between excitement and overpromising?

One of the biggest mistakes that we see BD or partnership professionals make is overselling the progress between their company and a partner. A BD team that has had one or two promising meetings with another company, but with no deal commitment, may share that information with the team without including the proper disclaimer. BD deals can be fragile at times and have the potential to fall apart. When deals do fall apart, you feel like a jerk for jumping the gun and sharing the deal with your team too early. It is one of the biggest no-no's in the BD handbook.

Richard Bloom, COO at Onswipe, says that oversharing with the team is almost always beneficial in moderation:

> I think it's great to share the deal pipeline with the entire company, but to make it clear that a deal isn't closed until it's live (not when the agreement is signed, but when it's actually live). I think it is good to overcommunicate on this. It also might help the product and engineering teams understand why certain features are being requested.
>
> However, it's also key to generally hold off on building new features specifically for a new deal until the agreement is executed and there is a clear date for the deal to go live. I learned this the hard way. On a similar note, I think that for a startup, it's key to be careful not to commit to build new products, features, or functionality for every potential big-name deal. The logic should be: (1) Is this feature already in the road map, but one that we'd move up? (2) If no, is it a feature that would be useful for other publishers (or partners)? (3) If no, as a one-off, is the deal so big or so impactful that it is worthwhile to do the work anyway? If the answer to any of these is yes, you still need to analyze the amount of time required and be mindful of what you're pushing back or giving up on the road map to make it happen.

When you're working on a big transaction, if you are at a point where you are sharing it with the team, make sure you explain to your team members that the deal is still not finalized (even if you are positive that it will happen) and that you will keep them up-to-date on its progress. It's better to overdeliver once it closes. Letting down your team members is an irreversible scenario.

CHAPTER 33

WORKING WITH BIG COMPANIES

THE NATURE AND life cycle of partnerships change depending on the size of your company and the size of the company with which you are seeking to partner. Regardless of the size of your company, however, working with large companies or conglomerates can be tricky to maneuver and involves more process than a peer-to-peer partnership.

Many professionals see working with big companies as a coveted experience. The right deal with the right big company can take your company or product to the next level faster than fund-raising and good press combined. Partnerships with big companies ordinarily necessitate large-scale implementation, a broadening of the product, and, as a result, an expansion of your user base. Working with a big company comes about through a mixture of persistence, patience, and intrigue on behalf of the larger company.

Large companies usually are publicly traded and make substantial revenue. You can find big companies in a variety of industries. There are big tech companies like Apple, Google, Amazon, Facebook, and eBay. There are big media companies like Comcast, Disney, Viacom, Condé Nast, Hearst, and Time Warner. There are big clothing brands like Gucci, Burberry, Louis Vuitton, Dolce & Gabbana, and Dior. We could go on and on.

Since working with big companies means taking a step toward legitimizing your company or can be seen as a validating factor for your product, maintaining a level of professionalism and organization is critical. In addition, conducting research on how that company works with other partners can help you structure your own partnership. For example, most big companies have long business cycles. If you talk to a company like Microsoft in October, the team might tell you to reconnect with it in February and work on an implementation in June.

Another nuance to be aware of when working with large companies is that they usually want to work with the "hottest startups" that they hear about in the news or other public forums. As a result, it is generally easier to partner with big companies if you have good press or an already-formed reputation in the space. If you do not have the kind of sizzle that makes you a hot company, but your technology is innovative and is something that the big company wants or needs, you are also a strong candidate to partner with one, but it will all boil down to the success and persuasiveness of your pitch.

Eric Batscha of Knewton has had experience facilitating partnerships at both large and small companies and describes the differences between business development strategies at the two types of companies:

> The biggest surprise when I switched from doing business development at a big company to working at a startup was how much harder it was to get meetings. Everyone knew the Yahoo! brand and name. Even though we were competing with Google and Microsoft, Yahoo! could command attention. More often than not, to line up partnerships at startups, I had to demonstrate the credibility of my company's brand before I could even start to talk about the value of our solution. Understandably, no one wants to partner with a company they think might be belly-up in six months, no matter how special the product.
>
> I had to change almost everything about my approach to building partnerships when I moved into startups: the text and format of my emails, what I said and how I said things on phone calls. I started attending different events and networking differently. I even kept different hours to account for the new paradigm I now found myself in at a startup.

In order to navigate the bureaucracy of a large company, you should either have a product that the company wants or needs (meaning that the company has reached out to you) or convince the company that you have something that is critically valuable for it. The way to achieve either of these options is to build something valuable that other people need. When you execute on that mission, customers and partners alike will evangelize your product, the press will cover you, investors will want to back you, and new partnership leads will come in frequently. The problem will become a positive one: being able to distinguish strong, qualified leads from irrelevant ones. Kristal Bergfield, formerly of StellaService and American Express, also notes that patience is critical when partnering with substantially larger or more established companies than your own. It takes longer to execute, and big companies are inevitably busier.

To entice large companies by proving that you have a product that is crucial to their development, use all of the aforementioned tactics, but tailor pieces of the product and pitch to the needs of that specific company. You will use existing partnerships and the metrics that were gained from them to excite potential new big companies.

CHAPTER 34

WORKING WITH THE PRESS

WORKING WITH THE media is a fact of life when you are pioneering partnerships. Without any coverage, the partnership can get overlooked, and you will miss the opportunity to capitalize on the momentum that press coverage can bring. But the press can be your best friend or your worst enemy, and you must be very careful and meticulous when working with it. Here are some best practices for interacting with the media and content producers.

At a small company, the person given the task of liaising with the press could be the founder or CEO, the marketing and communications lead, or the BD and partnerships lead. This person's duties include reaching out to those in the press, giving them the materials they need in order to cover you, communicating with them about the story, and ultimately getting them to write about you. At this early a stage, dealing with journalists is really a relationship game. If you don't know the journalists, but you want to do a product release or funding announcement right, your best bet is to hire a small PR firm to help you out. The right people there can do wonders.

When your company has something to announce to the public, the best way to disseminate that information is to put together a company blog post. This post should include all the information about your release and exactly how you would like the news to be viewed and consumed by the outside world.

Once you have your blog post ready, it is time to start talking to various outlets. Often, you can cherry-pick which media you would like to have showcase your story by granting interviews or exclusive access, but you ultimately cannot control who covers the story. In general, you should have concrete goals concerning why you want to solicit press coverage and what the outcome should be. You should understand the audience you are trying to reach and have a target in mind. Are you seeking to attract investors? Potential hires for the company? New consumers or users? Every stage of the press process should be premeditated.

In addition, you want to work with the press to ensure that you receive the best and most exposure for your company. "Best," in this case, can be defined as most revealing or enlightening, with as positive an angle as possible. Having the press reveal your weaknesses is not necessarily all bad, but positive reviews are usually more helpful. You also want to see variations of the same story, rather than exactly the same story, across various media. In practice, you should enable the various authors to tailor the story to their unique readership so that their audiences understand your story on their terms.

Best Practices for Writing a Press Release

The blog post can often serve as a press release. This may seem obvious, but the reason for a press release is so that the media can cover your announcement. After you have spoken with an outlet about what you have coming out, and it has committed to covering the news, you should share a password-protected unpublished blog post with that outlet.

In the initial blog post revealing your company's news, you should tell the thesis of your story and include most of the details that you plan to reveal publicly. Tell the story behind your announcement, describe the product, discuss changes in the product or partnership details, and find an audience to target.

If you are releasing a new product, explain what the new product is. Show examples of companies or people that are using the product. Discuss why they are using it, what they gain from it, and how other companies or people can gain the same thing. If you are announcing a partnership, explain why this partnership is important. Make sure you find an outlet whose readers will care about the announcement. When thinking about your announcement, whatever the news may be, you need to understand what you are announcing, who may care, and what press outlets have the right readers to maximize the effect of the announcement.

You should give the reporters who are interested in covering you an unpublished finished blog post for a few reasons:

1. They can refer to it when they are writing up their piece if they don't catch something or if you don't have enough time to give them the entire story on the phone or in person.
2. Journalists write many stories a day while covering their respective beats. You are making their lives easier by helping them to cover you (taking down any barriers for them is key).
3. You can publish the post and then let them link to your company, driving traffic to your website and your news.

Best Practices for Working with the Press

First, give your press contacts at least three business days to write an article. When they are covering a beat, it is easy for them to miss something that they might otherwise write about if they are not given enough time to put together a respectable piece on whatever it is you are announcing. If you are afraid to give it to them with enough time because you think they will "break" the embargo, then you are not close enough to them to ask for an embargo.

Next, you should provide your contacts with a clear story. You should be able to summarize the theme or announcement in one sentence. Synthesizing the story in a clear and concise manner will win you brownie points with the reporters and will also allow you better control of the message. This helps remove any barriers for the press people covering you.

Finally, after they write the article, thank your press contacts for covering you. Try to help them out by sending them cool and interesting stories that come your way. They will be appreciative and want to continue to cover you down the road.

Pitfalls to Avoid

Make sure you do not give the same exact story to 10 different outlets. If you can't spin the story for different audiences, then you should probably go the route of offering one big outlet an exclusive.

In addition, don't try to sell the idea of your company's existence as news. Unless you are a previously successful entrepreneur who is just starting a new company, you need to actually be launching your product to get coverage.

Also, don't blindly email the same story with the same text to every tech reporter. If you do, it is easy to tell that you did not do the legwork required to craft an original email that is relevant to each specific reporter and her overall readership demographic. Reporters also mostly move in the same circles, so they might even chat about it. Each tech outlet usually shares a chat group (often on Skype or Yammer), and they talk to one another about things that come in. In addition, try not to email multiple folks at the same outlet if you don't know them.

CHAPTER 35

"Launch Partner" Strategy

For a company, launching a product or a strategy can take months (or years), vast resources, and a sizable percentage of the firm's personnel. In an effort to ensure that these labors do not fall flat or go unnoticed, most companies engage other companies or individuals to help them launch their product. These are known as *launch partners*, and they are cultivated during the months and weeks before a product is planned to launch.

Instead of simply pushing a new feature into the abyss and hoping that it garners notoriety or traction, you should try to weave in a few companies to become stakeholders in that launch by becoming inextricably linked to the new product, most frequently by having these companies use your product or integrate it into their own offerings. This works only if you can presell these companies on what you intend to build, and getting someone to commit to integrating something before it is ready is not an easy task. But if it is done well, it can turn your medium-size announcement into a mushroom cloud type of ripple effect. Having great examples to point to from the get-go can make all the difference.

Finding a Launch Partner

Approaching a prospective launch partner is a tricky thing to master. Not every product launch necessarily needs a launch partner, and not every company is appropriate for the job, but the primary purpose for having such an arrangement is to create a symbiotic relationship between two pieces of technology. Ordinarily, a launch partner will have early access to the product that you are planning to release. Having a "sneak peek" into a product can be enticing for certain entities, and can give them creative license to build something that enhances both sides or that has a functionality that makes their product better.

Once a potential launch partner has agreed to meet with you, you should treat the meeting as you would any other form of partnership arrangement. As we described in Chapter 12, "Four Golden Rules of Partnerships," you must understand what is important to the other side from either a road mapping or a product enhancement perspective. If there is a fit, target this company for a launch partnership. The only difference between pitching for launch partnership opportunities and ordinary BD deals is that with a launch partnership, the idea is not yet fully hatched and the technology is not yet developed.

Some companies relish the opportunity to work through the technology development and provide hands-on product attention and feedback in real time. Usually, these are smaller companies that have the flexibility to adapt to a product as it gets built. Larger companies tend to shy away from the launch partnership track, especially when the partnership involves a technological enhancement.

The difference between a launch partner and any other partnership is the timing. "In retrospect, the main difference with the launch partnership is that you have some leverage you can use to inspire urgency," says Scott Britton. "This can be other partners, a press opportunity, or even a holiday, as in the case of the Valentine's Day partnership between SinglePlatform and Foursquare."

Benefits of Being a Launch Partner

Launch partnerships would not happen unless there were incentives on both sides of the deal. First, the promotion that comes with being a launch partner can be greatly beneficial to both companies. Often, launch partners showcase the other company's product on their own blogs, social media, or even native platforms. This is a distribution partnership in itself.

Launch partnerships also provide another opportunity for your company to be showcased in the media, especially if your partner garners a great deal of media attention. If your product went relatively unnoticed before, but you have the correct, high-profile launch partner, your product could get picked up by large news sources.

As with any partnership, a launch partnership provides two user bases' worth of users, meaning that the launch partners can mutually benefit from tapping into each other's pool of consumers. The effect can be multiplied by the fact that the combination of two products can attract the attention of entirely new users.

A good example of approaching a company and asking it to be a launch partner is telling the company that you have a new product coming out that is going to save it a bunch of money. On top of that, you will be bringing it your user base and the press that comes along with the launch. If you are a small-but-growing company with a few hundred or a few thousand users, this might be a great partnership and something that another company would want to be a part of.

Launch partners can be small or large, and ordinarily a large name brand or an easily recognizable company is helpful when you are trying to gain credibility. But, as we discussed previously in Chapter 33, "Working with Big Companies," large companies can be hard to maneuver, even when they have a time constraint attached to the deal. When Andy Ellwood was the head of business development at Gowalla, he brokered the deal between the geolocation check-in platform and Disney. "For our 3.0 release at the end of 2010, Disney was the prize partner we as a team wanted to lock in. But any time a company the size of Disney is involved, it is mayhem to attempt to get anything done. For just about all of our conversations, it was me on one side of the table and an army of folks from all different divisions on their side of the table. The deal was called off at least three different times because of circumstance beyond my control, but because we knew we had a competitive advantage and we'd allowed enough time to pull it off, we eventually got it launched and had a tremendous response that led to ongoing initiatives and Gowalla/Disney success all the way through to our acquisition."

How Many Launch Partners Are Enough?

When executing the launch partner strategy, you want to strike a good balance between quality and quantity of partners. We've been involved with launches with tons of companies, as well as some with a few select companies. Some have been successes, and some have been failures. One thing we've learned is that when you don't have a big team, launching with too many companies is almost unmanageable. It always depends, but we believe it's usually best to launch with less than 10 super-high-quality companies. Anything more than that can be difficult to juggle.

What Is Expected of a Launch Partner?

On your side of the launch partner strategy, you should ask a few things from your launch partners. The first is that the partner have everything up and running at least one or two weeks before the launch announcement, especially if the product will be public or consumer-facing. The reason for this is to ensure that the product has been completely tested and is ready to be rolled out on the day of the launch. The second thing to ask is that all launch partners involved in a strategic partnership post blog entries on their own corporate blogs explaining the launch and why they are involved. This is a very successful strategy and helps to compound the launch announcement.

36

TURNING A NICE TO HAVE INTO A NEED TO HAVE

ONCE YOU HAVE determined the right type of partnership, the desired outcome, and the correct person with whom to liaise, and you have received product feedback, it's time to actually make a partnership deal happen. The most effective way to ensure this is to make your product not only something that would benefit another company, but something that is essential to another company or its users.

In partnerships, a "nice to have" is a product, feature, or integration that is gravy for a company. Often these extra efforts are benefits, but not necessities, pertaining to integrating a technology, engaging in a joint branding promotion, or a variety of other cross-collaborative efforts. In this world, this can be thought of as a nonessential partnership that is not a priority for a company. It could be a product that a company doesn't need, but that would be *nice to have*. Any kind of company can come across these types of partnerships, and companies at all stages are both pitching and being pitched these additional features.

As a BD professional pitching an offering that is considered to be a nice to have, you need to figure out a way to get some urgency into the equation, turning a nice to have into a "need to have." There are many ways to do this. The most effective and best types of nice to haves involve a launch scenario, as we discussed in Chapter 35, "'Launch Partner' Strategy." Alternatively, a competitor may be using a similar product and has garnered a great deal of financial or consumer reward in a short period of time.

On the other hand, if you are the recipient of a pitch for a nice to have, you need to actively seek the nugget of urgency or the special element that would compel you to need to have it. The barrier to entry for a nice-to-have product is substantially higher, since you are not necessarily looking for that type of partnership.

In the launch scenario when you are pitching a company, you are offering it the opportunity to take part in something that is bigger than just your offering. It will be featured or highlighted in a press release and user promotion. If you have a proven track record of generating press for your product releases, having companies see the potential reach by participating in the launch can be an effective way to turn a nice to have into a need to have.

In the scenario in which the company's competitor is already using your product, you need to showcase how this competitor is using your product and why this company is missing out because it is not. This can go both ways. Some companies get jealous of their competitors, while others get resentful and don't want to work with you specifically because you work with their competitor. This is a touch-and-go tactic that you should use only if you feel comfortable with it. It can also be a way to turn a nice to have into a need to have.

The third scenario is when you are offering a short window and monetary gain for a user. This could mean doing a user promotion: for example, every user who uses a certain app receives a free credit toward something. When offering a short window, you need to figure out what will get the prospective partner to move quickly. This can be another valuable way to turn a nice to have into a need to have.

For example, Aviary has planted the idea that in the photo ecosystem, photo-editing is critical, and that to do this well, you need to devote an entire company to it. Photo-editing and manipulation tools are Aviary's focus; this allows its partners to focus on whatever is core to them. As a result, Aviary has made itself indispensable in the photo space, and as a result, many photo- and image-related companies want to partner with Aviary.

The goal of any partnership is to turn these nice-to-have initiatives into need to haves on behalf of the other partnership company. The first and primary mechanism of making this change is to think about what you're really offering and figure out how to make yourself absolutely essential.

PART 5

WAR STORIES

CHAPTER 37

INTRODUCTION TO WAR STORIES

CONGRATULATIONS! YOU'VE learned enough about business development and partnerships to be a bit dangerous.

The last part of this book is titled "War Stories." In it, we have some of the business's best and brightest share their experiences in BD, partnerships, operations, and entrepreneurship. In the previous four parts of this book, you have been absorbing information about the mechanics of business development, tactics for pitching, and strategies for closing a deal, with best practices interspersed. But it's been exactly that: a ton of information! BD tactics are best understood in context, and in Part 5, we will allow the experts to demonstrate these principles from firsthand experience and stories. We cover topics such as how to partner with large companies and navigate bureaucracy, how to use your network to do deals, and how to move from BD to founding a company or vice versa.

We asked a diverse group of BD professionals, as well as COOs, founders, lawyers, and those generally affiliated with partnerships, to describe their experiences and elaborate on their expertise. They explained how they got to where they are now, how they cultivated their specialty, and what their go-to partnership tactics are.

You will notice some commonalities among the people featured. Many of them had an entrepreneurial spirit from a young age or even parents who instilled these "startup values" into them. Some of them have technical backgrounds; others were formally schooled or trained in fields unrelated to BD. All of them are gregarious and tenacious, willing to talk about their love for networking and meeting others to create and/or add value. And all of them have heeded advice from their peers and mentors to make themselves better BD professionals and company founders. BD tends to attract individuals with a particular set of professional and interpersonal skills.

But don't be alarmed if your profile doesn't match those of the people highlighted here. We (Alex and Ellen) have very different backgrounds and skill sets, as do many of these professionals. Some have engineering backgrounds, while most do not. Some thrive at big, established companies, whereas others work best without major structure. Some were born to entrepreneurial parents and learned about entrepreneurship from a young age, while others explored that skill set for themselves. The moral is that there is no standard profile for a business development professional or an entrepreneur.

CHAPTER 38

LARGE-COMPANY BD:
KRISTAL BERGFIELD

Key Notes

Name: Kristal Bergfield

Companies: StellaService, American Express, Waggener Edstrom
  (Microsoft Account)

KRISTAL BERGFIELD most recently served as the vice president of BD at Stella-Service, a business analytics company that evaluates and rates customer service performance. StellaService, a business-to-business (B2B) company that provides a platform as well as data analytics, hired Bergfield because of her longstanding expertise in partnerships and marketing. She got her start at a small advertising agency in Portland, Oregon, where she used her undergraduate degree in advertising to learn the fundamentals of business. She moved on to a PR agency called Waggener Edstrom as an account manager working on the Microsoft account for three years in the late 1990s. As she says, "Those years had the biggest impact in terms of learning how to create strategies, seize opportunities, build relationships, roll with change, and fake it till you make it."

On Business School and Making the Move from Marketing to BD

Bergfield attended NYU Stern School of Business after a few years in the workforce, and this shaped her career in several ways. She is best known for her eight years of service at American Express, where she got her start in BD. How did she make the move from PR and marketing to BD?

"After working on a partner marketing team [a team that worked with American Express's partners to market card products worldwide] for a few years, I moved to a team that was establishing [American Express] card distribution partnerships with banks. I had no idea that this was BD. I was just attracted to doing something new that hadn't been done before, and I knew that my relationship skills would be an asset. We built a distribution program from the ground up: product, pricing, relationships, and so on. Ultimately, it wasn't a profitable card acquisition channel for American Express, but I loved being an intrapreneur." In the world of startups, an intrapreneur is someone who is able to create and develop something new within the confines of his company's structure or resources.

When talking about moving from a marketing position to a BD position, Bergfield recommends focusing on your network.

"If you are going from marketing to BD, I would highlight that BD is a lot about relationships: connecting them, building them, managing them. We all partner with people every day—internal partners, vendors, advertising agencies—regardless of whether or not that is in our job description. If that's something you enjoy, that's something you should highlight. And you're probably right for the role." If you have been successful at making marketing relationships or even marketing deals, this can serve you well when you are trying to make the move into BD or any other partnership role.

On the Nuances Between BD at Large Companies

Part of BD at larger companies is finding a balance between working within the confines of the company's culture and history, and trying to remain innovative.

Bergfield explains, "At a 150-year-old company, you will find pockets of innovation and pockets of status quo. The president of American Express, Ed Gilligan, tries to be innovative and takes it upon himself to really learn the technology and integrate it. The company has programs that encourage innovation. When you are trying to be innovative, you also have to work with a lot of different departments that say, 'We've always done it this way, and we can't change.'"

Larger companies receive more incoming requests from companies that want to partner than they make outbound to create lead-generating partnerships. As a result, if you are at a large company, the process for selecting deals can sometimes seem opaque or confusing. Some large companies have very stringent criteria for selecting potential partners, especially when they are working with smaller companies. But Bergfield talks about her team at American Express dealing primarily with companies that they actively solicited rather than the other way around.

"We decided that we wanted to find companies to work with that could help small businesses market themselves differently. We had a category we wanted to target; it was very strategic and consultinglike. We identified a need and a growing market segment, and we targeted only that universe. So we focused on products that helped with that. We found 20 startups that did search engine management software (at the time a fairly new and growing industry) and narrow(ed) it down to one." This happened to be a growing segment of the market largely because of Google and other search engines' massive successes.

"In addition, we took into account whether companies were well funded enough that working with American Express wouldn't pull them under. As far as whom we partnered with, it was all outbound and very intent-driven."

On Smaller Companies Navigating Large-Company Bureaucracy

Bergfield has worked on behalf of both small and large companies. In her time at American Express, she partnered with many small businesses as part of American Express's Small Business Saturday campaign. The advice she gave to these small businesses was this:

When working with smaller companies, I always tell people to go into it with their eyes open. Don't promise the world to a big company and get into a situation where you are burning your cash by trying to please that company. It can also be a great thing; at StellaService we have a great partnership with Google that has helped us get involved with other big companies and grow our company.

As far as navigating bureaucracy, it's sometimes hard for people to understand and be patient with the big company. When we don't call you back, it is most likely because we need to talk to multiple internal stakeholders, and that takes a few weeks to schedule before we can get back to you with anything worthwhile. You can't take it personally. On top of that, if we end up not working with you immediately, it's not that we don't ever want to work with your company; it's usually the case that there are higher priorities in our queue than what you are offering.

She likes to remind smaller companies that the priorities of larger companies are often scattered or disparate. The unfortunate reality is that partnerships are often a bigger deal for smaller companies than for larger ones.

On Creative BD

One of the phrases that Bergfield used when describing her passion for BD is "creative BD," which is the notion of inventing a partnership that has never been done before. Bergfield herself is a master at this, both at large corporations and at startups:

There are so many times when you are working on a deal in which you have to write a contract that hasn't been done before: between two kinds of companies with technologies that have never been paired. I have to structure a whole new type of relationship. It is a lot about starting with two companies that know that they want to work together because they have a similar mission or customer set. Let's look at our assets and what we can accomplish and then figure out how to do so.

A prime example of creative BD was the partnership deal that Bergfield led on behalf of American Express with Clickable, a search engine marketing and management and intelligence platform.

"The Clickable deal was the first of its kind; we were going to help market a product to small business owners. We would combine American Express's strength in marketing with Clickable's product strength, or the first Small Biz Saturday with Facebook. We know small businesses will grow if they advertise on Facebook, so how can American Express help them do that? Things that had never been done before." Creative BD is not necessarily exclusive to big companies working with smaller companies, but according to Bergfield, it is helpful when one side of the deal is innovative and can easily manipulate its product to work with another.

On Being a Work-Outside-the-Home Parent

Bergfield is also known for being steadfast about spending time developing both her professional and her personal passions, a question of balance that comes up frequently in the world of pitching and closing deals. The concept of "having it all" or having a "work-life balance" is one that troubles Bergfield, but she does focus on the notion of "work-life integration":

> I have a husband who is a true partner and splits parenting 50/50. We work it out, and we instilled in our kids the idea that we both have to work, and that's a part of life. But I hate the phrase "work-life balance." My old boss from American Express is a mom, and she used to always say, "You have only one life." I'm a big believer in that. Work and family are each part of your life, and there are times when some of those things are out of balance. This concept of work-life integration is also true for people who don't have a family. Anyone who wants to have a career must figure out work-life integration: if you want to run a marathon or play an instrument, the same trade-offs must be made.

Bergfield's professional trajectory, from PR to marketing to business development and partnerships, has laid the foundations for making her a well-known business development professional. Her experiences at both large and small companies have made her savvy about navigating the corporate world of connecting companies and products.

CHAPTER 39

ENTREPRENEURSHIP AND BD: SCOTT BRITTON

Key Notes

Name: Scott Britton
Companies: SinglePlatform, Constant Contact, Sfter, CollegeOnly

WHILE AT PRINCETON, Britton's academic interests were in political policy and economics, but after he graduated, his entrepreneurial passion took hold. He worked for a college classmate's company called CollegeOnly, which pivoted to be called YouAre.TV and created online game shows in which any-one could become a contestant. It was at YouAre.TV that he got his first taste of BD. After that, he started his own company called Sfter, "A social news cura-tion application similar to many other ones that still exist today." According to Britton, it became evident that this was a saturated space, so he joined Single-Platform six months later as its first nonexecutive business development hire. SinglePlatform is a service that connects local businesses with users searching for products.

On Learning BD

According to Britton, taking the time to learn BD by getting your hands dirty is crucial for anyone who is interested in becoming an entrepreneur or starting her own company. BD combines elements of sales that are important for understanding how to start your own business:

> Your ability to build a successful company is contingent upon building a great team. This means that you have to attract and hire world-class talent. This to me is a sales and marketing challenge, which is why mastering critical BD skills like persuasion and likability are so powerful for aspiring CEOs. There's no doubt that the best engineers want to work with the best engineers, and so on, but all you need to be able to do is sell one marquee engineer for that waterfall effect to happen. Maybe it's because I don't gravitate toward programming or design naturally, but I think the best thing aspiring CEOs can do is get great at sales and marketing, and BD in many ways fulfills that.

On Networking

Britton had the unusual experience of having worked for a friend's startup. There, he learned many tricks before setting out on his own entrepreneurial pursuits. He also leveraged his network to understand how to navigate the startup world and ultimately landed at SinglePlatform, where he helped build the company from the ground up:

> I ended up at SinglePlatform through joining Charlie O'Donnell's softball team. I didn't know him before I asked to play, but he was a well-known New York venture capitalist, and I thought the relationship would be a good one to have. When my company wasn't doing so hot and I decided that I needed some mentoring, Charlie introduced me to the guys at SinglePlatform, who were looking to bring on their first nonexecutive BD hire. The rest was history.
>
> This instance demonstrated to me the power of relationships and how you never know where your next opportunity is going to come from. I'd recommend that anyone who is looking to break in should invest in building relationships with as many helpful people that have it together as you can.

He also learned the art of networking to master a skill. "SinglePlatform was an amazing experience that taught me a lot of things. First and foremost, if you want to get good at something, go and find the best people at that particular skill and work for them. Calibrating with experts is the absolute fastest way to learn, and I was fortunate to mentor and learn under what I believe are some of the most talented BD and sales professionals around."

On Mastering the Vapor Sale

As we discussed in Chapter 18, "Vapor Sales," part of mastering BD is learning the ability to sell a product that does not yet exist. Britton is the master of this skill:

> Preselling is the ultimate strategy for validating that someone actually wants a product or feature that you're considering. Mastering this skill saves you an incredible amount of time and energy, which is why it's a superpower.
>
> The key to preselling is understanding what someone wants. You need to ask a lot of questions to develop a deep understanding of what the other party wants before you can truly craft a hypothetical offer that has legs. Once you craft your offer, you want to make it as easy as possible for this person to say yes, and ask him to put some skin in the game before you invest any time or resources in going further. This can be money, resources, or access to something that no one else gets. Never move forward if all you have is a soft verbal commitment.

On His Favorite Deal at SinglePlatform

Britton is known for orchestrating deals with well-known, established companies at SinglePlatform before Constant Contact acquired the company. His tactic for achieving success involved persistence and finding solutions via partnership to issues that hit close to home:

> I'd say I'm most proud of my deals with TomTom and Yellowbook for different reasons. I'm proud of TomTom because it was our first interna-

tional deal and it's a global data provider that powers everything from the navigation system in my dad's car to the maps on the iPhone.

Yellowbook had a lot of meaning for me because I approached it through at least three different channels over the course of a year and a half before getting the deal done. It was a valuable lesson in persistence and resilience, which made it rewarding. It doesn't hurt that it's also one of the biggest Internet yellow pages companies out there either.

On Moving to Brazil and Postacquisition BD

A company's being acquired can mean different things for different people. Sometimes BD professionals want to quickly jump to something new or take the first thing that is offered to them after an acquisition (regardless of whether they are asked to remain at the company). For Britton, the decision became apparent after conversations with various mentors:

When I was looking for something new, I thought I wanted to go run BD at another startup. I was having a conversation with Andy Dunn, the CEO of Bonobos, and told him about a few offers I had had. He looked me straight in the eye and said, "You're not taking any of those, are you?"

"What do you mean? These are good gigs," I remember saying.

He replied with something I'll never forget that dramatically hit home.

"Whatever it is you do next, you should be jumping out of your seat . . . it doesn't seem like you're jumping out of your seat about these opportunities."

He was right. And when I looked at everything I had in front of me—joining another startup, starting a company with someone from SinglePlatform, or moving to Rio with some of my best friends to go full time on my growing digital product business, the last one was by far and away what I was most excited about.

I plan on being in Rio through August 2014 to stick around for the World Cup, and I honestly have no idea whether I'll be back after that.

One thing I've realized is that I'll probably never want to completely stop working. I enjoy it. That being said, I'm not in any rush to get it over with, which empowers me to live out many dreams like living abroad while I'm in my prime. There's no doubt that I want to eventually build something huge, but I feel like I have time to do it. Right now I have a lifestyle business where I sell online courses that I create. I have five different courses in the market that pay me a comfortable salary with limited maintenance. I'd say that I probably spend anywhere from 5 to 20 hours a week working on it, depending on how aggressive I want to be in growing it. It's really cool because I have all this time to pursue other interests like surfing, learning a language, romance, and reading all the books I ever wanted to.

On BD and Blogging

As we discussed in Chapter 10, "Digital Identity," building a digital identity is very important. This has been an important part of Britton's major BD success. Britton has a blog titled *Life-Long Learner*, and he has been building his online presence at least as long as he has been building his professional career.

"Having an online presence is hugely important, and my blog is the core of that. I always tell people that if the only people who know that you do an awesome job are the ones at your company, then you're probably missing out on opportunities, even if it's just the chance to connect with cool people who can add to your current company's growth. If you have awesome insight and experiences, share it with the world. You'll reap the benefits tenfold."

On Mentorship

BD and mentorship go hand-in-hand. Every great BD professional has at least one mentor to whom she can turn in times of need, either professional or personal. Britton has had invaluable experiences with several mentors and has received some useful advice:

Kenny Herman, executive vice president of BD at SinglePlatform, is definitely my biggest mentor. He taught me two things that I'll never forget:

1. "It's not about where you are, it's who you're with." I've realized that the company I keep is much more important for my personal

happiness than things like geographic location or even what the company I work for does.

2. "People buy from people they like." There are a lot of things in life that basically mirror a sale. Understanding that given two remotely equal products, the person who is more likable is always going to win has been an empowering mindset that I've seen hold true time and time again."

CHAPTER 40

The Ultimate Connector: Charlie O'Donnell

Key Notes

Name: Charlie O'Donnell
Company: Brooklyn Bridge Ventures
Role: Founder, venture capitalist
Previous companies: General Motors, Union Square Ventures,
    First Round Capital

CHARLIE O'DONNELL is a New Yorker through and through. He has spent most of his storied career working in venture capital. After college, he worked with VCs from the pension fund side while working at GM. While he was there, he met Fred Wilson and Brad Burnham of Union Square Ventures (USV), who were pitching to his team. O'Donnell wasn't able to secure an investment from GM for USV, so instead he joined the firm at the height of the resurgence of New York City's tech community. He is best known for having discovered Twitter at the South by Southwest festival in 2007 and being very involved in USV's investment in the site. O'Donnell is currently the founder of Brooklyn Bridge Ventures, an early-stage VC firm.

On Silicon Alley

Silicon Valley has produced offspring all over the country (and all over the world!), but none have been quite as prolific as Silicon Alley. New York City has been a hotbed for new technology over the past decade. The city has opened its doors and actively solicited and courted companies to set up in New York. The initiative was spearheaded by former mayor Michael Bloomberg to infuse both creativity and capital into the city, and O'Donnell has been at the forefront of that movement.

"NYC has such a diversity of people and industries that a curious person can quickly learn a little bit about a lot of things. I think that's one of my best skills: the ability to quickly grasp how a lot of different businesses work. Growing up in Brooklyn gave me a bit of a 'Who do they think they are?' mentality when it comes to competing with the Valley. Screw those guys; we're going to build startups right here."

From the VC vantage point, O'Donnell has also had a big hand in shaping the tech companies that have come out of New York. "I gained some notability for helping Foursquare get recognized by the VC community. It's what led to me getting hired by First Round to help grow its NYC presence. While at First Round, I also led investments in SinglePlatform and GroupMe, both of which had quick exits. SinglePlatform was sold to Constant Contact, and GroupMe was sold to Skype." O'Donnell has helped put New York on the map as a second technology hub, serving as a major connector for companies started and head-quartered in New York.

On Networking, BD, and the Cycle of Connecting

O'Donnell is an incredible connector and is well known in the venture capital space for making introductions to appropriate parties. "I like feeling useful and enabling others to be successful," he says about connecting two people. "Plus, I've always had help from others as well—so I feel like I'm just giving back what I've already gotten from others."

How do you become great at making introductions? O'Donnell says that there are two keys to being a connector:

First, I think you need to keep the bar really high for who gets your time and attention. I just don't have time for assholes. Everyone that I introduce someone to is pretty great—and that's highly intentional. Second, I have a knack for remembering people's stories and histories, and I'm really curious about what they do for a living. This makes it feel like my brain has a direct connection to my LinkedIn account. In this way, I can very quickly bring to mind someone that I should introduce you to.

O'Donnell has been savvy enough to capitalize on his ability to connect and his network, parlaying them into investing opportunities as well. When it comes to investing or partnerships, he focuses on learning about people to understand what they want, as opposed to just their ideas or products:

> I put myself out there, both online and off. Instead of seeking deals, I just seek interesting people, and that leads me to deals. I went to SXSW [South by Southwest] because of the people in attendance and the speakers. I was just as interested in meeting danah boyd [social media scholar, youth researcher, and advocate working at Microsoft Research] there as I was in finding the next big thing.
>
> With Foursquare, I got to know Dennis and Naveen before they started the business, reaching out to them separately just because they seemed like people I should know. They were builders of interesting things, well respected and well liked in the NYC community. It's my job to know people like that.
>
> I got to meet Raul from Tinybop at an under the radar conference in Brooklyn called Brooklyn Beta, and I simply asked him how I could be helpful. That's how I got into the sold-out conference in the first place: by asking what help the organizers needed.

On Helping People Get Jobs

O'Donnell also puts his master networking skills to use when helping people find jobs. He is well known in Silicon Alley for placing people at burgeoning tech companies. He has placed about 40 people at startups and has built up a reputation for helping with recruiting. His advice when soliciting jobs or reaching out is to be clear and succinct:

> I don't think contacting anyone for help is the way to go. Instead, contact people with a clear offer. You do X thing for Y companies as evidenced by

Z successes. Once you've nailed what your value proposition is, anyone with a big network can get you in front of the right folks. More than helping individuals seeking work, I'm trying to help founders build great teams. If you're not sure why someone should hire you and what makes you great, it's going to be pretty hard to put you in front of a founder who has his whole net worth tied up in this company.

On VC and Blogging

O'Donnell is also an active blogger, and says he does so to keep his mind fresh. He also credits his blog, *This Is Going to Be Big*, with helping him break into the world of VC:

I started blogging because I got into the daily practice of writing for a career advice book geared toward college kids. When no one wanted to publish it, I didn't want to just stop writing, so I turned to blogging.

Blogging is definitely part of why USV hired me. More than as a marketing channel, blogging benefits me as a mental exercise. Taking all the disparate data I consume every day in pitches, news, discussions, conferences, and so on and trying to make a coherent narrative out of it is an important developmental tool. I wouldn't be insightful enough about the market to be in VC if I didn't blog.

His blog is all about getting in front of opportunities early and his thoughts on trends that he foresees taking off.

CHAPTER 41

BD AND THE
LEGAL WORLD:
RICHARD BLOOM

Key Notes

Name: Richard Bloom
Company: Onswipe
Role: COO
Previous companies: Hearst, UGO Networks, 5min Media, AOL,
    Simpson Thacher, Hogan Lovells

RICH BLOOM, currently the chief operating officer for Onswipe, grew up in
Princeton, New Jersey. The Internet boom was just beginning to blossom when
he graduated from college, but he never really considered it and decided to pursue a law degree instead. His legal career, which he spent at the New York City
law firms Simpson Thacher and Hogan Lovells, was focused primarily on the
world of technology and news media. But eventually, Bloom moved away from
the legal realm into partnership roles and made the transition to the BD side of
the technology industry. He parlayed this experience and oversaw two successful
mergers and acquisitions (M&A) exits: UGO Networks, an online media site,
which was sold to Hearst, and then 5min Media, a platform for instructional
videos, which was sold to AOL in 2010.

On His Transition into BD

A move from law to BD is not rare, because some deal negotiating skills are broadly applicable for both. Bloom made the transition after five years in the legal world:

> I thought my next move would be to a legal/business affairs job with a large media company. In 2005, I randomly stumbled into an opportunity at UGO Networks in a dual role as sole in-house counsel and BD. A week in, I knew that the startup environment was an ideal spot for me. And shortly after that, I knew that I wanted to focus on BD, as opposed to law, as much as possible. My BD role involved our vertical ad network, M&A (we did six- and seven-figure acquisitions), and typical content/technology partnerships.
>
> After 2.5 years, we sold to Hearst. I was very involved in the process of selling the company on the business side and led it from the legal side. After the sale, I knew that I wanted a role at an earlier-stage startup and that I wanted to completely drop the legal role (it's difficult and dangerous to play the dual role of deal maker on the business side and ensuring that we're buttoned up on the legal side). I joined 5min Media shortly after it raised its Series A round from Spark Capital. I ran BD and opened the New York office along with the CEO/founder and a more junior BD person. We had 12 people in Israel and 3 of us in New York. BD consisted of content partnership deals and publication distribution deals (we were a one-stop video solution: we distributed video content along with a proprietary player that used technology to contextually match video to text on every page of a site and/or via the publication's editorial selection of videos).

The startup world beckoned to Bloom when he was in the legal profession. "I enjoyed the less formal environment, the ability to have more of an impact, and the ability to be less of a specialist (I went from being a litigator to overseeing all legal issues plus spending half my time on BD)."

On His Experience with M&A

Two of the companies that Bloom helped to scale and grow were met with successful acquisitions.

"With UGO, we had a relatively mature business that had been around for a decade, and it was good timing to have an exit for investors and management." The company ultimately was sold to Hearst as part of a boost in that company's online media strategy.

Bloom argues that there is no particular sweet spot in terms of the timing of an acquisition:

> In general, most startups can't and shouldn't try to get acquired at a specific time. When 5min was acquired by AOL, the timing made sense, and we truly believed we could grow more quickly under the umbrella of a larger company.
>
> The experience of going through the process was very exciting both times. When you're at a startup, unless you're at something that realistically can have an IPO, then you know that success means a sale. In both my experiences, employees were excited by the exit and felt a real sense of accomplishment (separate and apart from any financial upside) from having built a company that a Hearst and an AOL wanted to buy for a material amount of money. In both cases, no one lost her job as a result of the acquisition. If that hadn't been the case, I'm sure the feeling would have been different.

According to Bloom, having been privy to and involved in the negotiations and transition plans were the most interesting professional experiences of his career. The sale of 5min to AOL was one of the most rewarding deals of his career, and indeed one that he is proudest of. "I'm most proud of the deal to sell 5min to AOL. I think it was the best M&A deal they've done, and frankly, dollar for dollar, one of the best M&A deals in the space of the past several years."

On Ad-Supported Publisher Networks and BD

Bloom's specialty within BD stems from his time focusing on the media and entertainment sectors as a lawyer. He is an expert when it comes to advertiser-supported publisher platforms and publisher networks, which are sites that aggregate content, like AOL or Yahoo!, especially from his time working at UGO and 5min. Advertiser-supported publisher platforms are a strong area for business development because partners seek to take advantage of the publisher platforms to enhance their own offerings. But how did this come about?

By accident. UGO was a group of owned sites plus a vertical ad network. 5min was an ad-supported publisher platform. At AOL, my responsibilities included continuing to run the 5min publisher platform plus taking over the Ad.com video network. And now, Onswipe is an ad-supported publisher platform. It's certainly not as if I set out to focus on this space, and happily (for me), my experience has included other areas.

On Deal Tactics, Both Good and Bad

Bloom says that some of the best deals he has ever done looked the worst on paper before the deal. Figuring out that these are going to be great involves having the BD vision, something that we discussed in Chapter 1, "What Is Business Development?". Bloom clearly has that edge, and explains his thinking:

> Hypothetical: I'm at a Series A–funded startup [meaning that the startup has received an initial round of funding] that is a publishing platform. My typical deal terms are a 50/50 revenue share, and at the high end I'll give a publisher a 60/40 revenue share. A big sports network (this is made up) is willing to do a deal with my company, but it will do it only for a 90/10 revenue share in its favor. On paper, the deal seems to be a horrible financial choice. I'm probably going to lose money on it, and it will hurt my margins. But by having that major sports network as a partner, I'm going to attract a lot of other publishers, and the brand name of that network alone will help with the next round of investment. Just having that deal is going to have a halo effect and a stamp of credibility that is generally well worth the hit in the margin.

The compounding effects of deals can have financial implications in addition to other potential partnership opportunities. On the other hand, Bloom also says that some of the best deals he has done are with less-glamorous brands that have a huge amount of traffic:

> I can give a real-life example of Answers.com, which I worked with at 5min, at AOL, and now at Onswipe. It has a huge amount of traffic and as smart a team at every level as at any company I've ever worked with. It is still a well-funded company with a large team. There are also

many sites out there with significant traffic (millions of monthly unique visitors) that are bootstrapped with small teams. They want partnerships to help with technology and revenue. You don't have to jump through hoops of several layers of management. You generally can close a deal quickly by pitching the CEO, owner, or cofounder, and they aren't afraid to try something new.

On BD and Negotiating

Bloom cites a law school negotiations class as giving him one of the most formidable learned skills he has used in his professional life:

> The two classes that provided me with the most practical skills that I use on a daily basis were a high school typing class and a negotiations class that I took in law school. In that negotiations class, I learned the very basic lesson that when you're negotiating a deal, you mustn't get stuck on the fact that you want something and your counterpart wants something else. Find out why your counterpart is making that demand and explain why you want whatever you have chosen. I think one of the biggest mistakes I see BD people make when they're trying to negotiate a deal is that they get caught up in the "what" without the "why," which makes it much harder to find a creative compromise.

As we saw in Chapter 21, "The Legality of Deal Making: Contracts and Beyond," mastering negotiation tactics is critical for a business development professional, given the back-and-forth nature of generating partnerships. Bloom's advice is to dig into the assumptions you are making about those on the other side, and truly understand why they believe the partnership makes sense on their terms. Then, use that to your advantage.

CHAPTER 42

TRENDSETTER PARTNERSHIPS: GARY VAYNERCHUK

Key Notes

Name: Gary Vaynerchuk
Company: VaynerMedia
Role: Founder and CEO
Previous companies and books: VaynerMedia, *Wine Library TV*, *Crush It*,
The Thank You Economy, *Jab, Jab, Jab, Right Hook*

GARY VAYNERCHUK, the founder and CEO of VaynerMedia, is an "entrepreneur through and through." He learned from his parents, who came to the United States with his whole family from Belarus when he was three years old. They owned a wine store, which Vaynerchuk digitized as winelibrary.com in 1996 (very early for e-commerce, especially for a one-store liquor store business). He turned the business into a $45 million company by putting the wine online, cataloguing it, and building one of the first online wine businesses.

Ten years later, Vaynerchuk began creating video shorts about wine and got clued into Facebook and Twitter very early. He gained notoriety as a tech trend-spotter. "I got involved in using Facebook and Twitter and things of that nature to build up that show, which I parlayed into actually investing in certain things like Twitter and Tumblr early on. It was the gain that led me to start building up my personal brand as a businessman; I started making videos about business and technology, which led to me writing a book called *Crush It* that went viral and allowed me to become a public speaker."

It was eventually his investments in social media, in addition to his personal brand and building winelibrary.com, that allowed him to start VaynerMedia with his brother.

Vaynerchuk's specialty is his ability to get into deals early. "I got into tech deals early, and I did so by doing what I do best: playing the long game and actually building relationships. Quite frankly, the best wine buys I've made and contracts I've signed for VaynerMedia are predicated on me making the deal in the long term. My specialty in deal making is that I'm thinking about making deals 20 years down the line rather than right now."

On Spotting Trends Early On

Vaynerchuk is prescient when it comes to new trends. Like many other entrepreneurs, he is willing to take risks on products or trends early on. He began selling wine on the Internet in the mid-1990s, before e-commerce was a phenomenon. It was risky because making sales online was still a relatively unproven concept, and people still preferred a physical shopping experience to a virtual one. He spent money putting his inventory online, which could have been a risk had the site not taken off. When asked about how he is able to identify trends early, he said, "I think the world replays itself over and over. If I see something that I've seen before, and/or if I intuitively feel that people are really going to do it, I'll do it."

Vaynerchuk was an early investor in Facebook, Twitter, and Tumblr. Some might say that was luck, but he trusted his instincts.

"I invested in Tumblr in the Series B round [the second round of funding]. I was right about that company before most people; I saw that before most people. Twitter and Facebook were totally relationship-based."

On His Favorite Return on Investment

Through what is better known as "the dollar story," Vaynerchuk learned the value of seeking early marketing opportunities from a young age. "In 1992, the dollar store got starting lineup figures for European soccer teams that were not available in the United States. This was pre-Internet, and I was able to buy a bunch of them from one specific store. These figures were worth anywhere from $70 to $200 apiece, and I was buying them for a dollar. Two weeks after I bought them, I went to the mall to a baseball shop and went to a dealer and sold 14 of them for $3,000 in cash and $3,000 in 1986 basketball rookie cards! That was my favorite deal of all time."

On Developing Relationships in the Field

A BD professional is only as strong as his relationships, as we have seen throughout this book. Vaynerchuk's advice on networking is to reach out and listen, then talk.

"The best way to network is to listen and to put yourself in the best position to succeed. Meaning, my big thing is that you should go to as many conferences as possible and walk the halls, and reach out to as many people as possible on Twitter. One of the best ways to network with somebody is to ask. Also listen: read a lot and leave comments on blogs. You need to talk, but the best way to talk smartly is to listen first."

CHAPTER 43

FROM BD TO FOUNDER: TRISTAN WALKER

Key Notes

Name: Tristan Walker
Company: Walker & Company
Role: Founder and CEO
Previous Companies: Twitter, Foursquare, Andreessen Horowitz

TRISTAN WALKER, founder of Walker & Company, a consumer products life-style brand, was born and raised in Queens, New York. When he was in college, he decided that he wanted to make as much money as possible as quickly as he could. He determined that he could do so by either becoming a professional athlete, working on Wall Street, or becoming an entrepreneur. The first was quickly ruled out, so he opted for the second and went to Wall Street. When he graduated from college (in only three years and as valedictorian), he took a job working as an oil trader and absolutely loathed it.

After two years, he set out to get as far away from Wall Street as possible, both literally and figuratively, and went to Stanford to get his MBA. While he was at Stanford, he interned at Twitter and got to experience some of that early hypergrowth magic. Walker says that seeing the Twitter founders on Oprah while he was at the office is a surreal memory that's etched in his mind. Walker is also Internet famous for his blog post about blindly reaching out to Dennis Crowley and Naveen Selvadurai, the cofounders of Foursquare, via email (eight times until they responded) and receiving a job offer.

He spent two and a half years as the first business development employee at Foursquare, leading it into partnerships with some of the largest U.S. brands, like Bravo, CNN, and the *New York Times*. After his notable tenure at Foursquare, Walker worked as the entrepreneur-in-residence at Andreessen Horowitz before founding his own company, Walker & Company, which seeks to create consumer products that will rival those of companies like Procter & Gamble.

On Doing Deals to Reflect What Your Company Will Become

Walker recognizes the pattern of doing deals that will benefit your company now, but says that it is more important to be forward-looking when it comes to creating partnerships. Instead, strive to secure partnerships that will help you define what your company can become:

> When I started at Foursquare, we received 600 to 700 new emails a day from people who were interested in doing something with us. I couldn't realistically respond to all of these requests, maintain my sanity, and appease everyone at the same time.
>
> So instead we decided to take inventory of the vertical segments and pick what the charter brands for each were. We wanted to partner with the biggest brands in each vertical segment, like the *New York Times* for media or Pepsi for consumer packaged goods, and we spoke to each one of those folks and said, "We don't know what this platform can become; help us." To everyone else, we told them to sit tight.
>
> When we opened up Foursquare for brands, we were in talks with a studio that had a popular television show that wanted to do something with us (and be the first on the platform). We had already made a soft agreement to work with that studio, but then Bravo came knocking, and we had this dilemma: one channel that was popular and had a lot of clout with what our user base looked like today versus a major TV network that wanted to showcase us in its shows and had great reach, but at the time felt slightly more off-brand.
>
> We were still trying to figure out who our user was. Although at that exact moment, Bravo was off-brand, it had a more diverse audience, and we wanted that diversity and that reach. We decided to go with Bravo, and we launched in February 2010 with commercials,

product integrations, and mentions in shows. We gave Bravo a week's exclusive, and then on February 15, we announced partnerships with the rest of the "vertical leads" like Starbucks, Warner Brothers, and 10 or 12 other large channel advertisers that we had. That entire January, I was so stressed out. But after all the announcements, the channel we burned bridges with ended up doing a partnership with us anyway. So it all worked out.

What's interesting about the lesson I learned, going back to the sanity thing: the thing that is fascinating is that every Pepsi has a Coke, and every Coke has a Pepsi. Inevitably, they aren't going to be mad at you for working with one brand and not another. They know you have only so much time in the day, and they don't fault you.

I learned to focus, focus, focus, and specifically focus on what you want to become more than on what you are.

On His BD Values

Walker had a value-altering experience when he spent time traveling with actor and comedian Tyler Perry to do a series of question-and-answer sessions for American Express in three different cities in the United States:

Two years ago, Tyler Perry and I went to three different cities and got to speak to entrepreneurs about their local entrepreneurial journey. Before Perry was famous, he was homeless and sleeping in a car, and now he's one of the highest-grossing people in all of Hollywood. There was a woman at one of the events who asked a question about "How you keep going," and Tyler said the words that I live by now: "The day that you realize that the trials you go through and the blessings you see are the exact same thing, you will be at peace. You get better from them and you learn from them and you hope they don't happen again." Cover that with a little bit of faith in whatever you believe in, and that makes a lot of sense! There are things that will be within your control, and there are some things that are grossly out of your control, and all you can do is keep hoping and understand that it's all a blessing.

Whenever anyone tells me no, I ask her why, and maybe she gives me a reason, and maybe she doesn't, but inevitably it'll work out. One thing a lot of people don't realize is that there are a lot of things that folks shouldn't be doing. People spend cycles chasing things that aren't the best things for them. It wasn't until I knew with conviction that Walker & Company was the right thing to do and had the volition to do something exceptional, coupled with faith, that I became persistent and made it happen.

CHAPTER 44

Day 1 Entrepreneur: Shaival Shah

Key Notes

Name: Shaival Shah

Previous companies: Hunch, eBay, TA Associates, Electronic Arts

Shaival Shah had integrity and entrepreneurial values instilled in him from day 1. He grew up outside of San Francisco in the East Bay, in a relatively homogeneous town called Danville. His parents had emigrated from India in the 1960s, and Shah wanted to fit into Silicon Valley culture. He learned about technology and entrepreneurship from both his parents, who owned a build-to-order PC company. His father taught him how to operate a business, and his mother instilled in him the skills of sales and finance.

After college, Shah put aside his schooling in biology and spent two years as a technology investment banker, after which he moved to TA Associates, a private equity firm focused on growth-oriented, self-funded businesses. He parlayed his experience in the banking sector into a corporate development role at Electronic Arts, which opened his eyes to the world of BD. He worked at several other startups, including serving as the general manager and head of BD at Hunch, "a predictive technology company forming correlations between people and things." Hunch was bought by eBay in 2011, and Shah spent some time working there.

On Entrepreneurship from a Young Age

Shah's family had a strong influence on both his personal and his professional development. His parents' business, which they started with only $10,000, was eye-opening for the young Shah and taught him about operating a business.

"I remember things happening fast, and I loved it. Back then, everything was largely done on paper and transferred into workbooks. I did a lot of the counting of parts, updating inventory levels, and adding up the dollar amount of inventory. I loved numbers. I loved feeling relied on."

He also talks about the different skill sets his parents taught him, which served him well in the business and startup world:

My father was all operational (buying and building), and my mother was all about the selling and finances. As I got older, I started doing more and more. I ran pick-ups from local distributors and deliveries to customers. My mother loved having customers pick up their orders in the store so that she could cross-sell. My father loved the idea of delivering the final products to the house or business, as he saw the importance of service. And I loved listening to them debate (argue!) the pros and cons of each. While they differed along the way, they always had one basic philosophy, which was to focus on the little things and do them right, no matter how small they felt.

On How He Learned BD

Although Shah had a sturdy foundation in understanding how to build a business from scratch, he had no formal BD training. He relied heavily on his various professional experiences to learn different BD skills that he uses today:

I think the BD function is one of the most misunderstood functions at a company. BD is a multidimensional function, requiring a diverse set of skills that touch on marketing validation, analytics, monetization/business modeling, sales, marketing, legal, negotiating, product, technology, and general management.

For me, there was no silver bullet in my BD experience. It was a range of experiences. Banking and private equity were heavy in negotiation, deal structuring, and legal contracting. At Electronic Arts, I learned how to develop co-marketing arrangements to drive user adoption and growth. In my startup experiences, my focus was heavily oriented around understanding the trade-off between user adoption and monetization, while being an extension of the product team to drive market feedback on third-party requirements. My startup experience has been the rounding environment that I desperately needed to put some of the other aspects that I understood better (legal, negotiation, deal structuring, and the like) into perspective so that I could see how BD can genuinely and appreciatively develop and grow a business.

On Moving from Banking to Corporate Development

Shaival made the coveted move from banking to corporate development and ultimately BD. While "business development" and "corporate development" can be buzzwords for members of the financial services industry looking to break into the world of startups, Shah knew exactly what he was doing:

When I left banking and private equity, I had no marketable operating skills whatsoever. I was five years out of college and living in the Bay Area, where all my peers had committed to the startup world well ahead of me. I realized that one of my strengths was around deal structuring, M&A, and investing. So, I decided that I needed a thin edge into an operating role. I was fortunate to land in a corporate development role at EA.

I knew that once I got into EA, it would be much easier for me to expand my responsibilities into more traditional operating roles. There are many trails that can take you to a particular point on a mountain, but for me, this was the avenue that made sense. At EA, I was able to step in and contribute immediately. At the end of the day, performing the task or job at hand is the fulcrum. Doing so allowed me to build some credibility inside of EA for being good at something.

From there, there was a longer rope extended to expand my development path. I want to believe that meritocracy alone rules in technology, but tech pedigree is also very important, especially in the Valley. Where you have worked is an indicator of the commercial success that you have surrounded yourself with. At the time, gaming was a scorching hot market, and it provided me with the knowledge base and credibility to expand beyond there. I never really looked at corporate development as a hedge. I looked at it as a necessary intermediate step to get to the operational roles that I was seeking. It was investing forward.

On APIs as the New BD

Fred Wilson (founder of Union Square Ventures) and Caterina Fake (cofounder of Flickr) predicted a few years ago that application programming interfaces (APIs) would make BD and partnerships obsolete. Shah, who had great success at Hunch launching its API and working with partners to ensure its success, believes that the API should be viewed as "a product within the organization to be built into the business" rather than as the whole package by itself:

I think many of those thoughts are very well warranted and justified. But, I think you need to strip it way down to fully understand the API versus BD relationship. In the past, enterprise technology required large-scale integration. Teams of project managers from both companies coordinated between functional heads and technology leads to implement software on the premises. The model was largely broken.

The expense of integration influenced the economics, leading to cost-based pricing, not value-based pricing. What SaaS [software as a service] has represented for enterprise tech [technology for companies] is analogous to what an API enables for products and services that third parties want to extend to their own customers. Think about how easy it is for third parties to integrate Twilio's API to enable telephony.

Before APIs, [a technical product] integration would have been much more time-consuming, and thus much more expensive, and would have priced itself out of the market. Besides that, it would have taken Twilio many more years to scale to the successful size it is today. The API solves the integration and scale problem for a BD and product organization. And with efficient integration, we see greater levels of testing new ideas, mashups, and experiences to drive innovation because it is easy to test, fail fast, and move forward.

And this should be a BD organization's biggest blessing. It should allow BD to focus on all the interesting aspects of new product/market fits, new business models, interesting co-marketing relationships, and the like. After all, self-serve and SaaS offerings that tend to be successful also tend to have very sophisticated sales organizations that focus on large clients, bigger deals, and new markets. APIs and BD are no different.

On Unique Partnerships and Specialized Products

Partnerships are generally done to scale, so that they can be repeated if necessary. There is often a need to create structure partnerships that are unique to the individual company. Shah has become a master at scaling these specialized partnerships:

> I typically start with the problems that I believe our product can solve. This is typically on a functional level initially, not an industry level. For example, at Hunch, we knew we had a powerful taste graph. At its core, user-user and user-item correlations and predictions were what we were really good at, and that fit most closely into the recommendations space. That was the problem that we could solve. From there, we spent a lot of time determining the problems a company is facing to see if a market existed.
>
> For example, when I did the deal with Gifts.com at Hunch, the company had an interesting problem. Its customers were not buying for themselves. They were buying for friends and family, but they didn't have a mechanism to get any personalized predictions for them. It was not a use case that we had considered. It was starting at the top, understanding the firm's key business challenges, and getting people's impressions on what would move the needle. From there, it was a question of whether or not you can support those challenges. From there, I always try to join forces with the partners' product team.
>
> You have to effectively see the world from these people's perspective and help them think through how to think about the user experience, while managing expectations of your own capabilities. Once you have ways to help solve functional problems, you can certainly specialize in particular vertical segments. At Hunch, we had a sweet spot within e-commerce and media. There were numerous other categories, but this is where an open API can help inform you of the vertical segments where prospective partners see a need.

On the Best BD Advice He Has Received

Shah values leadership in a BD executive, and he is very careful about whom he hires and why. He likes to focus on the distinction between sales and BD, as we outlined in Chapter 4, "Business Development Versus Sales," and ensure that the person exemplifies the nuances that are important to BD:

> Know why you are hiring a BD person. A BD person isn't a salesperson. A BD person is required to define, validate, and develop new markets. A BD person, at his core, is strategic in nature, with a strong desire to execute. You need to seek people who can see the business from multiple aspects, not just product, not just sales, and not just marketing. You need an executive leader who can help define new products, can clearly communicate the message to the market, and can help establish the economic model.

CHAPTER 45

DORM ROOM DEAL MAKER:
ANDREW N. FERENCI

Key Notes

Name: Andrew N. Ferenci

Role: Angel investor

Previous companies: Spinback (sold to Buddy Media), Buddy Media
   (sold to Salesforce), Salesforce

ANDREW FERENCI, an entrepreneurial wunderkind, began pursuing his entrepreneurial passions by starting a company at the age of 19. But it really started
long before that for him.

"Growing up in Minnesota, my childhood best friend (Ben Glaze) and I were
always running some kind of enterprise, from screen printing apparel for high
school lacrosse teams to selling snacks to hungry students before Hebrew school."

His first company, called thecollegeshack.com, was an e-commerce retailer
of collegiate apparel that taught him the skills of building and designing websites
but also faced heavy market competition. Ferenci sold his company a year after
graduation, then immediately turned around and used the proceeds to start the
social media analytics platform Spinback, which provided conversion tracking
from sharing web-based content to purchase intent to sales. While he was raising money, an acquisition offer came. Spinback was sold after a year to Buddy
Media, and within another 12 months, the whole package (that is, Buddy Media
with the Spinback team) had been sold to Salesforce. Now, Ferenci is an angel

investor working on a whole different side of tech: "An idea that uses textile nanosensors to provide low-cost point-of-care diagnostics for people with physiological disorders."

On Product, BD, and Sales Strategy

Ferenci's specialty in BD is leveraging his knowledge of product design and sales, and he has been able to keenly marry the two to find monetary success and create partnerships:

> I've found my design/product experience to be critical in closing deals. When you're passionate and informed about the product, it shines through in meetings. No one wants to buy something if you're not super excited about it and can answer only some of the questions. This also helps push deals forward because you can speak on the technical integration side while also negotiating business terms. If you have to shuffle different people through a BD deal to answer different questions at different times, it's likely that a lot of information will fall through the cracks.

At Spinback, Ferenci focused on making deals a symbiotic relationship to ensure equal success and hard work from both parties:

> We knew from our past experience that doing deals can easily become a black hole of time and energy. Many deals may be well intended and synergistic . . . but they are difficult to make materialize. We decided to set three criteria for deals to ensure that they would make a big impact and have a high probability of being realized:
>
> 1. There should be an equal amount of value added for both companies.
> 2. The BD partnership should help us scale in areas that we lacked because of resource constraints.
> 3. The partnership should provide value to our clients.

They also had a large number of high-profile clients using the product at an early stage in Spinback's life. Ferenci credits having a data-driven approach to courting clients and laying the foundation for ROI before the company was able to make such targets:

Before we went to sell to the big brand names, we made it a priority to have at least 10 customers and data that clearly outlined our value. As a startup, you're at a significant disadvantage when you don't have a recognizable brand that people are familiar with. It was important for us to have glowing recommendations from early clients with the data to back them up. We created case studies from our earliest clients and managed to get a positive review of our product in Forrester's annual e-commerce report. We realized that selling a polished and feature-rich product that would generate clear return on investment [ROI] wasn't enough; it needed to be backed up by tangible and social proof.

On Working at Small, Medium, and Very Large Enterprises

Spinback was sold to Buddy Media, a supplier of "social enterprise software" that enables enterprises to maintain relationships in a content resource management system. Within a year's time, that company was sold to Salesforce. Ferenci had gone from working at a small, scrappy company to an empire and found value in each step along the way.

The founders chose to sell Spinback rather than take additional venture capital money because they felt that the acquisition would benefit both the product and the individuals working on it.

"In our scenario, we felt that the acquisition was a great fit and could help us grow and stay autonomous while providing a healthy liquidity event for our team members, employees, and investors. The timing also played a role, as many social networks were getting closer to IPOs, and we felt that this had driven up our value."

Ferenci believes that in order for a small company to be successful in both BD and other areas, the team members must be scrappy and resilient.

"A small team has to be willing and able to jump over countless obstacles that inevitably come up. It's like getting punched in the face repeatedly and always being able to get back up. This is also the period of time where the first 10 employees should all be extremely talented and really believe in the company."

Medium and large companies, on the other hand, have slightly nuanced versions of success. Ferenci says, "[In] medium/large teams, I've found that organizational structure and management are key. It's important to start developing processes for things that you used to do yourself, so that others can have a blueprint. You want dependable and self-sufficient managers that can take the blueprints, make a set of keys, and start unlocking doors for everyone."

On the Best Piece of Advice for Entrepreneurs

Although Ferenci is young, he has seen it all when it comes to the building and life cycle of companies. The best piece of advice he has for both BD professionals and entrepreneurs is to trust yourself.

"Everyone has an opinion or advice for how you should be running your business. Ignore almost all of it; you are the only one who really understands what will work and what won't. So trust your gut!"

CHAPTER 46

Sports, Private Jets, and Philanthropy: Jesse Itzler

Key Notes

Name: Jesse Itzler

Company: 100 Mile Man Foundation

Role: Cofounder

Previous companies: 100 Mile Man Foundation, ZICO, Marquis Jet,
    Vowch, Sheets, Alphabet City Sports Records

Jesse Itzler, a major influencer in several different industries, proudly boasts that he has never created a résumé in his life. He has never worked for anyone other than himself. He began his career by signing a recording contract with Delicious Vinyl in 1991, and quickly parlayed that into inventing a personal brand of writing team-specific NBA songs. You probably know him best for his anthems "Go NY Go," written for the Knicks, and "I Love This Game," written for an NBA campaign (winning him an Emmy).

But he didn't stop when he had a Billboard Hot 100 single or a top video on MTV. He decided instead to switch gears and cofounded Marquis Jet, a Zipcar-for-private-jets service by the hour that disrupted the private plane industry. He orchestrated banner deals, like working with NetJets to supply the planes for Marquis Jet.

As if that weren't well-rounded enough, Itzler embarked on a 100-mile non-stop run, pursuing philanthropic endeavors (the 100 Mile Man Foundation) at around the same time that he learned about the benefits of coconut water. He fueled his major run (and also his training sessions) with it and turned that into ZICO. He then struck a partnership with Coca-Cola and ultimately sold a majority stake in the company.

Jesse's deal specialty is his ability to identify trends very early and utilize his access to influencers and star power to achieve success. His ultimate BD talent is being a major connector who, as he says, can get along with everyone from "thugs to billionaires." And if Jesse doesn't have an impressive enough résumé, his wife just might. Jesse is married to Sara Blakely, an entrepreneurial legend and founder of SPANX.

On Turning a Nice to Have into a Need to Have

As we discussed in Chapter 36, the best accomplishment in BD is the ability to turn a nice to have into a need to have. Itzler's experience with the NBA perfectly exemplifies how he was able to make other teams jealous by writing a custom-tailored theme song for the Knicks:

> I was really into writing lyrics and making music at that time, and I was also way into sports. So I decided to marry those two passions and approached the Knicks with an idea for a new theme song. My thought was, people are at a basketball game for 2.5 hours, but the game is only 48 minutes. Teams need to keep those fans entertained and engaged. So I wrote "Go NY Go" for the Knicks as a "call and response" anthem. We filmed all the celebs at the arena singing the song . . . and it took off. Every team that came into Madison Square Garden asked two questions, "Why don't we have a song like that?" and "Who did that?"

Even more clever was Itzler's ability to carve out a niche and own his specialty:

> Since I was the only one doing custom team theme songs at the time, I was the only one the teams called. I literally went from being a recording artist competing against thousands of artists in a record store to being the *only* one doing sports music. So the NBA had only a short list of folks to call when it wanted to do the "I Love This Game" campaign.

On Combining Musical Talents and BD

Itzler says that being a great writer is helpful for entrepreneurs, but not critical. He was, however, able to use his songwriting talents for the benefit of winning business and closing deals.

"When I first started out on my own in business, I used to write a custom song for anyone I was trying to close a deal with. I would surprise them with a song about them and their journey. They loved it, and it helped me stand out. Bob Sillerman at SFX (Entertainment) got one. Steve Koonin (president of Turner Entertainment Networks) got one. Richard Santulli (founder of NetJets) got one."

On Private Jet Partnerships

Marquis Jet was one of the first companies to sell smaller intervals of time on private jets, a market deficiency that Itzler identified early on:

My partner [Kenny Dichter] and I were guests on someone's private jet in the late 1990's. No luggage issues. No removing shoes. No lines. We immediately were like, "How do we do this private jet thing more often?" After a little investigating, we learned there were only three ways to fly private at the time.

1. Buy a plane (that was out of the question).
2. Buy a minimum of 250 hours of flight time in a fractional program (way too much of a commitment).
3. Charter a plane (which raised all kinds of questions like, 'Who is the pilot?' and, 'Whose plane is this?').

Plus, we were only 29 at the time, and we took only three or four trips a year; we didn't want a big commitment. So we thought: why isn't there a program that offers all the benefits of owning a plane with *none* of the hassles or high cost, and we came up with the idea for Marquis Jet Partners, a 25-hour card.

But coming up with the idea was the easiest part, says Itzler.

"The hard part was convincing NetJets to partner with two 29-year-old guys and allow us to sell 25-hour jet cards on its fleet." The standard business model for private jet partnerships is to sell a certain number of hours with a commitment to use the private jets for a minimum number of years. Marquis Jet's business model was to allow people who did not want to purchase a full share of a jet to pay by the hour instead. Ultimately, they sold Marquis Jet to NetJets in 2008, an acquisition that stemmed from a partnership arrangement. To this day, NetJets allows you to purchase a Marquis Jet card that entitles the user to a certain number of hours on a private jet.

On the ZICO/Coca-Cola Partnership

Itzler's ability to marry all his interests served him very well when he branched out into coconut water. He was using his running hobby for philanthropic endeavors when he stumbled upon coconut water and its benefits.

"I was early to the coconut water party. I discovered the benefits of coconut water while training for a 100-mile nonstop run that I did for charity. I literally was the human guinea pig, having run 100 miles powered by coconut water. I knew it was going to be a big hit and the 'next thing' in beverages."

But instead of keeping it to himself, Itzler knew that he wanted to explore the commercial possibilities of coconut water. So he leveraged his network to work with Mark Rampolla, the founder of ZICO, and forged a partnership between the new company and Coca-Cola. In 2009, the Venturing and Emerging Brands unit of Coca-Cola invested in ZICO, and in 2012, it formalized its equity commitment by buying a majority stake in ZICO.

On His Ability to Spot Trends Early

From team-specific songs to private jets to coconut water, Itzler has a knack for spotting trends early and creating successful partnerships to ensure their longevity. How does he do it?

"I just pay very close attention to things that I genuinely like and want to share with other people. I like to look on the shelves at stores to see what is new, what is starting to catch on, and what packaging is different. I ask a lot of questions and try a lot of new products. You can spend an hour in Whole Foods and get a bunch of new ideas just by looking on the shelves."

On Being Patient

Entrepreneurs have a tendency to want to see results immediately. But with BD deals, Itzler advises that you must have a long-term horizon in mind.

"I think the best thing I have learned is that almost everything takes time. It is not easy to start something from scratch. The folks at Coca-Cola told me that it takes about eight to ten years to build a meaningful and great brand. So have a long road map and plan and be patient. Be prepared to call audibles as needed along the way."

On Whether He Still Raps/Sings

"Only in the shower or when driving alone!"

CHAPTER 47

MUSIC BD AND INTERNATIONAL RELATIONS: ZEESHAN ZAIDI

Key Notes

Name: Zeeshan Zaidi

Company: Host Committee

Role: Cofounder

Previous companies: Sony BMG, LimeWire, a band called The Commuters, Council on Foreign Relations, Oneblue.org

ZEESHAN ZAIDI has always let his heart follow his interest in music. He was born in Canada to parents of Pakistani origin, but he grew up in the Philippines, giving him an unusual international perspective in both his work and his "extracurricular" interests. Zaidi serves as a term member of the Council on Foreign Relations and a board member of Oneblue.org, in addition to running circles around others in the music partnership space.

He is a cofounder and director of Host Committee, an Internet startup in the nightlife industry that offers inside access to nightlife venues in New York during hours that are usually sleepy. He served as Host Committee's CEO from its founding in 2011 until September 2013. He also currently serves as strategic advisor to the president of Ticketmaster, a division of Live Nation, the world's largest concert promoter.

Zaidi got his start in the music industry at Sony BMG in various operating roles, where he built the careers of budding artists and formed partnerships between those artists and several major technology media outlets.

On Getting into the Music Space

"All my life, I've loved music and been a musician. I played the piano and the guitar from an early age, as well as a few other instruments," says Zaidi. After graduate school, he gravitated toward the music industry and took a job at Sony. But his personal interest in creating music didn't stop. "One day in late 2008. I said to myself: 'Some day I will die. And when that day comes, I don't want to look back on my life and kick myself for not doing what deep down inside I've always wanted to do: make music.'"

A friend, Uri Djemal, a music producer in New York, helped Zaidi assemble a band, which they ultimately called The Commuters:

> We self-released our first EP on a label that I created in August 2011 and put out the full album in April 2012. It was surprisingly well received, getting very strong reviews. The first single got a lot of college radio play, and the first video was added to the rotation at mtvU. We got a lot of cool online features too, including *Guitar World*, *PureVolume* (a major music blog that picked one of our songs as song of the day), and many others. We developed a large international online following pretty quickly. We've also played a lot of local gigs, the highlight being the album release show, where we packed a major Lower East Side rock club."

The experience, according to Zeeshan, has "literally been a dream come true."

On Music Digital Marketing and BD

Zaidi broke into the music industry at a time when digital activity was focused on marketing rather than sales. He wanted to change that by helping to build what he calls "digital street teams: fans who volunteered to help spread the word online about artists in blogs, chat rooms, and the like. Internet users were less jaded back then; people tuned out less and clicked through more, so these campaigns were very effective."

At a time when the Internet was less fragmented, there were a few key sites where having a plug for your artist or band could garner a great deal of attention. "When we started the campaign for Avril Lavigne's first album—when she was completely unknown—we did an extensive partnership with AOL to feature her new videos, do an in-studio performance, and create other exclusive content—all of which AOL would promote aggressively throughout its network. This really helped put her on the map. For her second album, this turned into a mall tour sponsorship as well as a release night concert at Webster Hall in New York, which AOL live-streamed to its network."

Changing the digital music landscape through partnerships was no easy feat. Zaidi was one of the first to help artists launch online campaigns to market and sell their albums.

On Changing Sides: Sony to LimeWire

In 2006, while Zaidi was working at Sony, LimeWire was sued by all of the major record labels, including Sony. But he turned the tables when he joined LimeWire as its COO:

> For me, it was an intriguing opportunity. As an attorney and a musician who had spent much of his career battling downloading and its impact, I had (and still have) never downloaded a song on a file-sharing network in violation of copyright laws. At the same time, I have always been pragmatic about the impact of technology on media consumption. The reality is that digitization has made content easy to reproduce, obtain, and share, and young music consumers were going to do so. The best path forward, I always felt, was one in which technology companies worked with content owners to create compelling licensed offerings that were attractive to consumers. That's exactly what LimeWire wanted to do: LimeWire's goal at the time was to settle the lawsuit, license content from the major labels, launch a new paid streaming service (similar to what Spotify did, although this was before Spotify launched in the United States), and steer the 150 million users of its file-sharing software towards this service.
>
> So I decided to sign on and, surprisingly, my friends in the music industry were very supportive. Everyone was positive about it because they knew that my intentions were to help the industry from a different

angle. We had a killer product and engineering team (when LimeWire was shut down, many of them were hired by Spotify to start its New York office), and we actually developed the streaming service application—the people at the major record labels who saw it said that it was the most impressive music app they had seen.

On Creating Valuable Assets Through BD Rollups

My main piece of advice is to build an asset (or create a plan to build an asset) and then leverage that asset (or the promise of your future asset). At its essence, that is what BD is about. Figure out what the business is going to create (even if it hasn't created it yet), and then figure out who (beyond end customers) can benefit from the results. Figure out what they can offer you and what you can offer them.

First, it starts with picking the right market. Rollups obviously work best in fragmented markets with lots of small players. It also helps if these small players have no obvious path for growing their individual businesses to serve the market's full needs. For example, when we were at Nabbr [a business he worked at in between Sony BMG and Lime-Wire], we rolled up a network of dozens of smaller websites serving the market. Second, you need to develop an understanding of the asset you're trying to create. How is the whole—the network of partners—greater than the sum of its parts? More important, what will creating the rollup allow you to achieve in terms of value that you can pass on to the individual members of the network? How will scale help them? This is key. You need to determine how the partners you're targeting are going to be made so much better off by joining the network than they are now that joining it is a no-brainer for them. Is it access to better rates for services? Is it access to a customer base they cannot service on their own?

As part of that, you have to decide how much value to pass on to the network and how much to keep for yourself. My advice is to make it worth the partners' while and then some. Leave some value on the table to make the network strong.

Finally, you need to structure a standard deal that is easy to understand so that you can do lots of deals quickly. If you can secure exclusivity (the partners can't participate in a competing network), that's better for you. But an exclusivity provision in a deal is no substitute for providing so much value in your offering that your partners won't risk losing that by going elsewhere.

I don't think you need a particular skill set to do this well—I've seen people with all sorts of backgrounds pull this off. The key is answering the key questions that I've outlined here.

On His Interest in Foreign Policy

I have always had a strong affinity for international affairs. I was born in Canada to parents who were originally Pakistani, and I grew up in the Philippines, where my father worked in international development and I attended an international school. While I was an undergraduate and graduate student, I was deeply involved in public affairs and progressive national security issues. However, after graduating, I pursued a career in the media and technology industry, and while I remained passionate about national security, my level of engagement was limited. A few years ago I applied to the term member program at the CFR [Council on Foreign Relations] and was fortunate enough to be accepted.

Because of my involvement in media and technology, but also in international affairs issues, I'm frequently approached by nonprofits in this space looking for help with social media or technology. I often have to say no, but in the case of Oneblue.org [a new-media nonprofit devoted to international conflict resolution and interfaith understanding], theirs was a cause that I believe in. I grew up in an international community where my classmates were from all corners of the world, so I learned early that learning about different cultures and establishing personal bonds at an early age can overcome any barriers created by international conflicts. My parents are originally from Pakistan, but many of my closest friends from high school are Indian and Israeli. In a social media–driven world, we need to take advantage of the ability to connect and educate people from different communities that are in conflict from an early age.

On His Proudest Deal

My favorite deal is one I did when I was at Arista Records with Starbucks for Sarah McLachlan. Sarah's album *Afterglow* was coming out in 2003 after a hiatus during which she was out of the public eye, and we were looking for partners to leverage their marketing muscle for relaunching her career. I figured that Starbucks would be the perfect partner in terms of brand fit, demographic, and reach. At the time, Starbucks was just beginning to dip its toes into the music waters, and it had not done very much with music partnerships in its stores. A classmate of mine from business school worked at Starbucks Corporate; she put me in touch with an executive named Tim Ziegler from the company's music division, and we spoke over a few months about the possibilities. We finally crafted a comprehensive marketing partnership that included Starbucks selling Sarah's new CD in its stores, Starbucks selling her music digitally on its website, Sarah creating a special "Artist's Choice" playlist of some of her top influences that would be sold as a CD in Starbucks stores, and lots of print advertising by Starbucks pushing the promotion.

There are many reasons I'm proud of this deal. First, it solved a major problem that my company was facing—how to amplify our marketing push given our limited resources. Second, it was a huge win for both sides. We got lots of marketing support from a major retail force where our target audience lived. Starbucks got exclusive content and an association with a superstar artist that not only generated a halo effect, but drove traffic into its stores. Third, we created such a compelling partnership that Starbucks turned it into a formal program that it then repeated with many other major artists. Finally, it was just massive. I love being involved with deals and campaigns that have a major impact on popular culture.

CHAPTER 48

BANKING TO BD:
NICOLE COOK

Key Notes

Name: Nicole Cook
Company: Dwolla
Role: Director of strategic partnerships
Previous experiences: BMO, Wharton Business School

NICOLE COOK, director of strategic partnerships at Dwolla, rose swiftly at the company, moving from MBA summer intern to running the BD team in less than a year. She began her career in investment banking, where she spent six years learning about financial services transactions. She then switched gears and used her understanding of corporate financial structures to persuade Dwolla's BD team to hire her as a summer intern.

On Leaving the Banking Industry

Many young professionals are intrigued by the possibilities that the investment banking industry has to offer. Nicole spent six years working for BMO Capital Markets and left shortly before she became a vice president:

At BMO, I'd learned about numerous companies, engaging directly with their senior management to provide integrated financing solutions. What inspired me, even on the longest days, was knowing that obtaining financing was critical to their success. Further, as one of a small group of University of Iowa graduates who had "made it" to Wall Street, and as one of its first two formal recruits to BMO, I took great pride in forging tighter bonds between my school and the company. As cochampion of BMO's Iowa recruiting, I'd helped to hire 20 bankers, continuing my support through training and ongoing mentorship. My mentees looked up to me, and my managers saw me as being "on track for senior management." This is what I would be giving up.

But there was also a great deal to be gained. When my only sibling got married, I spent most of my "vacation" working, missing several wedding events. It nearly killed me. Sadly, this was one of several important occasions that I had only half-attended. Upon hearing of my promotion to vice president, I looked around, and I didn't envy the lives of those who were in positions above me. I don't mind hard work, and I expect to work hard throughout my life, but I wanted more for myself, including an opportunity to do something that really mattered, while reconfirming the values that are important to me.

I know with tremendous confidence that I made the right decision to leave investment banking, start business school, and pursue a lead role in BD at a startup.

On Getting an MBA

As we discussed in Chapter 9, "A Career in BD," the trajectory of a startup career doesn't necessarily involve going to business school or getting an advanced degree. After her time in banking, Cook decided that she wanted to pursue a graduate degree in business for three reasons:

1. To make a career transition to a business or operating role at a smaller company. I believed that returning to school for an MBA would teach me how to think in a different environment, and not what to think, which would be especially critical when I moved into a new role at a smaller organization.

2. To expand my network, professionally and personally. I had spent my entire professional career at one organization (albeit in several different roles). During my first year of business school, I was exposed to more than 800 talented professionals and amazing human beings. In a very short time following school, I was connecting with many of them regularly for business (and to grab beers after work).

3. To use this time to build my case, while earning an advanced degree (it couldn't hurt, right?). Given the hours that I had been working before my departure from banking, I hadn't devoted much time to figuring out the type of small company I'd be interested in joining. I knew I wasn't ready to start my own.

On Transferable Skills from Banking to BD

Pure investment banking and BD don't necessarily have a high correlation in terms of skills. Yet some people are able to make the transition rather seamlessly. Cook was able to parlay her time in leveraged finance to learn how to structure deals and the flow of the corporate cycle. She uses that knowledge to build a foundation for the partnerships she creates at Dwolla:

> In [banking], I structured financings for corporate clients, and in doing so, interacted with management at the company, as well as serving as the intermediary between multiple internal groups. In BD at Dwolla, it's very similar in that I structure our partnerships.
>
> In leveraged finance, I wrote the underwriting memo for approval of the use of the firm's capital for the financing and offering memorandums to get other investors to participate in our financings; in BD, I am constantly selling to our company's internal stakeholders, including product and developments teams. In both, I structure(d) and negotiate(d) any contracts needed.

On Public-Sector Partnerships

Cook had the experience of working as a private-sector employee of Dwolla on a deal with the Iowa state government. While many partnership professionals may have an idea of what it might be like to work with the public sector, Cook dispels many of those myths:

When I started exploring partnerships at every level of government, I didn't have any prior government experience. However, I certainly had a few (mis)perceptions about how difficult it was going to be to get anything accomplished. For a startup, it's often difficult to balance between short-term partner wins and having the patience to build long-term partnerships that can take months (and sometimes years) to complete. I was proved very wrong. And not only once, but a few times.

In January 2012, Dwolla and the governor of the State of Iowa announced a partnership with the state. It meant that any agency in the state could begin accepting payments through Dwolla. The initial use case was built with the Iowa Department of Revenue and would provide an opportunity to put thousands of dollars of savings back into the economy. For one specific tax payment, businesses in the state were sending checks amounting to an estimated $130 million annually. There was no electronic payment option. By replacing checks with Dwolla, the government would save thousands of dollars in fees and administrative costs, and the taxpayers would receive the credentials they needed to operate their businesses much more quickly.

From the time I began connecting with parties at the state level, it took about four months to establish why partnering with Dwolla was smart for government, determine what opportunities existed, negotiate a new contract, and go live with the partnership. I found champions inside of government who wanted to use Dwolla's technology to inject savings, time, and resources back into the economy. And by many standards, they moved relatively quickly.

CHAPTER 49

BD AND SALES: ERIC FRIEDMAN

Key Notes

Name: Eric Friedman
Company: Foursquare
Role: Director of revenue and sales
Previous Companies: Union Square Ventures, MediaCom, Reprise Media

ERIC FRIEDMAN, currently director of sales and revenue at Foursquare, got his career start at the advertising behemoth MediaCom. He was immediately attracted to digital advertising and worked on an internal startup within MediaCom that allowed him to learn about the world of digital ads. He grew frustrated by the bureaucracy of a large company and began anonymously blogging about ideas that he had for disrupting the space.

He noticed a blog post for open positions at Union Square Ventures, one of New York City's top-performing venture capital funds, and realized that the only way to apply was to link to your digital presence. Friedman's blog was a hit among USV partners, and he got the job and spent the next two years shadowing the partners and learning from the entire team. "I can honestly say that it was one of the greatest learning experiences of my life," he says.

From USV, he moved to one of the firm's portfolio companies, Foursquare, which was just beginning to take off. He started as a director of BD and has moved into a role that focuses on monetization and revenue.

"If my first two years at Foursquare were about building a merchant network, the following two years were about building the machine that builds a real business. Being able to instrument the systems, processes, and people that can generate significant revenues for a company has been one of the most challenging and rewarding things I have done so far."

On Lessons from VC

Friedman spent two years working for USV. He applied using his strong digital presence (at the time, his blog), and he did not shy away from sharing his opinions about the changing nature of the digital advertising world. While at USV, he kept his eyes and ears open and learned a lot about the world of startups, investing, and leadership:

> One of the most important lessons I learned was pattern recognition. It sounds obvious in hindsight, but pattern recognition helped me understand why we invested in and did follow-on financing in the portfolio. Looking at how communities rallied around or abandoned a site or service during a change, upgrade, or outage could tell you many things. I also learned to recognize the patterns of strong leaders. One of the benefits of getting to shadow a partner on her deal and go to many different board meetings was that I was able to understand the makeup of a great CEO and leader through actual execution. The public perception of a leadership team is not always the actual reality that happens behind closed doors, and this pattern matching helped me identify the winners.

On "You Don't Get What You Don't Ask for" BD

Friedman abides by the words, "You don't get what you don't ask for," especially when it comes to partnerships. Indeed, he was able to get a Foursquare check-in from space simply because he had the gumption to ask someone at NASA to make it happen:

> The NASA deal taught me a very important lesson: you can't get what you don't ask for. Basically, aim for the moon (sorry, I couldn't resist!).

When I first started speaking with NASA via an agency, I knew we wanted to do something big: have someone check in from space. Asking for this over the phone and hearing silence on the other end was definitely a memorable moment. We talked for weeks about what was possible, and I learned that it was really about understanding NASA's goals and objectives, and what the key stakeholders were trying to accomplish for their team. This is critical in any deal, because while everyone wants a "win-win," it's really about making sure everyone is doing a great job for his respective company.

I also learned that pulling off something like this requires a ton of buy-in from the larger organization, as well as from the astronauts themselves. My killer hook was reminding the NASA team that [Mike Massimino] got to do the first tweet from space, and this astronaut could own the first check-in from space.

It ended up being Commander Wheelock who was interested in taking the honor.

The setup and prep for this task was enormous. I needed buy-in from Dennis (the CEO), Harry (the CTO), and the engineering and product organizations because we had to set up a lot of custom work. It was a cross-functional team effort, and we had a lot of fun with it. Getting multiple organizations within a startup on board was a valuable lesson. You can always be working on another feature or product, and conducting a proper effort regarding impact analysis is necessary. This was definitely worth the effort, and the residual results put Foursquare into the hearts and minds of more people—either introducing them to the service or showing them that we were continuing to do innovative things with a product that didn't even exist before.

On His Best Piece of Advice

"I think the best advice I give to my team is, 'Make the people around you shine.' You will become an indispensable team member and show that you are focused on your team's goals. If you can achieve this, it will mean success."

CHAPTER 50

Intern to VP: Erin Pettigrew

Key Notes

Name: Erin Pettigrew
Company: Gawker Media
Role: Vice president of business development

Erin Pettigrew spent her childhood in Kentucky dancing and coding. She became fascinated with coding at a young age when she learned how to program her calculator to create games or shortcuts. Always striving for personal growth, she went from being clumsy on the first day of first grade to graduating as the valedictorian of her class before heading to Yale.

Professionally, she has been able to combine her two passions: dancing and technology. In the arts, she started training in ballet, jazz, and tap dance at age two. All through her youth, she competed in forums like America's Junior Miss and Miss Dance of America. Pettigrew even made it all the way to the semifinals of FOX TV's *So You Think You Can Dance*!

After college, she challenged herself to work for a brand-new company, Gawker Media, where she served as one of its first interns. She has spent the past nine years working her way up, and she now serves as the vice president of BD.

On Her "Growth" Years

Pettigrew has never been satisfied with following the status quo.

"In academics, school [posed a great many challenges for me]. By the end, I fought my way from knowing nothing about colleges to being determined to go to Yale while most of my classmates stayed home. Luckily, I was admitted, and I spent four years at Yale, finally opening my mind to everything I had yearned for as a young student in Kentucky."

But she had the desire to express herself in several other critical ways beyond academics, namely, arts and technology, which became her channel for self-expression:

In the arts, I started training in ballet, jazz, tap, and other forms of dance at age two and competed my way to performing in national competitions like America's Junior Miss and Miss Dance of America. This was no small feat, since I had come from a state with less than professional dance training. I capped my dance career as a semifinalist on FOX TV's *So You Think You Can Dance*. Most people would say that dance is how I expressed myself. But I would also add something more thoughtful: dance is how I tested the push/pull between growing my abilities (more pirouettes, higher leaps, and the like) and structuring that growth (it takes time, research, and bravery to build proper technique for improvement). The best thing about dance is that progress within it is asymptotic. You can get better and better and better, but because you're human, you can never be perfect. There is always some growing to do.

In technology, I began my obsession with tinkering on my dad's laptop in fifth grade, while I pretended to do my English homework. Absolutely taken with computers, I emerged from high school having taught myself how to program my graphing calculator and to code HTML/CSS, Basic, Java, and C++, and having made numerous Internet message boards and content sites. [In college], I worked as a university computing technician, and eventually I used all this technology knowledge to land my first "real job" . . . at a tech company. I had grown myself from a secret computer enthusiast to an educated technologist.

On Climbing from Intern to VP

Pettigrew has had a well-deserved meteoric rise in her career. She began working at Gawker Media when it was a small company and served as one of its first interns after graduating from college. She worked tirelessly and now serves as vice president of BD:

> I have spent most of my professional life bringing my same fire for growth to Gawker Media. The company was founded in 2002, and I joined as an intern shortly after, in 2005. Since then, I've climbed the ladder from intern to VP, and we've grown our audience from a few niche readers to more than 100 million monthly unique visitors. We started with our first banner ad a decade ago, and we have now run thousands of successful campaigns with most of the world's top brands in advertising and e-commerce. Many in the industry credit us with originating the news delivery style, content management system, and advertising programs that inspire most publishers today.

In her professional life, as with her personal pursuits, Pettigrew has pushed herself to spend time going beyond the world of Gawker.

"I spend time at conferences and associations as well as speaking and presenting my ideas to my colleagues. BD requires strong market knowledge and an unending appetite for new ideas. Reading, meeting, and networking ensure that I am always generating new thinking."

On BD and Advertising

To Pettigrew, BD is synonymous with growth. It often manifests itself as partnerships or launching new markets, but it's really "anything that increases a company's capacity, overall or in a particular area. I focus in particular on growing our capacity to drive top-line revenue." To do so, she likes to take one of two approaches:

> The first is the buildout of core advertising effort: As the first staff hire on the business side, I was quickly set to building and hiring nearly every business department from scratch. That included building up BD, sales operations, advertising technology, sales marketing, and creative production. I would move into an area and then figure out how to build the team, the processes, and the workflows from the ground up. It was a lot

of learning by doing, researching, and getting advice from senior peers in the industry. You can't beat that sort of supported entrepreneurial experience just out of college. I dove into the trenches and worked my heart out. Many of the processes and missions that I laid out for the business teams in those early days still guide them years later.

Next, there is the buildout of BD effort. In the last few years, as I have focused more specifically on BD, I built a BD team that is charged with growing top-line revenue outside of our core advertising practice in smart, efficient ways that protect the integrity of our news product. This is not an easy task. The digital media world is rife with bad ideas for "bad revenue," as we call it. I feel very strongly that our business should generate "good revenue." That's revenue that is not derived from interruptive partnerships or bolted onto monetization products, but arises from carefully identified areas of the business that yield native growth. I am less concerned with whether these are internal business launches or external arrangements, but instead much more intent on making sure that we're growing the business in the best possible way for our readers and our editorial mission as a news organization.

On Advice When Starting in BD

When I first took a role in BD, I spent time researching ways to approach the discipline. Sage people in the industry noted that it is the responsibility of a good BD person to know the product first and the business second. Of course, both are required, but you absolutely cannot build successful (defined as revenue-generating, not just fancy-sounding) business deals around a product that you do not understand. And that includes both development of the product and the market response to the product. With a knowledge of technology and an understanding of how markets receive technology products, I am always able to know the product first and the business second. And that makes my business acumen very, very strong.

*   *   *

We hope that these stories have put the theories from the first four parts of the book into context, and have given you the courage to get out there and start closing some deals!

Sources

Part 1

People Interviewed for Part 1

Eric Batscha: Knewton, Yahoo!
Kristal Bergfield: StellaService, AMEX
Andy Ellwood: BOND, Waze, Gowalla
Lars Fjeldsoe-Nielsen: Dropbox
Jared Hecht: GroupMe, Tumblr
Brian Kil: Dwolla
Tanuj Parikh: Estimote, GroupMe
Laurie Racine: Startl
Itai Ram: Vidyo, Apple
Matt Van Horn: Path, Lyft
Zeeshan Zaidi: Host Committee, LimeWire

Secondary Sources

Besson, Taunee. "Six Tips for Successful Networking." *Career Cast*, http://www.careercast.com/career-news/six-tips-successful-networking, accessed September 22, 2013.

Birch, Mark. "BD vs. Sales: What Is the Difference?" *Strong Opinions@marks birch*, July 1, 2011, http://birch.co/post/7122117064/bd-vs-sales-what-is-the-difference, accessed September 22, 2013.

Dixon, Chris. "Business Development: The Goldilocks Principle." ChrisDixon.org, November 28, 2011, http://cdixon.org/2011/11/28/business-development-the-goldilocks-principle/, accessed September 22, 2013.

———. "B2B, B2C, B2B2C and B2S." *CDixon Posterous Blog*, September 16, 2011, http://cdixonposterous.wordpress.com/2011/09/16/b2b-b2c-b2b2c-and-b2s, accessed September 22, 2013.

———. "The Ideal Startup Career Path." ChrisDixon.org, October 22, 2009, http://cdixon.org/2009/10/22/the-ideal-startup-career-path/, accessed September 22, 2013.

Dumont, Andrew. "The Difference Between Sales and Business Development,"
AndrewDumont.me, http://andrewdumont.me/the-difference-between
-sales-and-business-development, accessed September 22, 2013.

Elman, Josh. "'How Will They Make Money' Is the Wrong Question."
I.M.H.O., June 10, 2013, https://medium.com/i-m-h-o/a5890c2c2cc0,
accessed January 13, 2014.

Ganelius, Susan. "What Is an API and Why Does It Matter?" *Sprout Social
Insights*, October 31, 2011, http://sproutsocial.com/insights/api-definition/,
accessed September 22, 2013.

Gerber, Scott. "How to Find a Mentor for Your Startup." *ReadWrite*, July 22,
2013, http://readwrite.com/2013/07/22/how-to-find-a-mentor-for-your
-startup#awesm=~orsmihJ97Anoiq, accessed September 22, 2013.

Godin, Seth. "Understanding Business Development." *TypePad* (Seth's blog),
September 21, 2009, http://sethgodin.typepad.com/seths_blog/2009/09
/understanding-business-development.html, accessed September 23, 2013.

Hewlett, S. A. *Forget a Mentor, Find a Sponsor: The New Way to Fast-Track Your
Career*. Boston: Harvard Business Review Press, 2011.

Lowry, Josh. "Business Development Versus Sales." *Josh Lowry Blog*,
http://joshlowryblog.com/2012/04/25/business-development-versus-sales/,
accessed September 22, 2012.

Luedorf, Holger, via Fred Wilson. "Guest Post: Startup Business Development
101." *AVC*, January 16, 2013, http://www.avc.com/a_vc/2013/01
/guest-post-startup-business-development-101.html, accessed September
22, 2013.

MobileIron. "Box Adds Secure Mobile Collaboration to MobileIronApp
Connect Ecosystem." Press release, May 16, 2013, http://www.mobileiron
.com/en/company/press-room/press-releases/box-adds-secure-mobile
-collaboration-mobileiron-appconnect, accessed January 12, 2014.

Nielsen, Lisa. "Controlling Your Digital Identity Is as Easy as 1-2-3." *Lisa
Nielsen: The Innovative Educator*, July 18, 2010, http://theinnovative
educator.blogspot.com/2010/07/controlling-your-digital-identity-is-as
.html, September 22, 2013.

O'Connor, Shawn. "Step 7 for a Successful Startup: Seek a Mentor." *Forbes*,
September 10, 2013, http://www.forbes.com/sites/shawnoconnor
/2013/09/10/step-7-for-a-successful-startup-seek-a-mentor-3/, accessed
September 22, 2013.

Pollack, Scott. "What, Exactly, Is Business Development?" *Forbes*, March 21, 2012, http://www.forbes.com/sites/scottpollack/2012/03/21/what-exactly-is-business-development/, accessed September 22, 2013.

Roos, Dave. "How to Leverage an API for Conferencing." *HowStuffWorks.com*, November 23, 2007, http://money.howstuffworks.com/business-communications/how-to-leverage-an-api-for-conferencing1.htm, accessed September 22, 2013.

Twilio. About Twilio, http://www.twilio.com/company, accessed January 10, 2014.

Van Grove, Jennifer. "How To: Land a Business Development Job." *Mashable*, November 13, 2010, http://mashable.com/2010/11/13/biz-dev-tips/, accessed September 22, 2013.

Wong, Victor. "Difference Between Business Development and Sales." *I Am Victorious*, 2012, http://iamvictorio.us/post/26979018144/difference-between-business-development-and-sales, accessed September 22, 2013.

Part 2

People Interviewed for Part 2

Kristal Bergfield: StellaService, AMEX
Scott Britton: SinglePlatform
Kenny Herman: SinglePlatform
Tirath Kamdar: Fab.com
Nam Nguyen: Aviary
Tanuj Parikh: Estimote, GroupMe
Eli Portnoy: ThinkNear, Amazon
Itai Ram: Vidyo, Apple
Julie Vaughn Ruef: MessageMe, AOL
Tristan Walker: Twitter, Foursquare, Andreessen Horowitz, Walker & Co.

Secondary Sources

"American Express OPEN Launches SearchManager, an Online Solution That Helps Businesses Harness the Power of Search Engine Advertising." June 22, 2010, http://www.enhancedonlinenews.com/portal/site/eon/permalink/?ndmViewId=news_view&newsId=20100622005657&newsLang=en, accessed January 14, 2014.

Brown, Philip. "How to Make Product Partnerships Work." *Pando*, July 6, 2013, http://pando.com/2013/07/06/how-to-make-product-partnerships -work/, accessed October 23, 2013.

Desmarais, Christina. "5 Tips on Exponentially Growing Your Customer Base." *Inc.*, http://www.inc.com/christina-desmarais/5-tips-on-exponentially -growing-your-customer-base.html, accessed January 14, 2014.

Dudas, Michael. "New Technology Products and Promise-Driven Sales." *Just Dudas*, December 9, 2013, http://mikedudas.com/2013/12/29/new -technology-products-and-promise-driven-sales/, accessed January 14, 2014.

Greenwald, Michelle. "The Secrets of Successful Co-Brands." *Inc.*, November 11, 2011, http://www.inc.com/michelle-greenwald/innovative-co-branding -and-creative-partnerships.html, accessed October 23, 2013.

Porter, Kyle. "The 15 Essential Ingredients of Sincere Selling." *SalesLoft*, March 26, 2013, http://blog.salesloft.com/ingredients-sincere-selling, accessed October 23, 2013.

Selley, Nicole. "The Importance of Understanding Cultural Differences in Business." *Inside Business: 360*, October 17, 2007, http://www.insidebusiness 360.com/index.php/the-importance-of-understanding-cultural-differences -in-business-9-29147/, accessed October 23, 2013.

Taub, Alex. "The Four Golden Rules of Partnerships." *Forbes*, March 25, 2012, http://www.forbes.com/sites/alextaub/2012/03/15/the-four-golden-rules -of-partnerships/, accessed January 13, 2014.

"Understand Your Competitors." Info Entrepreneurs, http://www.infoentre- preneurs.org/en/guides/understand-your-competitors/, accessed October 23, 2013.

Part 3

People Interviewed for Part 3

Scott Britton: SinglePlatform
Jared Cohen: Kickstarter
Andy Ellwood: Marquis Jet, Gowalla, Waze, BOND
Phillip Eubanks: Spotify

Lars Fjeldsoe-Nielsen: Dropbox
Eric Friedman: Foursquare
Maxine Friedman: Contently, Syncapse, Clickable
Mike Ghaffary: Yelp
Jeremy Schwartz: Squarespace
Rob Weiss: RentHop

Secondary Sources

Fenn, Donna. "How to Manage a Sales Pipeline." *Inc.*, October 28, 2010, http://www.inc.com/guides/2010/10/how-to-manage-a-sales-pipeline .html, accessed December 13, 2013.

Llopis, Glenn. "5 Ways to Earn Respect and Get Noticed in a Meeting." *Forbes*, March 4, 2013, http://www.forbes.com/sites/glennllopis /2013/03/04/5-ways-to-earn-respect-and-get-noticed-in-a-meeting/, accessed December 13, 2013.

O'Grady, Don. "3 Ways to Build Your Sales Pipeline." *SalesForce Search*, August 13, 2013, http://web2.salesforcesearch.com/bid/150645/3-Ways -to-Build-Your-Sales-Pipeline, accessed December 13, 2013.

Tumblr. Tumblr Blog Network, November 26, 2012, http://staff.tumblr.com /post/36598494153/top-10, accessed January 14, 2014.

Part 4

People Interviewed for Part 4

Rick Armbrust: angel investing, Facebook
Eric Batscha: Knewton, Yahoo!
Richard Bloom: Onswipe
Scott Britton: SinglePlatform
Andy Ellwood: BOND, Waze, Gowalla
Lars Fjeldsoe-Nielsen: Dropbox
Maxine Friedman: Contently, Syncapse, Clickable
Alex Guttler: AppNexus
Jeremy Lermitte: Uber
Nam Nguyen: Giphy, Aviary
Gary Vaynerchuk: VaynerMedia

Secondary Sources

Caprino, Kathy. "How to Successfully Reach Out to a Stranger and Make a Connection." *Forbes*, March 25, 2013, http://www.forbes.com/sites /kathycaprino/2013/03/25/how-to-successfully-reach-out-to-a-stranger -and-make-a-connection/, accessed December 3, 2013.

Doyle, Alison. "Follow Up Letter to a Contact Met at a Networking Event." *About.com*, http://jobsearch.about.com/od/samplenetworkingletters/a /networking-event-letter.htm, accessed December 3, 2013.

"Email Follow Up After Networking Event." *Undergrad Success*, March 15, 2013, http://undergradsuccess.com/email-follow-up-after-networking -event/, accessed January 13, 2014.

Evans, Teri. "Taking On Risk, Embracing Rejection and Other Startup Lessons from the Trenches." *Entrepreneur.com*, http://www.entrepreneur.com/video /225925, accessed December 3, 2013.

Gaertner-Johnston, Lynn. "How to Follow Up on Networking Contacts." *Business Writing*, September 5, 2009, http://www.businesswritingblog .com/business_writing/2009/09/how-to-follow-up-on-networking -contacts.html, accessed December 3, 2013.

Galpert, Michael. "Fearlessness." *The Michael Galpert Experience*, March 18, 2011, http://www.michaelgalpert.com/post/5610779761/fearlessness-is -like-a-muscle-i-know-from-my-own, accessed December 3, 2013.

Gil, Elad. "Ask Before You Intro." *Elad Blog*, August 3, 2012, blog.eladgil .com/2012/08/ask-before-you-intro.html, accessed November 29, 2013.

Graham, Paul. "What Startups Are Really Like." *Paul Graham*, October 2009, http://www.paulgraham.com/really.html, accessed December 3, 2013.

Haney, Porter. "Persistence and Startups Go Hand in Hand." *What I Learned Building*, https://medium.com/what-i-learned-building/ea174db8a0b6, accessed January 13, 2014.

"How to Follow Up After Meeting Someone in Person." *The Art of Manliness*, August 8, 2013, http://www.artofmanliness.com/2013/08/08/how-to -follow-up-after-meeting-someone-in-person/, accessed December 3, 2013.

Huffington, Arianna. *Startupquote*, 2012, http://startupquote.com/ post/5594363469, accessed December 3, 2013.

Kammel, Liz. "Re-Starting Your Startup—or, How to Overcome Rejection." *Forbes*, July 6, 2012, http://www.forbes.com/sites/zipfitme/2012/07/06

/re-starting-your-startup-or-how-to-overcome-rejection/, accessed December 3, 2013.

Legge, Deborah. "Reach Out and Touch Someone You Don't Know (But Should!)." *Influential Therapist*, December 16, 2013, http://www.influential therapist.com/reach-out-touch-someone-you-dont-know-but-should/, accessed January 13, 2014.

Sprouter, "Why Persistence Is Necessary for Startup Success." *Business Insider*, May 19, 2011, http://www.businessinsider.com/why-persistence-is-necessary -for-startup-success-2011-5, accessed December 3, 2013.

Wilson, Fred. "The Double Opt-In Introduction." *AVC*, November 3, 2009, http://www.avc.com/a_vc/2009/11/the-double-optin-introduction.html, accessed December 3, 2013.

Winch, Guy. "Ten Surprising Facts About Rejection." *Psychology Today*, July 13, 2013, http://www.psychologytoday.com/blog/the-squeaky- wheel/201307/ten-surprising-facts-about-rejection, accessed December 3, 2013.

———"Rejection Is More Powerful Than You Think." *Salon*, July 23, 2013, http://www.salon.com/2013/07/23/rejection_is_more_powerful_than _you_think/, accessed December 3, 2013.

Part 5

People Interviewed for Part 5

Kristal Bergfield: StellaService, American Express
Richard Bloom: Onswipe
Scott Britton: SinglePlatform
Nicole Cook: Dwolla
Andrew N. Ferenci: angel investor
Eric Friedman: Foursquare
Jesse Itzler: 100 Mile Man Foundation
Charlie O'Donnell: Brooklyn Bridge Ventures
Erin Pettigrew: Gawker Media
Shaival Shah: Hunch
Gary Vaynerchuk: VaynerMedia
Tristan Walker: Twitter, Foursquare, Andreessen Horowitz, Walker & Co.
Zeeshan Zaidi: Host Committee, LimeWire

Secondary Sources

http://www.crunchbase.com/company/buddymedia.
http://www.hostcommittee.com/about.
http://www.stellaservice.com/business/team/.
http://stories.twitter.com/en/mike_massimino.html.
"In the News: Syncapse to Acquire Clickable, Adding Social & Search
    Advertising into Leading Social Performance Management Platform."
    Syncapse, June 14, 2012, http://www.syncapse.com/syncapse-acquires
    -clickable-integrates-social-search-advertising-into-leading-social-
    performance-management-platform-for-global-enterprises/#.
    UtR3v2RDtMY, accessed January 13, 2014.
Perez, Sarah. "Foursquare Biz Dev VP Tristan Walker Leaves Company,
    Heads to Andreessen Horowitz as EIR." TechCrunch, May 2, 2012,
    http://techcrunch.com/2012/05/02/foursquare-biz-dev-vp-tristan-walker
    -leaves-company-heads-to-andreessen-horowitz-as-eir/, accessed January
    13, 2014.

INDEX

ABOUT THE AUTHORS

Photographer: Melissa Taub

Alex Taub

Alex is the cofounder of SocialRank, a tool that helps brands find out more information about the people that follow them on social networks.

Alex previously led business development and partnerships for online integrations at Dwolla, a payments startup based in Iowa, and at Aviary, a New York–based startup that provides a photo-editing API for web and mobile devices.

Alex is active in the New York tech scene as the creator of the BD Meetup and an advisor to early-stage companies. He has been featured in *Business Insider* as one of the "Top 20 Under 25" on the New York tech scene. Alex writes a popular blog called *Alex's Tech Thoughts*; has been published in *Fast Company*, the *New York Observer*, The Next Web, and VentureBeat; teaches business development classes; and has been quoted on many tech websites, including TechCrunch, Gigaom, the *New York Times*, *Business Insider*, Mashable, and *PC Magazine*. He is also a contributor to the *Forbes* Entrepreneur section.

Alex holds a BA in economics from Yeshiva University. He is married and lives on the Upper West Side of Manhattan with his talented, amazing, drop-dead gorgeous wife, Liz (and their dog, Bart).

Photographer: Melissa Taub

Ellen DaSilva

Ellen was born and raised in New York and currently lives in San Francisco. She works on the business operations team at Twitter, which finds and targets strategic revenue opportunities for the company. She also served on the promoted operations team at Twitter.

Previously, she worked at Barclays on the Equity Syndicate and Capital Markets team. In her tenure there, she priced more than $10 billion worth of initial public offerings and other equity origination for technology and media/telecommunications companies.

Ellen holds a BA in English literature with honors from Brown University.

In her spare time, she also coleads the Business Development Meetups in San Francisco and is the founder and leader of the Super Women at Twitter organization, a group focusing on the advancement of women in technology. She is also a trustee of the Brown University Hillel.

For more, please follow up:

pitchingandclosing.com
alexstechthoughts.com
ellenjdasilva.com
@pandc